✕

**PARK LEARNING CENTRE**
The Park Cheltenham
Gloucestershire GL50 2RH
Telephone: 01242 714333

UNIVERSITY OF
GLOUCESTERSHIRE
at Cheltenham and Gloucester

## NORMAL LOAN

### NORMAL LOAN

D1357742

# Logical Reasoning
# with
# Diagrams

# Studies in Logic and Computation

**D. M. Gabbay**, Series Editor

# LOGICAL REASONING
# WITH
# DIAGRAMS

*edited by*

GERARD ALLWEIN

*and*

JON BARWISE

*with contributions by*

| | |
|---|---|
| GERARD ALLWEIN | ERIC HAMMER |
| JON BARWISE | STEVE JOHNSON |
| NORMAN DANNER | ISABEL LUENGO |
| JOHN ETCHEMENDY | ATSUSHI SHIMOJIMA |
| KATHI FISLER | SUN-JOO SHIN |

New York      Oxford
Oxford University Press
1996

Oxford University Press

Oxford   New York
Athens   Auckland   Bangkok   Bogota   Bombay
Buenos Aires   Calcutta   Cape Town   Dar es Salaam
Delhi   Florence   Hong Kong   Istanbul   Karachi
Kuala Lumpur   Madras   Madrid   Melbourne
Mexico City   Nairobi   Paris   Singapore
Taipei   Tokyo   Toronto

and associated companies in

Berlin   Ibadan

Copyright © 1996 by Oxford University Press, Inc.

Published by Oxford University Press, Inc.
198 Madison Avenue, New York, New York 10016

Oxford is a registered trademark of Oxford University Press

All rights reserved. No part of this publication may be reproduced,
stored in a retrieval system, or transmitted, in any form or means,
electronic, mechanical, photocopying, recording, or otherwise,
without the prior permission of Oxford University Press.

Library of Congress Cataloging-in-Publication Data
Logical reasoning with diagrams / edited by Gerard Allwein and Jon Barwise;
with contributions by Gerard Allwein . . . [et al.].
p.   cm.—(Studies in logic and computation; xxx)
Included bibliographical references and index.
ISBN 0-19-510427-7
1. Logic, Symbolic and mathematical—Charts, diagrams, etc.
2. Knowledge representation (Information theory)
I. Allwein, Gerard, 1956–   . II. Barwise, Jon.   III. Series.
QA9.L624   1996
511.3—dc20     95-41885

1  3  5  7  9  8  6  4  2

Printed in the United States of America
on acid-free paper

*To*

*Ariel, Genny, and Tinkerbell,*
*little people with fur, fangs, and claws.*

# Preface

About three years ago, while in Washington, D.C. for a meeting, I came across a bookstore specializing in used books on logic and literature. Inside, I came across a thin volume by Martin Gardner called *Logic, Machines, and Diagrams*. Opening that book brought about a small epiphany.

How many hours had I spent in Kansas City Central High School's library reading Gardner's *Scientific American* columns those many years ago, I wondered? And how large a hall would it take to hold everyone whose career was influenced by those monthly features? But these thoughts were only the backdrop against which my psychodrama played itself out. To explain, I must go back several more years.

Logic is the science of reasoning. In this regard it is at the very heart of all rational inquiry, transcending any particular branch of engineering, science, or mathematics. I became interested in logic in high school in the late 1950's and have happily spent my professional life in its pursuit. In the early 1980's, when I was on the faculty at Stanford University, the first Macintosh computers came on the market with a whopping 128K of memory. A friend and colleague, John Etchemendy, and I were inspired by the visual power of the Macintosh to try to develop programs for it that would help our students visualize and understand some of the more abstract notions of logic. This collaboration has over the past decade led to the development of *Turing's World*, *Tarski's World*, and most recently, *Hyperproof*. Each of these is a courseware package that teaches some basic notions in logic by exploiting diagrams one way or another.

While our motivation was pedagogical—to provide better ways for our students to learn standard material from logic—something unexpected happened. We found our students using the diagrams of *Turing's World* and *Tarski's World* in ways that did not fit within the confines of logical theory as we knew and taught it. They were using diagrams to reason in ways that were clearly logically valid but that just were not accounted for within the very theory we were teaching. The reason for this was that the existing logical theory took the sentence as the basic unit of reasoning and analyzed valid methods of reasoning solely in terms of relationships among sentences.

The discovery of empirical data that does not fit within existing theory is (or should be) an exciting occurrence in any science. Our initial observation opened our eyes to a treasure trove of unexplained methods of reasoning used pervasively in every branch of engineering, science, mathematics, and even in everyday life. A small sample includes hardware design diagrams, blueprints, the Minkowski diagrams of relativity theory, Feynman diagrams, molecular bond diagrams, Cartesian graphs in calculus, commuting diagrams of modern algebra, as well as good old everyday maps, photos and charts. We took up the challenge to expand the science of logic to account for the logical properties of these tools.

Over the past few years visual information has become even more important, and the graphic capabilities of modern computers allow us to visualize huge amounts of scientific data in new ways, to develop products using CAD systems, and to explore new places over the World Wide Web. It seems to us evident that it is important to understand the logical properties, good and bad, of these forms of visual presentation of information. What is it to use visual information in logically valid and invalid ways?

Etchemendy's and my discovery led to the first chapter of this book (written in 1989), a kind of gauntlet thrown down to the logic community. It also led to the development of the *Hyperproof* courseware package mentioned earlier, to the creation of the Visual Inference Laboratory at Indiana University, and to exciting work in this area by our students and colleagues, which brings me back to that June day in Washington, D.C.

What I realized as I opened Gardner's *Logic, Machines and Diagrams*, published in 1958, was that I had seen this book before. Not just that, I had *owned and read it* when I was still a high school student. That was where I first learned about Venn diagrams, Euler circles, Lewis Carroll's diagrams and other diagrammatic techniques. While I had no conscious memory of the book, the memory must have been there to be released by the presence of that slim book. And it must have played some role in my part of the "discovery" with Etchemendy of the importance of diagrams in reasoning. It was then that I decided to help create a new book about logic and diagrams in the hopes that it would inspire others to pursue the topic. The chapters of this book advance the theoretical frontiers of the study of the logic of diagrams. But if truth be told, the subject is still in its infancy. My hope is that this book's appearance will encourage scientists and mathematicians to be more up front about the use of diagrams in their own reasoning, teachers of logic to use them in their teaching, and future logicians to contribute to the development of the logic of diagrams.

*Indiana University*                                                    *Jon Barwise*
*4 July* 1995

## Acknowledgments

This volume was made possible by the Visual Inference Laboratory at Indiana University. This laboratory is a multi-disciplinary institute devoted to the study of the logical and cognitive properties of diagrams in reasoning, and to the development of computational tools to facilitate such reasoning. It is a cooperative endeavor involving the Departments of Computer Science, Mathematics and Philosophy, and the Cognitive Science Program. The VI Lab is directed by Jon Barwise; Gerard Allwein is its assistant director. Most chapters of this book were written by members or former members of the laboratory as described in detail below. More information on the VI Lab can be found at on the World Wide Web at http://www-vil.cs.indiana.edu, or by contacting Barwise at barwise@indiana.edu and Allwein at gtall@indiana.edu. Other books of interest in this area include *Hyperproof* by Jon Barwise and John Etchemendy, *The Logical Status of Diagrams* by Sun-Joo Shin, *Diagrammatic Reasoning: Cognitive and Computational Perspective* edited by J. I. Glasgow, N. H. Narayanan and B. Chandrasekaran, *Logic and Visual Information* by Eric Hammer, and *Logic, Machines, and Diagrams* by Martin Gardner.

The creation of the VI Lab was made possible by support of the College of Arts and Sciences and the Research and the University Graduate School at Indiana University, and especially Dean Morton Lowengrub. In these times of constrained budgets, it is difficult for a university to support new research initiatives that do not fit within established boundaries. We appreciate the confidence in this effort evidenced by the support of our Indiana University's leaders.

We also owe a debt to Ruth Eberle, Isabel Luengo, and Mary Jane Wilcox for helping to copy-edit and produce the index for this book.

Some of the chapters, or earlier versions of them, in this book have appeared elsewhere. We appreciate the permission to reprint these articles as chapters of this book.

Chapter I, by Barwise and Etchemendy, originally appeared as *Visual Information and Valid Reasoning*, in MAA Notes number 19, Mathematical Association of America, 1991.

Chapter V, by Hammer and Danner, originally appeared as *Towards a Model Theory of Venn Diagrams*, to appear in Journal of Philosophical Logic, Kluwer Academic Publishers. Copyright ©1991 Kluwer Academic Publishers.

Chapter IV, by Shin, originally appeared as *A situation-theoretic account of valid reasoning with Venn diagrams*, in Situation Theory and its Applications, vol. 2, edited by Jon Barwise, Jean Mark Gawron, Gordon Plotkin, and Syun Tutiya. CSLI Publications, 1991. 581-606. Copyright ©1991 CSLI Publications.

Chapter VIII, by Barwise and Etchemendy, originally appears as *Heterogeneous Logic*, in Diagrammatic Reasoning: Cognitive and Computational Perspectives, edited by J. I. Glasgow, N. H. Narayanan, and B. Chandrasekaran, published by AAAI/MIT Press. Copyright ©1991 American Association for Artificial Intelligence.

# About the Contributors:

**Gerard Allwein** is a logician-computer scientist and was a main engineer behind the *Hyperproof* program. He received his Ph.D. in computer science and logic from Indiana University in 1992 and is assistant director of the VI Lab and an adjunct member of the I.U. Computer Science Department.

**Jon Barwise** is COAS Professor of Philosophy, Mathematics, Computer Science and Logic at Indiana University. He moved to I.U. in 1990 and founded the Visual Inference Laboratory, of which he is the director. He also directs the I.U. Program in Pure and Applied Logic.

**Norman Danner** is currently a graduate student in the Indiana University Bloomington Mathematics Department. His current interests include feasible computation in classical mathematics and notions of recursion.

**John Etchemendy** is Professor of Philosophy and Symbolic Systems at Stanford University, where he is Senior Associate Dean for the Humanities. Etchemendy is the author of *The Concept of Logical Consequence* and coauthor with Jon Barwise of a number of books and courseware packages, including *Hyperproof.*

**Kathi Fisler** is a Ph.D. candidate in the Department of Computer Science at Indiana University. She is a joint member of the Visual Inference and Hardware Methods Laboratories. Kathi currently holds a Ph.D. Fellowship from AT&T Bell Laboratories, where she has studied hardware verification.

**Eric Hammer** is a Postdoctoral Fellow at the Center for the Study of Language and Information at Stanford University. He recieved his Ph.D. in Philosophy from Indiana University and was the first Ph.D. of the Visual Inference Lab.

**Steven D. Johnson** is an Associate Professor of Computer Science at Indiana University. His research interests include formal methods for specification and verification of systems, programming languages, and logic. He is a faculty participant in the Visual Inference Laboratory.

**Isabel Luengo** is a former member of the Visual Inference Lab. She received her Ph.D. in Philosophy from I.U. in 1995 and is currently a Philosophy Instructor at MiraCosta College.

**Atsushi Shimojima** is a Ph.D. candidate in the Department of Philosophy at Indiana University. He is a research assistant of the Visual Inference Laboratory. Atsushi's research is mainly in the theory of information originated in situation theory and operational constraints in reasoning.

**Sun-Joo Shin** received her Ph.D. from Stanford University and is an assistant professor of philosophy at Notre Dame University. She is currently working on the philosophy and logic of C.S. Peirce.

# Contents

## Part C.     Heterogeneous Systems

# Part A

# Theoretical Issues

*Chapter I*

# Visual Information and Valid Reasoning

Jon Barwise and John Etchemendy

## 1   Introduction

Psychologists have long been interested in the relationship between visualization and the mechanisms of human reasoning. Mathematicians have been aware of the value of diagrams and other visual tools both for teaching and as heuristics for mathematical discovery. As the chapters in this volume show, such tools are gaining even greater value, thanks in large part to the graphical potential of modern computers. But despite the obvious importance of visual images in human cognitive activities, visual representation remains a second-class citizen in both the theory and practice of mathematics. In particular, we are all taught to look askance at proofs that make crucial use of diagrams, graphs, or other nonlinguistic forms of representation, and we pass on this disdain to our students.

In this chapter, we claim that visual forms of representation can be important, not just as heuristic and pedagogic tools, but as legitimate elements of mathematical proofs. As logicians, we recognize that this is a heretical claim, running counter to centuries of logical and mathematical tradition. This tradition finds its roots in the use of diagrams in geometry. The modern attitude is that diagrams are at best a heuristic in aid of finding a real, formal proof of a theorem of geometry, and at worst a breeding ground for fallacious inferences. For example, in a recent article, the logician Neil Tennant endorses this standard view:

> [The diagram] is only an heuristic to prompt certain trains of inference; ... it is dispensable as a proof-theoretic device; indeed, ... it has no proper place in the proof as such. For the proof is a syntactic object consisting only of sentences arranged in a finite and inspectable array (Tennant [1984]).

It is this dogma that we want to challenge.

We are by no means the first to question, directly or indirectly, the logocentricity of mathematics and logic. The mathematicians Euler and Venn are well known for their development of diagrammatic tools for solving mathematical problems, and the logician C. S. Peirce developed an extensive diagrammatic calculus, which he intended as a general reasoning tool. Our own challenge is two-pronged. On the one hand, we have developed a computer program, *Hyperproof,* that follows in the tradition of Euler, Venn, and Peirce. The program will allow students to solve deductive reasoning tasks using an integrated combination of sentences and diagrams. On the other hand, we are developing an information-based theory of deduction rich enough to assess the validity of heterogeneous proofs, proofs that use multiple forms of representation. In this task, we do not want to restrict our attention to any particular diagrammatic calculus; rather, our aim is to develop a semantic analysis of valid inference that is not inextricably tied to linguistic forms of representation.

Our aim in this chapter is just to sow a seed of doubt in the reader's mind about the dogma mentioned above. In the next section we give a number of examples of heterogeneous inference, showing the wide range of types of reasoning that we think fall under this heading. In the third section, we give an example of the way *Hyperproof* can be used to solve a simple problem. In the concluding section, we present some thoughts about what it is that makes diagrams and other forms of visual representation so useful for mathematical discovery, proof, and pedagogy. Later chapters will present particular diagrammatic logics.

## 2    The Legitimacy of Heterogeneous Inference

Valid deductive inference is often described as the extraction or making explicit of information that is only implicit in information already obtained. Modern logic builds on this intuition by modeling inference as a relation between sentences, usually sentences of a formal language like the first-order predicate calculus. In particular, it views valid deductive proofs as structures built out of such sentences by means of certain predetermined formal rules. But of course language is just one of the many forms in which information can be couched. Visual images, whether in the form of geometrical diagrams, maps, graphs, or visual scenes of real-world situations, are other forms.

A good way to appreciate the importance of nonlinguistic representation in inference is simply to look at some everyday examples of valid deductive reasoning. This exercise serves two purposes. First, it convinces us of the ubiquity of nonlinguistic representation in actual reasoning. Second, it calls

into question some of the basic assumptions that have led to the theorist's
disdain for such reasoning.

## On the universality of linguistic representation

The modern account of inference given to us by logic has an unstated
assumption, namely that all valid reasoning is (or can be) cast in the form
of a sequence of sentences in some language. This picture has been strongly
challenged by psychologists investigating visualization. An example tracing
back to Stenning [1977] and Kosslyn [1980] involves the use of maps and
map-like representations in human problem solving.

**Example 2.1** Suppose you are a tourist in San Francisco's Chinatown,
and a motorist stops and asks how to get to China Basin. You take out
your map, find both Chinatown and China Basin, and tell him what route
he could take.

Here there is a clear sense in which you have engaged in a valid piece
of deductive reasoning, one whose assumptions consist in part of the information provided by the map and whose conclusion consists of the claim
that a certain route will take the motorist to China Basin. But notice that
you do not simply "read" the map in the sense in which you might read
the same directions written out on a scrap of paper. The map contains
a vast amount of information, most of which is useless for any particular
use of the map. In particular, it contains information about how to get
from Chinatown to China Basin, the information also contained in your
subsequent directions. But this information has been extracted from the
map and expressed in a very different form.

Kosslyn uses such examples to argue that visual and linguistic representations of the same information have different properties. His point is
that one form may represent a given piece of information more efficiently
than another for a particular purpose. This same conclusion is reinforced
by Stigler (1984) in studying the role of visualization in mental calculation.
Noting Kosslyn, Stigler observes that "much of what we know can be represented in more than one format (e.g., images or propositions), and ... for
different tasks, different representational formats may lead to differences in
the nature, speed, and efficiency of the processing they support" (p. 175).

We think this is an important point. But we also think that in many
cases it is more than a matter of alternative representations of a given piece
of information. Consider another example.

**Example 2.2** Suppose you are at a large party and want to meet a visiting
mathematician (Anna, to give her a name) whom you know to be there.
You are told that Anna is in the next room talking to a man with a beard.
When you enter the room you see that, unfortunately, there are two bearded

men. Fortunately, though, they are both talking to the same woman. You conclude that she must be Anna.

Note that in this case your conclusion is based on two forms of information. One of these is the earlier statement (plus your knowledge that Anna is a woman), the other is information you get from the scene in front of you. Although some might claim that you translate the latter information into mental sentences of some sort, there is no obvious reason to think this is so.

For our purposes, the crucial feature of this example is that the conclusion associates a name with a person in a way that transcends each domain individually, both the linguistic and the visual. Because of this, the reasoning cannot be accurately modeled by deductions in a standard formal language. The nearest sentential analog to this conclusion might associate a name with some description ("Anna is the woman who . . . "), rather than with Anna herself. Alternatively, we might employ some deictic, demonstrative, or indexical element ("That woman is Anna"), but of course it is not this sentence, in isolation, that is the conclusion of your reasoning. Only when we interpret the demonstrative as referring to Anna have we captured the genuine content of your conclusion.

We also note that if this really is a case of heterogeneous inference, then it is clear that this kind of reasoning is ubiquitous in daily life.

## On the dangers of visual representation

The main reason for the low repute of diagrams and other forms of visual representation in logic is the awareness of a variety of ill-understood mistakes one can make using them: witness the fallacies that have arisen from the misuse of diagrams in geometry. By contrast, it is felt that we have a fairly sophisticated semantic analysis of linguistically based reasoning.

Our counter to this attitude is two-fold. First, we note the obvious fact that a wide variety of mistaken proofs and fallacious inferences do not use visual information. These range from the traditional informal fallacies, to the misapplication of formal rules (for example, inadvertently capturing a free variable in a substitution), to mistakes far harder to classify or categorize. And, as we all know, a simple diagram can often be used to pinpoint such an error. The mere existence of fallacious proofs is no more a demonstration of the illegitimacy of diagrams in reasoning than it is of the illegitimacy of sentences in reasoning. Indeed, what understanding we have of illegitimate forms of linguistic reasoning has come from careful attention to this form of reasoning, not because it was self-evident without such attention.

Our second reply is to point out that although one can make mistakes using various forms of visual representation, it is also possible to give perfectly valid proofs using them. We give some examples here. Later chapters present rigorous logical systems that employ diagrams in essential ways.

**Example 2.3** Recall that the Pythagorean Theorem claims that given any right triangle as follows,

the sum $a^2 + b^2$ is equal to $c^2$, the square of the hypotenuse. One familiar proof of this theorem involves a construction that first draws a square on the hypotenuse:

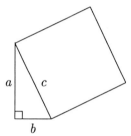

and then replicates the original triangle three times as shown:

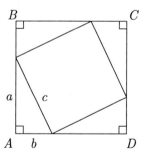

Using the fact that the sum of the angles of a triangle is a straight line, one easily sees that $ABCD$ is itself a square, one whose area can be computed in two different ways. On the one hand, its area is $(a+b)^2$, since the sides of the large square have length $a+b$. On the other hand, we see by inspection that its area is also $c^2 + 4x$, where $x$ is the area of the original triangle, i.e., $x = \frac{1}{2}ab$. This gives us the equation

$$(a + b)^2 = c^2 + 2ab,$$

which leads to the desired equation,

$$a^2 + b^2 = c^2.$$

It seems clear that this is a legitimate proof of the Pythagorean Theorem. Note, however, that the diagrams play a crucial role in the proof. We are not saying that one could not give an *analogous* (and longer) proof without them, but rather that the proof as given makes crucial use of them. To see this, we only need note that without them, the proof given above makes no sense.

This proof of the Pythagorean Theorem is an interesting combination of both geometric manipulation of a diagram and algebraic manipulation of nondiagrammatic symbols. Once you remember the diagram, however, the algebraic half of the proof is almost transparent. This is a general feature of many geometric proofs: Once you have been given the relevant diagram, the rest of the proof is not difficult to figure out. It seems odd to forswear nonlinguistic representation and so be forced to mutilate this elegant proof by constructing an analogous linguistic proof, one no one would ever discover or remember without the use of diagrams.

As we have noted, there is a well-known danger associated with the use of diagrams in geometrical proofs. The danger stems from the possibility of appealing to accidental features of the specific diagram in the proof. For example, if any piece of our reasoning had appealed to the observation that, in our diagram, $a$ is greater than $b$, the proof would have been fallacious, or at any rate would not have been as general as the theorem demands. Nevertheless, it is clear that we did not make use of any such accidental features in our proof. Further, it should be noted that a linguistically presented proof can have accidental features that lead to errors as well. For example, one of the constituent sentences may be ambiguous. More than one error has resulted from a valid step that is expressed ambiguously.

The potential for error in diagrammatic reasoning is real. But as we have noted, it is no more serious than the sorts of fallacies that can occur in purely linguistic forms of reasoning. The tradition has been to address these latter fallacies by delving into the source of the problem, developing a sophisticated understanding of linguistic proofs. It is not obvious that an analogous study of diagrammatic reasoning could not lead to an analogous understanding of legitimate and illegitimate uses of these techniques.

**Example 2.4** We are all familiar with the use of Venn diagrams to solve problems and illustrate theorems in set theory. Consider, for example, their use in proving the distributive law,

$$A \cup (B \cap C) = (A \cup B) \cap (A \cup C).$$

To prove this, we draw two copies of a diagram with circles used to represent the three sets. We successively shade in these diagrams, with operations corresponding to union and intersection, Figure 1 shows the derivation of the left-hand side of the distribution equation.

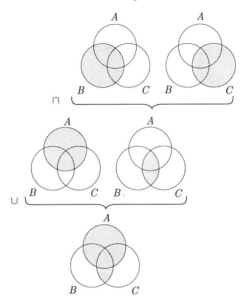

Figure 1: Derivation of $A \cup (B \cap C)$

Figure 2 shows the derivation of the right hand side of the distribution equation.

The fact that we end up with the same diagram in both cases shows that the distributive law holds.

Venn diagrams provide us with a formalism that consists of a standardized system of representations, together with rules for manipulating them. In this regard, they could be considered a primitive visual analog of the formal systems of deduction developed in logic. We think it is possible to give an information-theoretic analysis of this system, one that shows, among other things, that the demonstration above is in fact a valid proof.

In Venn diagrams, regions on the page represent sets, adding and intersecting regions correspond to union and intersection of sets. Shading a region serves to focus attention on that region. What makes our purported proof a real proof is the fact that there is a homomorphic relationship be-

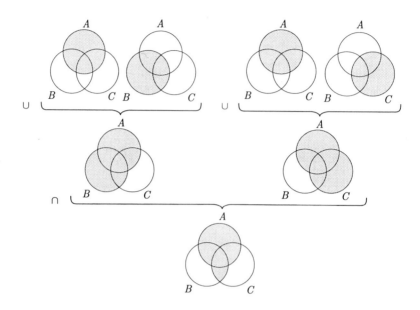

Figure 2: Derivation of $(A \cup B) \cap (A \cup C)$

tween regions (with the operations of addition and intersection of regions) and sets (with the operations of union and intersection of sets).[1]

As we have said, diagrams can lead us into error if they are used improperly. For example, if we were to take the nonemptiness of a region as indicating nonemptyness of the represented set, we would be led to conclude that the intersection of $A, B$, and $C$ is nonempty, which it might not be. Likewise, the size of a region carries no representational significant whatsoever about the represented set, any more than the size of the letter "$A$" indicates that the set denoted is larger than the set denoted by "$a$." The use of diagrams, like the use of linguistic symbols, requires us to be sensitive to the representational scheme at work.

Mathematics instructors know from experience that these sorts of diagrammatic proofs are much more helpful and convincing to students than more standard linguistic proofs. Frequently, they enable the student to see, in a way that formal proofs do not, just what the theorem is saying and why it is true.

The sort of reasoning we have examined most closely is typified by

---

[1]More precisely, given any three sets $A, B$, and $C$ we map the various regions in our diagrams to the obvious sets. This is a homomorphism relative to the operations mentioned, so any positive statement formulated in terms of adding and intersecting regions that is true of the diagram corresponds to a true statement about the sets.

problems found in puzzle magazines or on the analytical reasoning section
of the Graduate Record Examination. A very simple example of this kind
of problem is described in Example 2.5.

**Example 2.5** You are to seat four people, $A, B, C,$ and $D$ in a row of five
chairs. $A$ and $C$ are to flank the empty chair. $C$ must be closer to the
center than $D$, who is to sit next to $B$. From this information, show that
the empty chair is not in the middle or on either end. Can you tell who
must be seated in the center? Can you tell who is to be seated on the two
ends?

We urge the reader to solve this problem before reading on. As simple as
it is, you will no doubt find that the reasoning has a large visual component.
Probably you will find it useful to draw some diagrams. With more complex
problems of this sort, diagrams become even more essential.

One line of reasoning that can be used in solving this problem (the one
we analyze in Barwise and Etchemendy (1990)) runs as follows. Let us use
the following diagram to represent the five chairs.

Our first piece of information tells us that $A$ and $C$ are to flank the empty
chair. Let us use $\times$ to signify that a chair is empty. Then we can split into
six cases. Or, since the problem does not distinguish left from right in any
way, we can limit our attention to three cases, the other three being mirror
images of them.

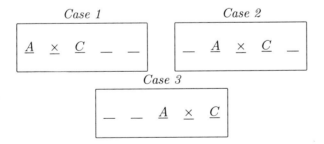

Using the fact that $C$ must be seated closer to the center than $D$, we can
eliminate Case 3, since $C$ is not closer to the center than any available
chair. Similarly, since $D$ must sit next to $B$, we can rule out Case 2, since
no contiguous chairs are available. This leaves us with the following two
possibilities:

Case 1.1

| $\underline{A}$ | $\times$ | $\underline{C}$ | $\underline{B}$ | $\underline{D}$ |

Case 1.2

| $\underline{A}$ | $\times$ | $\underline{C}$ | $\underline{D}$ | $\underline{B}$ |

In both of these cases, all of the stated constraints are satisfied, and so we know that neither case can be ruled out. This allows us to answer the questions posed in the puzzle. First, we see that in both cases the empty chair is not in the middle or on either end, as desired. Second, we see that $C$ must be seated in the middle. And finally, we see that $A$ must be on one end of the row, but that we do not know whether $B$ or $D$ is on the other end. Either one is possible.

We are convinced that, properly understood, the demonstration above is a valid proof of the conclusions reached, not just a psychological crutch to help us find such a proof, as the traditional account would have us believe. Moreover, we think that there are some parts of this proof that are missed in traditional accounts of inference. Notice, for example, that although our reasoning is all of a piece, the three parts of the problem have quite different characteristics when looked at from the traditional perspective. The first question asks us to prove that a specific fact follows from the given information. The second, in contrast, ask us whether a certain sort of information is implicit in the given information, and the answer is *yes*. The third question is of the same sort, but here, we end up showing that something does *not* follow from the given, namely, who is seated on the end opposite $A$. We show this *nonconsequence* result by coming up with models of the given, one of which has $B$ on the end, while the other has $D$. Normally, showing that something follows from some assumptions and showing that something does not follow are thought of as dual tasks, the first deduction and the second model building. This dichotomy seems unhelpful in analyzing the reasoning above, since there was no apparent discontinuity between the portions of the reasoning that demonstrated consequence and the portions that demonstrated nonconsequence. This occurence, in one reasoning task, of parts that are usually thought of as duals of one another (deduction and model construction) turns out to be typical of a whole spectrum of reasoning tasks. The desire to account for this dual nature of ordinary reasoning is an important motivation for some of the details of our theory of heterogeneous inference.

We have claimed that diagrams and other forms of visual representation can be essential and legitimate components in valid deductive reasoning. As we have noted, this is a heretical claim, running counter to a long tradition in mathematics, logic, and certain traditions within cognitive psychology. No doubt many readers will initially find it implausible. We invite such readers to work out a solution to Example 2.5 using a standard system of deduction, and to compare the complexity and structure of that solution with the original solution using diagrams. This sort of exercise has convinced us that even when syntactic analogs can be constructed, they are poor models of much actual valid reasoning.

## Various uses of visual information in valid reasoning

Looking back at these and similar examples, we see that there are at least three different ways that visual representations can be part of valid reasoning. (i) Probably the most obvious and pervasive form in everyday life is that visual information is part of the given information from which we reason. In the simplest case, this sort of reasoning extracts information from a visual scene and represents it linguistically. (ii) Visual information can also be integral to the reasoning itself. At its most explicit, such reasoning will employ an actual diagram, as in the examples above. In other cases, there may be no need for such an explicit diagram, since the reader will be able to visualize the steps without it. (iii) Finally visual representations can play a role in the conclusion of a piece of reasoning. Imagine replacing the story of Anna above by a similar story where the problem is to provide a caption for a photo identifying the people represented by the photo. In a given problem, visual information could play any or all of the above roles.

We suspect that visualization of sort (ii) plays a much bigger role in mathematical proofs than is generally acknowledged, and that this is in fact part of what accounts for the discrepancy between mathematical proofs and their formal counterparts. In calculus, for example, the concept of a continuous function is essentially a visual one, one that is linguistically captured by the usual $\epsilon - \delta$ characterization. But it seems clear that in giving proofs we often shortcut this characterization and rely more directly on the visual concept. Another example is the ubiquity of arrow diagrams in modern mathematics. As Saunders Mac Lane puts it in the first sentence of his classic book on category theory:

> Category theory starts with the observation that many properties of mathematical systems can be unified *and simplified* by a presentation with diagrams of arrows.[2] (Mac Lane 1971, p. 1)

If visualization plays a bigger role in mathematical proof than has been widely recognized by our accounts of proof, it would explain in part the difficulty of creating automated proof checkers, let alone automated proof generators, based as they are on the linguistic model of reasoning. And it could account for the trouble our students have in mastering the ability to prove things.

---

[2]We note that there are actually two sorts of diagrams in category theory, diagrams as physical parts of proofs, and abstract objects called diagrams used to model them.

It might be thought that visual representations would only be appropriate in proofs of results that can themselves be visualized or visually represented in a natural way. However, this is not the case. For example it has been suggested that what is paradoxical about the Banach-Tarski paradox rests in the fact that it is a result that defies our visual intuitions. This may well be right. However, it does not follow that one cannot use diagrams or other forms of visual representations effectively in giving its proof. Indeed, the most popular proofs of the result do use diagrams.

A striking feature of diagrammatic reasoning is its dynamic character. The reasoning often takes the form of successively adding to or otherwise modifying a diagram. This makes it a very convenient form for use in one-on-one discussions at a blackboard or in front of a class. However, it makes it very awkward to use in a traditional linguistically based document, say a book or research paper. Adding to this problem are the difficulties in getting even a static diagram into print at all. For example, each diagram in this chapter took us much more time and effort than a similar amount of text would have taken. However, this need not be so, and indeed it is changing all the time. Computer technology is making it ever easier to create and replicate diagrams and other forms of visual information in an accurate and relatively painless manner. As this process continues, it will become increasingly convenient for mathematicians to use static diagrams in papers and texts.

Of course it is also possible to think beyond the static printed documents of the past, to dynamic computer-driven documents of the future. In these documents, it is possible to create dynamic visual representations that unfold before the reader's eyes. It seems likely that such documents will lead to proofs that would otherwise be impossible to find or comprehend. In the next section, we turn to a discussion of *Hyperproof*, a tiny first step along that road. Unfortunately, we are confined to the printed page, but we will try to give a feel for the dynamic program.

# 3   Hyperproof

*Hyperproof* allows the user to reason based on two forms of information about a blocks world. At the top of the screen, there is a diagram of the blocks world. These worlds consist of objects of various shapes and sizes located on an $8 \times 8$ grid. The possible shapes are cube, tetrahedron, and dodecahedron; the possible sizes are small, medium, and large. A crucial feature of the visual representation is that the depicted information can be incomplete in a variety of ways. For one thing, the objects depicted in the world may be named, but their names may not be indicated in the diagram.

For another, an object's location, size, or shape may not be determined.[3]

Below the diagram, the user is given information by means of sentences in the usual first-order logical notation. This information will typically be compatible with, but go beyond, the incomplete information depicted in the diagram. It will also typically be the sort of information not easily incorporated in a diagram.

Given these two sources of information about a blocks world, the student is presented with some reasoning task or tasks. These come in a variety of forms, analogous to some of the examples in the preceeding section. In one type of problem, the student is asked to use the given information to identify one of the depicted objects by name. In another, the student is asked to determine whether some other claim follows from the given information. If it does, the student is required to demonstrate this by means of a proof, one that can use both sentences and diagrams that extend the original diagram. If it does not follow, the student is required to prove this by constructing an extension of the orginal diagram that depicts a world that falsifies the claim. More sophisticaed reasoning tasks that combine these can also be given, like "What is the most you can say about the number of cubes left of $d$?" Such a problem might involve identifying $d$, showing that in all worlds compatible with the given information, there are at least three and at most four cubes left of $d$, and finally showing that in some such worlds there are exactly three, while in others there are exactly four.

*Hyperproof* provides, in addition to the facilities for presenting the sorts of information described above, a system of inference rules that allows the student to manipulate the information. The rules include all the usual linguistic rules familiar from first-order logic, but also rules for dealing with the extralinguistic information provided by the diagram. A "keyboard" for use in giving proofs can be found on the right of the screen. Rather than go into detail about these rules, we will illustrate them by means of an example.

Figure 3 shows a sample problem that a student might solve using *Hyperproof.* The goal of this problem (stated at the lower left) is to prove that $d$ is either a cube or small. The given information comes in the form of four sentences plus the information in the diagram. The diagram indicates that one of the objects is named $c$ but does not indicate which objects are named $b$ or $d$. And, as it happens, there is not enough information given to determine which objects are named $b$ or $d$. Another way in which this diagram is incomplete has to do with the size of one of the tetrahedra. The "barrel" with a triangle on it represents a tetrahedron whose size is

---

[3]The one form of uncertainty that our program does not incorporate is uncertainty about the number of objects in the world in question. We allow the user to assume that he can see every object in the world.

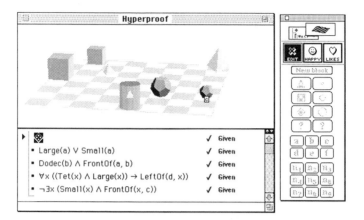

Figure 3: The initial screen.

unknown. (Similar graphical devices are used to represent other forms of partial information.)

The reader might like to solve this problem before reading on. To do so, one needs to know that *FrontOf* means further forward though not necessarily on the same file, and *LeftOf* means to the viewer's left, though not necessarily on the same rank. We will work through one possible solution to this problem.

We start by citing the second sentence to break into two cases (using the rule **Exhaustive Cases**), as shown in Figure 4. In the first of these cases, we have labelled the medium sized dodecahedron *b* and the tetrahedron in front of it *a*. In the second, we have labeled the other dodecahedron *b* and the tetrahedron in front of it *a*. The system permits this breaking into cases only because every blocks world compatible with the original diagram and the cited sentence must also be compatible with one of these two extensions of the diagram. So, for example, had there been another possible dodechahedron in the diagram, these cases would not have been exhaustive, and the program would have required the student to find the missing case or cases.

At this stage, we are in a situation analogous to the Anna example in the preceeding section. Namely, we are not sure which object is *b* but, in either case, we know that the tetrahedron of unknown size is *a*. This allows us to use the rule **Merge Cases** to regain a single diagram containing the information that *a* is the tetrahedron of unknown size. This is shown in Figure 5.

We are now in a position to use the information provided by the first sentence, that *a* is large or small, since we now know which object is *a*. We

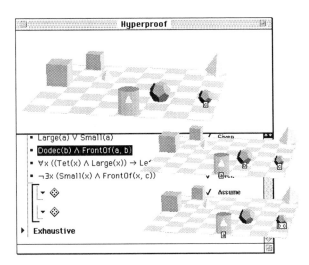

Figure 4: After breaking into cases.

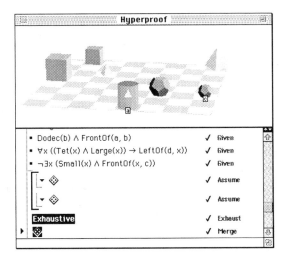

Figure 5: After merging cases.

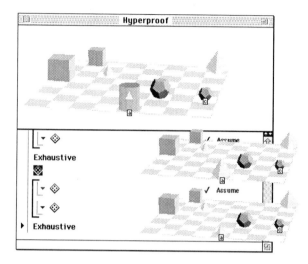

Figure 6: After breaking into cases again.

again use the rule **Exhaustive Cases** to break into cases, one where $a$ is large, the other where $a$ is small. The result is shown in Figure 6.

The second of these cases can be eliminated on the basis of the information contained in the last sentence. This sentence says that there is nothing small in front of $c$, but the diagram Figure 7 indicates that $a$ is both small and in front of $c$. We can thus apply the rule **Close Case** by citing the diagram and the fourth sentence, as shown. The program checks that the sentence is false in any blocks world compatible with the diagram, and so permits this closing, leaving us in the situation depicted in Figure 8.

We next cite the third sentence which says that $d$ is to the left of every large tetrahedron. This allows us to use the rule **Exhaustive Cases** again to break into the three cases shown in Figure 9.

Each of these cases is compatible with all the given information, so we cannot determine which object is $d$. But we observe that the desired conclusion, that $d$ is either a cube or small, holds in each of these cases. Thus, we can use the rule **Inspect**, which allows us to survey all the open cases, verifying that a particular claim holds in all of them. The program displays each open case in turn, evaluates the desired claim, and indicates whether it is true or not before going on to the next case. If the claim holds in all cases, the program indicates that the rule has been successfully applied. This leaves us with the final stage of our proof, as shown in Figure 10.

This example does not illustrate the use of several important rules avail-

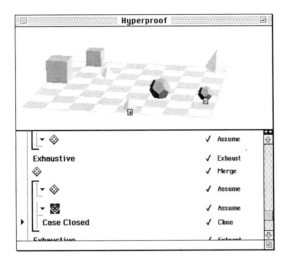

Figure 7: Closing case 2.

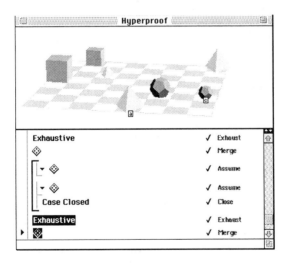

Figure 8: After closing case 2.

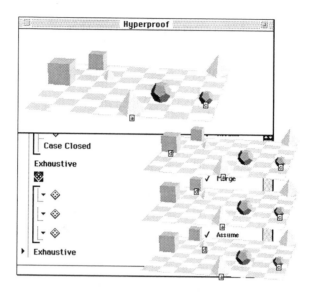

Figure 9: After breaking into cases yet again.

able to the student. For example, it does not show any of the traditional logical rules of inference at work. But it does give a rough feel for the sorts of things one can do using the diagrams.

We have never had the patience to work out a purely linguistic proof of this problem. We have done this exercise for a much simpler problem, where the resulting proof was over 100 lines long, and was quite unintuitive. This was a problem where one could think through the diagramatic solution in one's head with little effort. The present problem is more difficult. We suspect that a purely linguistic proof would be on the order of 200-300 lines, well beyond the reach of any but the most diligent logic student with no date for the weekend.

We believe that programs like *Hyperproof* will aid greatly in teaching students general reasoning skills of use both in mathematics and in everyday life. In part it works by forcing the student to focus on the subject matter of the problem, rather than to resort to purely formal manipulation of symbols. But it also works by exploiting the power of visual representations in reasoning.

The system currently available, (Barwise and Etchemendy [1994]), is restricted to reasoning about blocks worlds. However, a second generation program is in the planning stage. It will provide a toolbox for constructing diagrams of a more abstract and general sort, for use in solving a wide variety of puzzles and problems, typified by the analytic reasoning problems found on the Graduate Record Examination. In particular, it would allow

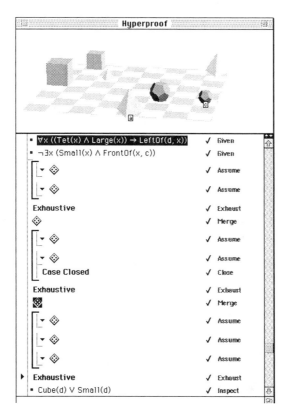

Figure 10: The completed proof.

us to carry out the solution given to Example 2.5.

# 4    Inference as Information Extraction

During the past hundred years, logicians have developed an arsenal of techniques for studying valid inference in the case where all the information is expressed in sentences of a formal language. On the one hand, there are many varieties of deductive systems, ranging from natural deduction to Gentzen's sequent calculus to Hilbert-style formalisms to semantic tableaux. On the other hand, semantic techniques have been developed that allow us to assess the adequacy of given deductive systems. The most widely accepted semantic analysis of consequence represents the information content of a sentence with the collection of structures in which the sentence is true, and declares one sentence to be a consequence of another if the information content of the first is contained in the content of the second, that is, if all the models of the second are models of the first. A deductive system is said to be sound provided that a derivation of one sentence from another is possible only if it is in fact a consequence of that sentence. The system is said to be complete if whenever one sentence is a consequence of another there is in fact a derivation of the one from the other.

These familiar techniques have been tailor made to the homogeneous, linguistic case. When we turn our attention to heterogeneous inference, we need to generalize them along various dimensions. On the one hand, it would be nice to exhibit something comparable to a deductive system that allows us to generate mathematical analogs of valid reasoning, but where the reasoning involves multiple forms of representation. But more importantly, we need a semantic touchstone to assess the adequacy of such reasoning.

In addition to our work on *Hyperproof*, we have been working on developing such a touchstone. There are several challenges to be met. One has to do with simply coming up with a framework that does not presuppose that information is presented linguistically, or, for that matter, in any particular medium. Thus, we need a notion of information and information containment that is independent of the form of representation. Given such a notion, we need to be able to say what it means for a given attempt at a proof to be a genuine proof. And we need a way to say all this without knowing in advance the form in which the information is going to be represented. Our first attempts along these lines are spelled out in the companion article mentioned earlier.

# 5   Conclusions

In the picture of inference that emerges from traditional logic, the vast majority of valid pieces of reasoning—perhaps all—take place in language, and this sort of reasoning is thought to be well understood. We think this picture is wrong on both counts. First, it is wrong in regard to the frequency with which nonlinguistic forms of information are used in reasoning. There are good reasons to suppose that much, if not most, reasoning makes use of some form of visual representation. Second, it is wrong in regard to the extent to which even linguistic reasoning is accounted for by our current theories of inference. As research in semantics over the past twenty years has shown, human languages are infinitely richer and more subtle than the formal languages for which we have anything like a complete account of inference.

When one takes seriously the variety of ways in which information can be presented and manipulated, the task of giving a general account of valid reasoning is, to say the least, daunting. Nevertheless, we think it is important for logicians to broaden their outlook beyond linguistically presented information. As the computer gives us ever richer tools for representing information, we must begin to study the logical aspects of reasoning that uses nonlinguistic forms of representation. In this way we can hope to do something analogous to what Frege and his followers did for reasoning based on linguistic information. Frege made great strides in studying linguistically based inference by carving out a simple, formal language and investigating the deductive relationships among its sentences. Our hope is that the tools we have begun to develop will allow something similar to be done with information presented in more than one mode.

## Comparing visual and linguistic representations

Looking at our theory and examples, we can summarize some of the ways in which diagrammatic representations differ from linguistic representations.

### Closure under constraints

Diagrams are physical situations. They must be, since we can see them. As such, they obey their own set of constraints. In our example from *Hyperproof*, when we represent tetrahedron *a* as large, a host of other facts are thereby supported by the diagram. By choosing a representational scheme appropriately, so that the constraints on the diagrams have a good match with the constraints on the described situation, the diagram can generate a lot of information that the user never need infer. Rather, the user can simply read off facts from the diagram as needed. This situation is in stark contrast to sentential inference, where even the most trivial consequence needs to be inferred explicitly.

## Conjunctive *vs* disjunctive information

It is often said that a picture is worth a thousand words. The truth behind this saying is that even a relatively simple picture or diagram can support countless facts, facts that can be read off the diagram. Thus a diagram can represent in a compact form what would take countless sentences to express. By contrast, sentences come into their own where one needs to describe a variety of mutually incompatible possibilities. For instance, in our *Hyperproof* example, the facts expressed by the various sentences could not themsleves be represented in our first diagram. It is only after we have used other information that we can take advantage of this information in subsequent diagrams.

## Homomorphic *vs* non-homomorphic representation

Another advantage of diagrams, related to the first two, is that a good diagram is isomorphic, or at least homomorphic, to the situation it represents, at least along certain crucial dimensions. In Example 2.5, there is a mapping of certain facts about our two dimensional diagrams to corresponding facts about the three dimensional arrangment of chairs and people. In our Venn diagram proof, there is a homomorphic relationship between regions and sets. This homomorphic relationship is what makes the one a picture, or diagram, of the other. By contrast, the relationship between the linguistic structure of a sentence and that of its content is far more complex. It is certainly nothing like a homomorphism in any obvious way.

## Symmetry arguments

As we have looked at the use of diagrams in solving various sorts of puzzles, we have been struck by the fact that in most such solutions, there is some sort of symmetry argument, either explicit or implicit. We have seen such an argument in the case of Example 2.5. Such arguments often result in a drastic lowering of inferential overhead, by cutting down on the number of cases that need to be explicitly considered. Diagrams often make these symmetry arguments quite transparent.

There are various ways to try to analyze this phenomenon. For instance, in Example 2.5, we can think of each diagram as admitting two distinct readings, and so as representing two distinct cases. Whether or not this is the best analysis of the phenomenon, it seems clear to us that the ability to shortcut the number of cases that need to be considered by appealing to symmetries in the diagrams and the situations they represent is a significant aspect of the power of diagrams in reasoning.

### Perceptual inference

Strictly speaking, the eyes are part of the brain. From the cognitive point of view, however, the perceptual apparatus is fairly autonomous. The sorts of things it does are fairly well insulated from the forms of reasoning we engage in at a conscious level. Nevertheless, the perceptual system is an enormously powerful system and carries out a great deal of what one would want to call inference, and which has indeed been called perceptual inference.

It is not surprising that this is so, given the fact that visual situations satisfy their own family of constraints. Indeed, it is the fact that visual situations do satisfy constraints that has made it possible for our perceptual system to evolve in the way that it has. And so it is not surprising that people use the tools this system provides in reasoning. Indeed, it would be incredible were this not so. Once the ubiquity of visual reasoning is recognized, it would seem odd in the extreme to maintain the myth that it is not used in mathematics.

## Two final remarks

We end by reminding the reader that we are not advocating that mathematics replace linguistic modes of representation by diagrams and pictures. Both forms of representation have their place. Nor are we advocating that logical proofs should be anything less than rigorous. Rather, we are advocating a re-evaluation of the doctrine that diagrams and other forms of visual representation are unwelcome guests in rigorous proofs.

As we have noted, our understanding of valid inference using linguistic modes of representation is far less advanced than is commonly supposed, since the language mathematicians use is far richer than that of first-order logic. This limitation has not blocked progress in mathematics. A full understanding of the power and pitfalls of visual representations is no doubt a long way off. But lack of understanding should not block their use in cases where it is clearly legitimate. Only time and dedication will provide anything approaching a full understanding of the power of visual representation in logic, mathematics, and other forms of human reasoning. But a major impetus for such work can come from the power the computer gives us to use graphical representations in our proofs. For once such tools are in wide use, we logicians will be forced to admit them into our model of mathematical reasoning.

# Chapter II

# Operational Constraints in Diagrammatic Reasoning

Atsushi Shimojima

## 1   Introduction

Diagrammatic reasoning is reasoning whose task is partially taken over by operations on diagrams. It consists of two kinds of activities: (i) physical operations, such as drawing and erasing lines, curves, figures, patterns, symbols, through which diagrams come to encode new information (or discard old information), and (ii) extractions of information diagrams, such as interpreting Venn diagrams, statistical graphs, and geographical maps.

Given particular tasks of reasoning, different types of diagrams show different degrees of suitedness. For example, Euler diagrams are superior in handling certain problems concerning inclusion and membership among classes and individuals, but they cannot be generally applied to such problems without special provisos. Diagrams make many proofs in geometry shorter and more intuitive, while they take certain precautions of the reasoner's to be used validly. Tables with particular configurations are better suited than other tables to reason about the train schedule of a station. Different types of geographical maps support different tasks of reasoning about a single mountain area. Mathematicians experience that coming up with the "right" sorts of diagrams is more than half-way to the solution of most complicated problems.[1]

Perhaps many of these phenomena are explained with reference to aspect (ii) of diagrammatic reasoning because some types of diagrams lets a reasoner retrieve a kind of information that others do not, or lets the

---

[1] Tufte [1984] collects and discusses wide varieties of diagrams used for different tasks of reasoning. Hammer and Shin [1995] discuss possible provisos that supplement Euler diagrams. Barwise and Etchemendy [1991a] cite a good example of a geometry proof shortened by the use of diagrams, and Luengo [1996] develops a proof theory for geometry that embodies the precautions used for geometry diagrams.

reasoner retrieve it more "easily" than others. In fact, this is the approach
that psychologists have traditionally taken. In this chapter, we take a different path and focus on aspect (i) of diagrammatic reasoning. Namely,
we look closely at the process in which a reasoner applies operations to
diagrams and in which diagrams come to encode new information through
these operations. It seems that this process is different in some crucial
points from one type of diagrams to another, and that these differences
partially explain why some types of diagrams are better suited than others to particular tasks of reasoning. The question is: what makes such
differences?

Our hypothesis is partly anticipated in the following passage from Barwise and Etchemendy [1991a]:

> Diagrams are physical situations. They must be, since we can
> see them. As such, they obey their own set of constraints....
> By choosing a representational scheme appropriately, so that
> the constraints on the diagrams have a good match with the
> constraints on the described situation, the diagram can generate
> a lot of information that the user never need infer. Rather, the
> user can simply read off facts from the diagram as needed.

We extract the following two points from this passage: (i) there exists a set
of *operational constraints* that govern the process in which a reasoner constructs diagrams, (ii) depending upon the representation system associated
with the diagrams, these operational constraints may or may not intervene
in the process in which the diagrams encode information.[2] In our view,
the interventions of such operational constraints explain the suitedness or
ill-suitedness of some types of diagrams to particular tasks of reasoning.

Exactly how, if ever, do operational constraints over diagrams intervene in the process of reasoning? This chapter aims to define as accurately
as possible two notions of intervention. In the next two sections, we will
illustrate these two notions with simple examples, and offer first tentative definitions of (i) the conditions in which an operational constraint on
diagrams gives a reasoner a "free ride" from information to information
(section 2), and (ii) the conditions in which an operational constraint imposes "overdetermined alternatives" upon a reasoner (section 3). Using the
notions of free ride and overdetermined alternatives, we will show why some
derivations with diagrams can be shorter than those without, and how some
diagrams end up with so-called "accidental features" that mislead a reasoner. In section 4, we invoke the theory of information being developed by

---

[2]The quoted passage of Barwise's and Etchemendy's also suggests a particular way
in which the constraints governing diagrams facilitate reasoning. We will later discuss
this process under the name of "free ride."

Barwise and others (Barwise [1991], Barwise [1993], Barwise, Gabbay, and Hartonas [1995], Devlin [1991]), and set up a formal framework in which we understand diagrammatic reasoning in general. We will then refine our tentative definitions of free ride and overdetermined alternatives in that formal settings (section 4).[3]

## 2 Free Rides

Let us start by looking at simple cases of free rides.

**Scenario 1**

We use Venn diagrams to check the validity of the following syllogisms:

($\theta_1$) All $C$s are $B$s.

($\theta_2$) No $B$s are $A$s.

($\theta_3$) (Therefore) no $C$s are $A$s.

We start by drawing three circles, labeled "$A$s," "$B$s," and "$C$s" respectively. On the basis of the assumptions $\theta_1$ and $\theta_2$ of the syllogism, we shade the complement of the $B$-circle with respect to the $C$-circle (Figure 1) and then shade the intersection of the $B$-circle and the $A$-circle (Figure 2). Observing that the intersection of the $C$-circle and the $A$-circle is shaded as a result, we read off the conclusion $\theta_3$ of the syllogism, and decide that the syllogism is valid.

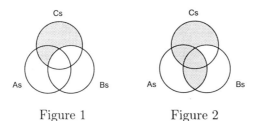

Figure 1                    Figure 2

**Scenario 2**

We use Euler circles to solve the same problem. On the basis of the assumptions $\theta_1$ and $\theta_2$, we draw a circle labeled "$C$s" inside a circle labeled

---

[3]Under the name of "surrogate reasoning," Barwise and Shimojima [1995] discuss reasoning whose task is partially taken over by operations on external aids in general, and present informal definitions of free rides and overdetermined alternatives found in such wider varieties of reasoning.

"*Bs*" (Figure 3), and then draw a circle labeled "*As*" completely outside the *B*-circle (figure 4). We observe that the *C*-circle and the *A*-circle do not overlap, and decide that the syllogism is valid.

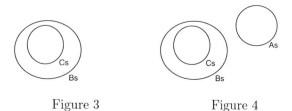

Figure 3                    Figure 4

Each of these scenarios involves a case of "free ride." Let us examine scenario 1 more closely.

Let us call a portion of paper (or of any surface) on which a diagram is drawn a "diagram site." In drawing a Venn diagram on a diagram site, we follow more or less explicit rules of operations. For ease of reference, let *Venn* be the particular method of operations that we adopt in drawing Venn diagrams[4].

We start the derivation by applying an operation of the following type to a blank diagram site:

($\omega_1$) Draw three (partially overlapping) circles, labeled "*As*," "*Bs*," and "*Cs*" respectively.

*Venn* allows this type of action "any time" since the semantic convention associated with it does not assign any semantic value to the resulting diagram. Next, on the basis of the assumption $\theta_1$, *Venn* allows us to:

($\omega_2$) Shade the complement of the *B*-circle with respect to the *C*-circle.

On the assumption $\theta_2$, the *Venn* allows us to:

($\omega_3$) Shade the intersection of the *B*-circle and the *A*-circle.

Now *in virtue of an operational constraint* governing Venn diagrams, this sequence of actions causes the following fact to obtain on the diagram site:

($\sigma_1$) The intersection of a circle labeled "*Cs*" and a circle labeled "*As*" is shaded.

---

[4]Shin [1991] develops a logical system that formalizes an operation method and a semantic convention associated with Venn diagrams. Our description of Scenario 1 assumes her system.

Notice that this fact is a "side-effect" of the actions that we have taken: none of the instructions $\omega_1, \omega_2, \omega_3$ orders us to shade the intersection of the $C$-circle and the $A$-circle. Yet, on the semantic convention associated with Venn diagrams, this fact has an independent semantic value, and lets us read off new information $\theta_3$, a piece of information different from the assumptions $\theta_1$ and $\theta_2$ with which we start. We get the information $\theta_3$ "for free," so to speak.

We find a similar case of free ride in scenario 2. Let *Euler* be the set of operation rules that we follow in drawing Euler circles. On the basis of the assumptions $\theta_1$ and $\theta_2$, *Euler* allows us to:

($\omega_4$) Draw a circle labeled "$C$s" inside a circle labeled "$B$s,"

and then to:

($\omega_5$) Draw a circle labeled "$A$s" completely outside the $B$-circle.

Again, in virtue of an operational constraint on Euler circles, this sequence of actions makes the following fact hold on the diagram site:

($\sigma_2$) A circle labeled "$C$s" appears completely outside a circle labeled "$A$s."

Although neither of the instructions $\omega_4, \omega_5$ entails the realization of the fact $\sigma_2$, the fact $\sigma_2$ has an independent semantic value, and lets us read off the conclusion $\theta_3$ of the syllogism in question. Again, we get the information $\theta_3$ for free.

In each of these scenarios, we get a "free ride" from the premises to the conclusion of the syllogism. The relevant constraints are different in the two scenarios—in Scenario 1, the relevant constraint is one that governs the shadings of different areas of overlapping circles, while in Scenario 2, the relevant constraint is one that governs the enclosure-disclosure relations among circles of different sizes. However, these different constraints spare us the same deduction steps—if we were using the standard first-order calculus, we would have to go through two applications of modus ponens and a universal generalization.

We tentatively define the notion of free rides in the following way:

**Definition 2.1 (Free Ride–Tentative).** We say that a method $\mathcal{M}$ of operations and a semantic convention $\Rightarrow$ provide a *free ride from* the information $\theta, \ldots, \theta'$ *to* the information $\theta^*$ iff the following conditions are satisfied:

1. On the basis of the assumptions $\theta, \ldots, \theta'$, the operation method $\mathcal{M}$ allows a sequence of operations of the types $\omega, \ldots, \omega'$ to be applied to a diagram site.

2. In virtue of a operational constraint governing the diagrams being drawn, any sequence of operations of the types $\omega, \ldots, \omega'$ realizes a fact $\sigma$ on the diagram site.

3. None of the instructions $\omega, \ldots, \omega'$ entails the realization of the fact $\sigma$.

4. On the semantic convention $\Rightarrow$, the fact $\sigma$ encodes the information $\theta^*$.

According to this definition, a free ride is where a reasoner attains a semantically significant fact $\sigma$ in a diagram site, while the instructions of operations that the reasoner has followed do not entail the realization of $\sigma$.[5] Thus, we can view the process as one in which the reasoner has attained the fact $\sigma$ *without taking any step specifically designed for it.* As free rides accumulate in a longer process of derivation, the diagram site encodes a large amount of information after relatively few steps of derivations.[6] This explains the often observed phenomenon that a derivation in diagrams has fewer steps than the corresponding derivation in sentences.

Notice that a free ride is essentially a case in which an operational constraint intervenes in the process of reasoning—a free ride cannot occur without an operational constraint of the kind specified in clause 2 of our definition. Of course, the occurrence of a free ride also depends on the operation method $\mathcal{M}$ and the semantic convention $\Rightarrow$ that the reasoner employs. But once $\mathcal{M}$ and $\Rightarrow$ satisfy the conditions above, the operational constraint intervenes in the process of reasoning, and lets the diagram encode the information $\theta^*$ "automatically," sparing the reasoner an inferential step that would be otherwise required.

It is, however, another issue whether the "free" information $\theta^*$ that the reasoner obtains actually *follows from* the initial assumptions $\theta, \ldots, \theta'$. That is, there may or may not be a constraint (pertinent to the target of the reasoning) that makes $\theta^*$ a consequence of $\theta, \ldots, \theta'$. We will, therefore, distinguish two cases of free rides in the following way:

**Definition 2.2 (Correctness of Free Ride–Tentative).** A free ride from the information $\theta, \ldots, \theta'$ to the information $\theta^*$ is *correct* iff there is a constraint (on the target of the reasoning) that makes $\theta^*$ a consequence of $\theta, \ldots, \theta'$. The free ride is *incorrect* otherwise.

---

[5] We will later give a precise definition of what it is for "an instruction to entail the realization of a fact." For now, let us understand the English phrase by relying on what it intuitively means.

[6] This is the situation that Barwise and Etchemendy characterize by saying, "...the diagram can generate a lot of information that the user never need infer."

Fortunately, both Scenarios 1 and 2 are cases of correct free rides in that there is a (logical) constraint, governing the sets $As$, $Bs$, and $Cs$, that makes $\sigma_3$ a consequence of $\sigma_1, \sigma_2$.

# 3   Overdetermined Alternatives

Barring incorrect ones, free rides are cases in which operational constraints governing diagrams facilitate reasoning. However, there are cases in which operational constraints impede reasoning by imposing what we call "overdetermined alternatives." We will illustrate the process of such interference with two simple examples.

### Scenario 3

We use Euler diagrams to see what conclusions can be deduced from the following premises:

($\theta_1$)  All $Cs$ are $Bs$.

($\theta_2$)  No $Bs$ are $As$.

($\theta_4$)  All $Bs$ are $Ds$.

Knowing that the first two premises are the same as what he had in Scenario 2, we start with drawing the same diagram as in Scenario 2 (Figure 5).

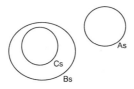

Figure 5

We now want to represent the premise $\theta_4$ in the diagram. This requires us to enclose the $B$-circle in a circle labeled $D$. However, such a $D$-circle must either have no overlap with the $A$-circle (Figure 6) or have some overlap with it (Figure 7). Given the semantic convention that we employ for Euler circles, the first alternative encodes the information that some $Ds$ are $As$, while the second encodes the information that no $Ds$ are $As$. Since neither follows from the given premises $\theta_1, \theta_2, \theta_4$, we cannot take an action required to represent the premise $\theta_4$.

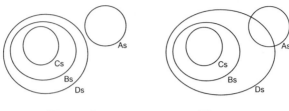

Figure 6                    Figure 7

## Scenario 4

This time, we are given the following set of premises:

($\theta_1$) All $C$s are $B$s.

($\theta_2$) No $B$s are $A$s.

($\theta_5$) All $A$s are $D$s.

We start with drawing the diagram in Figure 5 on the basis of the first two assumptions. Now we want to represent the premise $\theta_5$ in the diagram. This requires us to enclose the $A$-circle in a circle labeled "$D$s." However, such a $D$-circle must either have no overlap with the $B$-circle and the $C$-circle (Figure 8), or overlap only with the $B$-circle (Figure 9), or overlap with both (Figure 10). Again, each alternative indicates a piece of information that does not follow from the given premises $\theta_1, \theta_2, \theta_5$. We must give up representing the premise $\theta_5$ in the diagram.

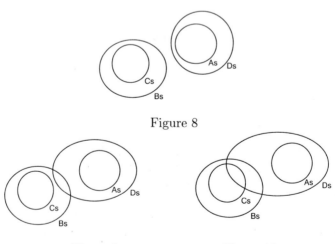

Figure 8

Figure 9                    Figure 10

In each of these scenarios, an operation constraint on diagrams imposes overdetermined alternatives to the reasoner. Let us look at scenario 3 more closely.

Following the operation method *Euler*, we take the following types of actions on the basis of the assumptions $\theta_1, \theta_2$.

($\omega_4$) Draw a circle labeled "$Cs$" inside a circle labeled "$Bs$."

($\omega_5$) Draw a circle labeled "$As$" completely outside the $B$-circle.

Now, on the basis of the assumption $\theta_4$, the *Euler* allows us to:

($\omega_6$) Enclose the $B$-circle in a circle labeled $Ds$.

However, *as a matter of operational constraints*, if an operation of this type is applied after the operations of the types $\omega_4, \omega_5$, one of the following facts comes to hold on the diagram site:

($\sigma_3$) A circle labeled "$Ds$" has no overlap with a circle labeled "$As$."

($\sigma_4$) A circle labeled "$Ds$" overlaps with a circle labeled "$As$."[7]

Both of these facts have independent semantic values—they indicate the following pieces of information respectively:

($\theta_6$) No $Ds$ are $As$.

($\theta_7$) Some $Ds$ are $As$.

Unfortunately, neither piece of information follows from the assumptions $\theta_1, \theta_2, \theta_4$. The alternatives $\sigma_3$ and $\sigma_4$ thus constitute "overdetermined alternatives," which are imposed as long as we try to apply an operation of the type $\omega_6$ after operations of the types $\omega_4, \omega_5$.

Scenario 4 is a similar story. After taking actions of the types $\omega_4, \omega_5$ on the basis of the assumptions $\theta_1, \theta_2$, we wish to represent the premise $\theta_5$ in the diagram. For this purpose, the operation method *Euler* requires us to:

($\omega_7$) Enclose the $A$-circle in a circle labeled "$Ds$."

---

[7]In fact, the alternative $\sigma_4$ has two sub-alternatives:

($\sigma_{4-1}$) A circle labeled "$Ds$" partially overlaps with a circle labeled "$As$."

($\sigma_{4-2}$) A circle labeled "$Ds$" encloses a circle labeled "$As$."

The previous picture for the alternative $\sigma_4$ is for the sub-alternative $\sigma_{4-1}$. For the purpose of illustrating the notion of overdetermined alternatives, however, we do not have to discuss these sub-alternatives.

*As a matter of operational constraints* governing Euler diagrams, however, any sequence of actions of the types $\omega_4, \omega_5, \omega_7$ gives rise to one of the following facts on the diagram site:

($\sigma_5$) A circle labeled "$Ds$" has no overlap with circles labeled "$Bs$" and "$Cs$."

($\sigma_6$) A circle labeled "$Ds$" overlaps with a circle labeled "$Bs$" but has no overlap with a circle labeled "$Cs$."

($\sigma_7$) A circle labeled "$Ds$" overlaps with circles labeled "$Bs$" and "$Cs$."[8]

On the semantic convention we adopt, these alternative states of affairs indicate the following pieces of information respectively:

($\theta_8$) No $Ds$ are $Bs$ and no $Ds$ are $Cs$.

($\theta_9$) Some $Ds$ are $Bs$ but no $Ds$ are $Cs$.

($\theta_{10}$) Some $Ds$ are $Bs$ and some $Ds$ are $Cs$.

Unfortunately, none of these follows from the given premises, $\theta_1$, $\theta_2$, and $\theta_5$. Thus, we must either give up representing the premise $\theta_5$ or tolerate that the diagram represents one of the above invalid conclusions.

We tentatively define the notion of overdetermined alternatives as follows:

**Definition 3.1 (Overdetermined Alternatives–Tentative).** We say that a method $\mathcal{M}$ of operations and a semantic convention $\Rightarrow$ impose *overdetermined alternatives on the assumptions* $\theta, \ldots, \theta'$ iff the following conditions are satisfied:

1. On the basis of the assumptions $\theta, \ldots, \theta'$, the operation method $\mathcal{M}$ allows a sequence of operations of the types $\omega, \ldots, \omega'$ to be applied to a diagram site.

2. In virtue of an operational constraint governing the diagrams being drawn, any sequence of operations of the types $\omega, \ldots, \omega'$ realizes at least one of alternative facts $\sigma, \ldots, \sigma'$.

3. On the semantic convention $\Rightarrow$, each fact in $\sigma, \ldots, \sigma'$ encodes a piece of information that does not follow from the initial assumptions $\theta, \ldots, \theta'$.

---

[8]Each of the alternatives $\sigma_6, \sigma_7$ has two sub-alternatives, concerning enclosure and partial overlapping between circles. Again, it is not essential to list them separately for the purpose of illustrating the notion of overdetermined alternatives.

As in the cases of free ride, the occurrence of overdetermined alternatives heavily depends on the operation method $\mathcal{M}$ and the semantic convention $\Rightarrow$ that a reasoner adopts. However, once $\mathcal{M}$ and $\Rightarrow$ meet the above conditions, an operational constraint governing diagrams interferes in the process of reasoning—it prevents the reasoner from taking a prescribed sequence of actions without thereby realizing a fact that encodes an unwarranted piece of information. This fact is "accidental" in the sense that (if ever realized on the diagram site) it is realized *by an arbitrary choice* from several alternatives. In many cases, it misleads the reasoner by letting us read off the unwarranted information that it encodes. These are the cases that are usually described as "appealing to an accidental feature of a diagram."

# 4    A Formal Model

Now that we have an intuitive grasp of free rides and overdetermined alternatives, let us polish our definitions by embedding them in a more formal framework.

## Framework

As we can see from the examples in our scenarios, diagrammatic reasoning consists of two kinds of activities: (i) operating upon a diagram site according to a set of operation rules, and (ii) reading off information from a diagram site according to a semantic convention. We see this process as an intentional one: there is always some object, a target, that the reasoner is reasoning *about*. Starting with the concept of *target of reasoning*, we will formalize the following concepts used in the previous sections: *diagram site, semantic convention, operation on diagrams, sequence of operations, effect of operation, methods of operations*, and *constraint*.

**The domain of targets**    The target of reasoning is the object about which the reasoner manipulates information in reasoning. We assume that the target $t$ of reasoning is a certain situation, which can be classified by *states of affairs*, or *infons*, holding in it.[9] Given a target situation $t$, we choose the set $\Theta$ of states of affairs that can *possibly* classify $t$ (members of $\Theta$ need not be true of $t$), and choose the set $T$ of situations that members of $\Theta$ can possibly classify. Let us call the pair $\mathcal{T} = \langle T, \Theta \rangle$ of these two sets the *domain of target situations*, and use the notations $Sit(\mathcal{T})$ and $Soa(\mathcal{T})$ to denote the sets $T$ and $\Theta$ respectively. If a state of affairs $\theta$ holds in a target situation $t$, we write $t \models \theta$ and say that $t$ *supports* $\theta$. We stipulate

---

[9]We use the notions of "states of affairs" and "infons" interchangeably.

that $Soa(\mathcal{T})$ is closed under the top $\top$, the negation $\neg$, the implication $\supset$, and the disjunction $\wedge$, with their usual truth-functional interpretations.

For example, the target situation of the reasoning in Scenario 1 is a fictional situation $t_1$ that has the classes of $As$, $Bs$, and $Cs$ as constituents. Although the existence of $t_1$ is merely postulated for the purpose of the logic exercise, we count $t_1$ as a member of $Sit(\mathcal{T})$ for a certain domain $\mathcal{T}$. The pieces of information $\theta_1, \theta_2, \theta_3$ are members of $Soa(\mathcal{T})$ since all of them can sensibly classify $t_1$ even though $t_1$ may not actually support ($\models$) some of them.

**The domain of diagram sites**   A diagram site is itself a situation in the world, and as such it belongs to its own domain of classification, just as a target situation does. Namely, we assume that every diagram site $s$ belongs to a class $S$ of diagram sites that a collection $\Sigma$ of infons classifies, and that the pair $\mathcal{S} = \langle S, \Sigma \rangle$ forms a domain of diagram sites. We use the same notations $\models$, $Sit$, and $Soa$ for a domain of diagram sites. The set $Soa(\mathcal{S})$ is closed under $\top$, $\neg$, $\supset$, and $\wedge$.

If a diagram site $s$ is used to reason about a target $t$, we write $s \rightsquigarrow t$, and say that $s$ *signals* $t$. Thus, $\rightsquigarrow$ is a binary relation from $Sit(\mathcal{S})$ to $Sit(\mathcal{T})$. If $s \rightsquigarrow t$, we say that the domain $\mathcal{S} = \langle S, \Sigma \rangle$ to which $s$ belongs is the *source domain* for the domain $\mathcal{T} = \langle T, \Theta \rangle$ to which $t$ belongs.

An example of a diagram site is the particular portion of the paper on which we drew a Venn diagram in Scenario 1. The portion of the paper *before* the first operation is taken to be a different diagram site from the same portion *after* the operation. This latter diagram site is in turn different from the portion of the paper after the second operation, which in turn is different from the portion of the paper after the third operation. Thus, if $s_0, s_1, s_2, s_3$ are diagrams sites divided by the three operations in Scenario 1, $s_0, s_1, s_2, s_3$ are all different members of $Sit(\mathcal{S})$. An example of infon in $Soa(\mathcal{S})$ is the state of affairs $\sigma_1$ that partially characterizes the portion of the paper after the third operation. Observe that $s_3 \models \sigma_1$ but neither $s_0 \models \sigma_1$ nor $s_1 \models \sigma_1$ nor $s_2 \models \sigma_1$, because the intersection of the $C$-circle and the $A$-circle gets shaded only after the third operation. Each of $s_1, s_2, s_3$ signals $\rightsquigarrow$ the target situation $t_1$, since we use these diagram sites to reason about $t_1$.

**The indication relation**   How can a reasoner read off a piece of information about the target situation from a diagram site? Usually, a reasoner perceives that a state of affairs $\sigma$ holds in a diagram site $s$, and with reference to a semantic convention associated with diagrams drawn on $s$, the reasoner reads off a piece of information that a state of affairs $\theta$ holds in the target situation $t$. Thus, the semantic convention must relate the states of affairs $\sigma$ that classify diagrams sites to the states of affairs $\theta$ that classify target situations. We thus model a semantic convention by a binary relation $\Rightarrow$ from the set $Soa(S)$ of infons in the domain of diagram sites to the set $Soa(T)$ of infons in the domain of target situations. We say that an infon $\sigma$ *indicates* an infon $\theta$ if $\sigma \Rightarrow \theta$.[10] A reasoner reads off a piece of information $\theta$ about the target $t$ from a diagram site $s$ only if $s$ is used as a signal for $t$ and there is an $S$-infon $\sigma$ such that $s \models \sigma$ and $\sigma \Rightarrow \theta$.

In Scenario 1, for example, we read off the information $\theta_3$ about the target situation $t_1$ from the diagram site $s_3$ because $s_3 \rightsquigarrow t_1$ while $s_3$ supports the infon $\sigma_1$ and $\sigma_1$ indicates $\Rightarrow$ the infon $\theta_3$.

**The domain of operations**  Consider the three actions that we take in Scenario 1. We draw three circles, labeled "As," "Bs," "Cs," shade the complement of the $B$-circle with respect to the $C$-circle, and then shade the intersection of the $B$-circle and the $A$-circle. These all involve starting with an initial diagram site $s_I$, performing some action $a$ (or sequence of actions) on it, and getting a new diagram site $s_O$. It is useful to think of these actions in realistic terms, as certain kinds of events in the world that start with an initial situation and result in another situation; we write this as $s_I \overset{a}{\longmapsto} s_O$, which is read "action $a$ has $s_I$ as input diagram site and $s_O$ as output diagram site." So, $\longmapsto$ is a tertiary relation on $Sit(S) \times Sit(A) \times Sit(S)$. We stipulate that each action has unique input site and output site.

Since actions are particular events in the world, they constitute their own classification domain, just as diagram sites and their target situations do. Thus, we assume that there is a domain $A$ of actions, consisting of a class $Sit(A)$ of actions and a class $Soa(A)$ of infons that classify these actions. We use the notations $\models$, $Sit$, and $Soa$ for a domain of actions too, and stipulate that the set $Soa(S)$ is closed under $\top$, $\neg$, $\supset$, and $\wedge$.

For example, if $a_1, a_2, a_3$ are the three actions taken in Scenario 1, then $a_1, a_2, a_3$ are all members of $Sit(A)$ for some domain $A$ of actions, and $s_0 \overset{a_1}{\longmapsto} s_1$, $s_1 \overset{a_2}{\longmapsto} s_2$, and $s_2 \overset{a_3}{\longmapsto} s_3$. Also, the *types* $\omega_1, \omega_2, \omega_3$ that classify these actions in Scenario 1 are members of $Soa(A)$, and $a_1 \models \omega_1$, $a_2 \models \omega_2$, and $a_3 \models \omega_3$. Other examples of infons for actions are $\omega_4, \omega_5$ in Scenario 2, $\omega_6$ in Scenario 3, and $\omega_7$ in Scenario 4.

**Sequences of operations**  The actions $a_1, a_2, a_3$ in Scenario 1 form a "sequence" of actions in that the output diagram site $s_1$ of the action $a_1$ is the input site for the action $a_2$, and the output site $s_2$ of the action $a_2$ is the input site for the action $a_3$. To model this notion of "sequence

---

[10]The pair $L = \langle \rightsquigarrow, \Rightarrow \rangle$ of a signaling relation and an indicating relation provides what Barwise [1991] has called a "link" between the domain of source situations and the domain of target situations.

of actions," we introduce a partial binary associative operation $\circ$, called *composition*, on the set $Sit(\mathcal{A})$ of operations, with $Sit(\mathcal{A})$ closed under $\circ$. We stipulate that for all actions $a, a'$ in $Sit(\mathcal{A})$ and for all diagram sites $s, s'$ in $Sit(\mathcal{S})$, $a \circ a'$ is defined and $s \xmapsto{a \circ a'} s'$ iff there is a diagram site $s^*$ in $Sit(\mathcal{S})$ such that $s \xmapsto{a} s^*$ and $s^* \xmapsto{a'} s'$. For example, $a_1 \circ a_2 \circ a_3$ is defined and $s_0 \xmapsto{a_1 \circ a_2 \circ a_3} s_3$, since $s_0 \xmapsto{a_1} s_1$, $s_1 \xmapsto{a_2} s_2$, and $s_2 \xmapsto{a_3} s_3$.

We also introduce a total binary associative operation $\circ$ on the set $Soa(\mathcal{A})$ of infons that classify actions, and stipulate that $Soa(\mathcal{A})$ is closed under $\circ$. Thus, for any infons $\omega, \omega'$ in $Soa(\mathcal{A})$, $\omega \circ \omega'$ is itself an infon that classify operations. Naturally, an action $a^*$ supports an infon $\omega \circ \omega'$ if and only if there are actions $a, a'$ such that $a^* = a \circ a'$ and $a \models \omega$ and $a' \models \omega'$. For example, the action $a_1 \circ a_2 \circ a_3$ supports the infon $\omega_1 \circ \omega_2 \circ \omega_3$, since $a_1 \models \omega_1$, $a_2 \models \omega_2$, and $a_3 \models \omega_3$.[11]

**Translation functions *in* and *out***  Notice that the classification of operations is *not* completely independent of the classification of the diagram sites to which they are applied. In many cases, we describe an action by specifying what it achieves. In Scenario 1, for example, we describe the action $a_3$ with the infon $\omega_3$, as "shading the intersection of the $A$-circle and the $B$-circle." In doing so, we are not referring to the type of movement involved in the action, but to the difference that the action makes to the diagram site to which it is applied. The action $a_3$ can be described as "shading the intersection of the $A$-circle and the $B$-circle" *because* the intersection of the $A$-circle and the $B$-circle is not shaded in the input site for $a_3$ and the intersection of the $A$-circle and the $B$-circle is shaded in the output site for $a_3$.[12]

In our framework, this means two things: (i) some infons $\omega$ in $Soa(\mathcal{A})$ work as the "translations" of some infons $\sigma$ in $Soa(\mathcal{S})$ in the sense that an action $a$ supports $\omega$ if and only if the *input* site of $a$ supports $\sigma$, and (ii) some

---

[11] The idea of composing actions by the operation $\circ$ is borrowed from Barwise, Gabbay, and Hartonas [1995]. Our operation $\circ$ on $Sit(\mathcal{A})$ corresponds to their operation $\circ$ on "channels," and our operation $\circ$ on $Soa(\mathcal{A})$ corresponds to their operation $\circ$ on "expressions" of a type language $L$. They also discuss the binary operations $\rightarrow$, $\downarrow$, and $\leftarrow$ in expressions of $L$, which can be used to describe actions (and their effects) in interesting ways.

[12] The distinction of these two different ways of classifying actions is originated in Israel, Perry, and Tutiya [1991] and Israel, Perry, and Tutiya [1993], although they characterize the distinction in a different theoretical setting. They see actions as properties of agents, and divide actions into the two categories: executions and accomplishments. In their framework, executions are properties of agents that are identified by the types of their movements, and accomplishments are properties of agents that are identified by the effects of their movements. In contrast, we use the term "actions" to denote concrete events rather than properties of agents, and conceive the two categories of actions simply as two different ways of classifying these events.

infons $\omega'$ in $Soa(\mathcal{A})$ work as the "translations" of some infons $\sigma'$ in $Soa(\mathcal{S})$ in the sense that an action $a$ supports $\omega'$ if and only if the *output* site of $a$ supports $\sigma'$. We model these two different schemes of translation by two functions *in* and *out* from $Soa(\mathcal{S})$ into $Soa(\mathcal{A})$. Naturally, the translation functions *in* and *out* satisfy the following conditions: for all infons $\sigma$ and $\sigma'$ in $Soa(\mathcal{S})$ and for all actions $a$ in $Sit(\mathcal{A})$, $a$ supports $in(\sigma)$ if and only if the input site for $a$ supports $\sigma$, and $a$ supports $out(\sigma')$ if and only if the output site for $a$ supports $\sigma'$. We stipulate that both functions preserve the operations $\top$, $\neg$, $\supset$, and $\wedge$, namely, $out(\top) = \top$, $in(\neg\sigma) = \neg in(\sigma)$, $out(\sigma \supset \sigma') = out(\sigma) \supset out(\sigma')$, $in(\sigma \wedge \sigma') = in(\sigma) \wedge in(\sigma')$, and so on.[13]

For example, we can model the $\mathcal{A}$-infon $\omega_3$, "Shade the intersection of the $A$-circle and the $B$-circle," as the conjunction of the *in*-translation of the $\mathcal{S}$-infon "The intersection of the $A$-circle and the $B$-circle is not shaded" and the *out*-translation of the $\mathcal{S}$-infon "The intersection of the $A$-circle and the $B$-circle is shaded." As we expect, an action supports $\omega_3$ if and only if the input site for the action supports the first $\mathcal{S}$-infon and the output site for the action supports the second $\mathcal{S}$-infon.

**Methods of operations**   Our notion of "method of operation" is a generalization of the notion of "rule of inference" in logic. Roughly speaking, a method of operations is a set of instructions that specify what types of actions can be taken under what circumstances. For the purpose of this chapter, we can model such a system of instructions by means of a class $\mathcal{M}$ of pairs $\langle \theta, \omega \rangle$ of infons from $Soa(\mathcal{T})$ and $Soa(\mathcal{A})$. Intuitively, an individual instruction $\langle \theta, \omega \rangle$ allows the following action: if the target situation supports $t \models \theta$, carry out any action $a$ such that $a \models \omega$. If $\Theta$ is a set of target infons, we say that the method of operations $\mathcal{M}$ *allows* an action *of the type* $\omega$ on the *assumptions* $\Theta$ if and only if (i) there is an action in $Sit(\mathcal{A})$ that supports $\omega$ and (ii) if $\omega$ is not a composition, then $\mathcal{M}$ contains a member $\langle \theta, \omega \rangle$ such that $\theta \in \Theta$ or $\theta = \top$, and (iii) if $\omega$ is a composition $\omega' \circ \omega''$, then $\mathcal{M}$ allows an action of the type $\omega'$ and an action of the type $\omega''$ on the assumptions $\Theta$. Due to condition (i), an operation method $\mathcal{M}$ can allow an operation of the type $\omega' \circ \omega''$ on the assumptions $\Theta$ without allowing an operation of the type $\omega'' \circ \omega'$ on the same assumptions.

The operation method $Venn$, for example, can be considered to contain members $\langle \top, \omega_1 \rangle$, $\langle \theta_1, \omega_2 \rangle$, and $\langle \theta_2, \omega_3 \rangle$. Thus, in Scenario 1, $Venn$ allows the first action $a_1$ of the type $\omega_1$ on the empty assumption $\emptyset$, allows the second action $a_2$ of the type $\omega_2$ on the assumption $\{\theta_1\}$, and allows the third action $a_3$ of the type $\omega_3$ on the assumption $\{\theta_2\}$. It also follows that $Venn$ allows all these actions on the assumptions $\{\theta_1, \theta_2\}$. Since there is

---

[13]The idea of using the functions *in* and *out* in modeling certain properties of actions is already suggested in Example 9 in Barwise, Gabbay, and Hartonas [1995]. The paper uses the notations $l$ and $r$, instead of *in* and *out*.

an action $a_1 \circ a_2 \circ a_3$ that supports $\omega_1 \circ \omega_2 \circ \omega_3$, we can say that the method *Venn* allows an operation of the type $\omega_1 \circ \omega_2 \circ \omega_3$ on the assumptions $\{\theta_1, \theta_2\}$.

**Constraints on target situations**   The reader may have wondered why we need the notions of *domain* of target situations, of diagram sites, and of operations, in addition to the notions of target situation, diagram site, and operations. The main reason is that the notion of classification domain lets us model the notion of constraint naturally.

Let us look at the case of target situations first. Given a domain $\mathcal{T}$ of target situations, we assume the set $Sit(\mathcal{T})$ of situations exhausts all the situations that are logically possible. Thus, we can use $Sit(\mathcal{T})$ to define the logical consequence relation $\models$ in the following way: for all subsets $\Theta, \Theta'$ of $Soa(\mathcal{T})$, $\Theta \models \Theta'$ iff for every situation $t$ in $Sit(\mathcal{T})$, if $t$ supports every infon in $\Theta$, then $t$ supports at least one infon in $\Theta'$. We can conceive $\models$ as the model of the weakest system of constraints governing target situations.

Now, take a subset $T_\ell$ of $Sit(\mathcal{T})$, and define a consequence relation $\models_{T_\ell}$ in the following analogous manner: for all subsets $\Theta, \Theta'$ of $Soa(\mathcal{T})$, $\Theta \models_{T_\ell} \Theta'$ iff for every situation $t$ in $T_\ell$, if $t$ supports every infon in $\Theta$, then $t$ supports at least one infon in $\Theta'$. This relation $\models_{T_\ell}$, which we call a "local" consequence, is stronger than the logical consequence relation $\models$ in the sense that $\Theta \models_{T_\ell} \Theta'$ implies $\Theta \models \Theta'$ for all $\Theta, \Theta'$. Thus, we can conceive $\models_{T_\ell}$ as the model of a stronger, extra-logical system of constraints that govern certain target situations.

What is the point of defining a local consequence relation $\models_{T_\ell}$ along with the logical consequence relation? Let $\mathcal{M}$ and $\Rightarrow$ be an operation method and a semantic convention adopted in a diagrammatic reasoning. Then, there is a range of "normal" target situations that $\mathcal{M}$ and $\Rightarrow$ are designed to cover, and there is a system of "target" constraints that reasoning with $\mathcal{M}$ and $\Rightarrow$ is supposed to capture. This system of target constraints often consists of special, extra-logical constraints, such as geometrical laws, physical laws, and social conventions, depending upon the application $\mathcal{M}$ and $\Rightarrow$ are designed for. We model the range of normal target situations by a subset $T_\ell$ of $Sit(\mathcal{T})$, and model the system of target constraints by the local consequence relation $\models_{T_\ell}$ defined by $T_\ell$. We assume that for any pair of an operation method $\mathcal{M}$ and a semantic convention $\Rightarrow$, there is a local consequence relation $\models_{T_\ell}$ associated with it. Thus, target situations outside $T_\ell$ are logically possible, but "abnormal" situations fall outside of the coverage of $\mathcal{M}$ and $\Rightarrow$. The local consequence $\models_{T_\ell}$ is usually stronger than the logical consequence $\models$, but when $\mathcal{M}$ and $\Rightarrow$ are designed to capture only the logical consequence governing target situations, $\models_{T_\ell}$ and $\models$ coincide. The operation methods *Venn* and *Euler* adopted in our scenarios are both such methods.

**Constraints on diagrams sites and operations**   We apply the same
technique to the domain $S$ of diagram sites and the domain $\mathcal{A}$ of operations
and define two consequence relations, logical and local, for each domain.
Thus, if $S_\ell$ is a subset of $Sit(S)$, $\models_{S_\ell}$ denotes the local consequence relation
over $S$ defined in terms of $S_\ell$. Similarly, if $A_\ell$ is a subset of $Sit(\mathcal{A})$, $\models_{A_\ell}$
denotes the local consequence relation over $\mathcal{A}$ defined in terms of $A_\ell$. We
use the same notation $\models$ to denote the logical consequence relations over
both domains.

Given an operation method $\mathcal{M}$ and a semantic convention $\Rightarrow$, there
is a range of "normal" operations for which $\mathcal{M}$ and $\Rightarrow$ are designed, and
a system of operational constraints under which $\mathcal{M}$ and $\Rightarrow$ are designed
to work. In our framework, a subset $A_\ell$ of $Sit(\mathcal{A})$ models the range of
such "normal" operations, and the local consequence relation $\models_{A_\ell}$ models
the system of constraints on which $\mathcal{M}$ and $\Rightarrow$ rely. Operations outside $A_\ell$
are logically possible, but "abnormal" operations constitute exceptions to
the given operation method $\mathcal{M}$. Furthermore, there is a range of normal
diagram sites for which $\mathcal{M}$ and $\Rightarrow$ are designed, and a system of constraints
on diagram sites under which $\mathcal{M}$ and $\Rightarrow$ are designed to work. As you may
expect, we model this range of normal diagram sites by a subset $S_\ell$ of
$Sit(S)$, and use the local consequence relation $\models_{S_\ell}$ to model the system of
constraints on diagram sites upon which $\mathcal{M}$ and $\Rightarrow$ rely.

We stipulate that every normal operation starts at and results in normal
diagram sites—namely, for all members $a$ in $Sit(\mathcal{A})$ and all members $s, s'$ in
$Sit(S)$, if $a \in A_\ell$ and $s \xmapsto{a} s'$, then $s, s' \in S_\ell$. Given this assumption, the
following proposition is easy to prove: for all $\sigma, \sigma'$ in $Soa(S)$, if $\sigma \models_{S_\ell} \sigma'$,
then both $in(\sigma) \models_{A_\ell} in(\sigma')$ and $out(\sigma) \models_{A_\ell} out(\sigma')$.[14] This means that
every local constraint on diagram sites is reflected in a local constraint on
actions taken on them and influences the effects of those operations.

Let us look at an example. In Scenario 1, we assumed that whenever we draw three (partially overlapping) circles, labeled "As," "Bs," and
"Cs" respectively, shade the complement of the $B$-circle with respect to the
$C$-circle, and shade the intersection of the $B$-circle and the $A$-circle, the
intersection of a circle labeled "Cs" and a circle labeled "As" is shaded.
In our framework, this means that there holds a *local* operational con-
straint: $\omega_1 \circ \omega_2 \circ \omega_3 \models_{A_\ell} out(\sigma_1)$. However, this is not a *logical* constraint:
$\omega_1 \circ \omega_2 \circ \omega_3 \not\models out(\sigma_1)$. There are some exceptional circumstances in which
it does not hold. Think of drawing the diagram with the toy pen whose
"magic" ink fades away a few seconds after it is put on paper, or imagine
drawing the diagram into a computer which automatically distorts, moves,
and sometimes erase what you draw. In these circumstances, even if you

---

[14]For readability, we omit the curly braces surrounding a singleton when it is the
antecedent or the consequent of a constraint. Thus, "$\sigma \models_{S_\ell} \sigma'$" is an abbreviation of
"$\{\sigma\} \models_{S_\ell} \{\sigma'\}$." Similarly for "$in(\sigma) \models_{A_\ell} in(\sigma')$" and "$out(\sigma) \models_{A_\ell} out(\sigma')$."

execute all the operations described above, there is no guarantee that the intersection of a circle labeled "$As$" and a circle labeled "$Cs$" gets shaded. Nevertheless, the operational constraint from $\omega_1 \circ \omega_2 \circ \omega_3$ to $out(\sigma_1)$ is fairly reliable—reliable enough for the operation method $Venn$ to depend on it in Scenario 1.

Even if we bar the above tricky circumstances, and assume that everything that we draw is preserved until the end of the derivation, the constraint from $\omega_1 \circ \omega_2 \circ \omega_3$ to $out(\sigma_1)$ is still not a logical necessity. The constraint holds because the following geometrical (or topological) constraint holds on the diagram site: if both the complement of the $B$-circle with respect to the $C$-circle and the intersection of the $B$-circle and the $A$-circle are shaded in a normal diagram site, the intersection of the $C$-circle and the $A$-circle is also shaded in the diagram site. This is a case in which a local constraint on diagram sites is reflected in a local constraint on operations and supports the working of an operation method.[15]

In clause 2 of our tentative definition of free ride, we used the sentence "None of the instructions $\omega, \ldots, \omega'$ entails the realization of the fact $\sigma$." We can now explicate this clause by means of the notion of logical consequence $\models$ upon operations. Intuitively, it means that none of the instructions $\omega, \ldots, \omega'$ logically implies the realization of the fact $\sigma$. Formally put, it means that for every infon $\omega^*$ in $\{\omega, \ldots, \omega'\}$, $\omega^* \not\models out(\sigma)$ for the *logical* consequence $\models$. For example, when we say that none of the instructions $\omega_1, \omega_2, \omega_3$ in Scenario 1 entails the realization of the fact $\sigma_1$, it means that for every infon $\omega^*$ in $\{\omega_1, \omega_2, \omega_3\}$, $\omega^* \not\models out(\sigma_1)$. For one thing, it is not the case that $\omega_1 \models out(\sigma_1)$. It is far from a logical necessity that an action of the type $\omega_1$ be an action that realizes the fact $\sigma_1$—in most cases, drawing three (partially overlapping) circles labeled "$As$," "$Bs$," and "$Cs$" does not result in a diagram site in which the intersection of the $C$-circle and the $A$-circle is shaded. Likewise, neither $\omega_2 \models out(\sigma_1)$ nor $\omega_3 \models out(\sigma_1)$.

To sum up, given a particular process of diagrammatic reasoning, there are several elements associated with it:

- a domain of target situations $\mathcal{T} = \langle Sit(\mathcal{T}), Soa(\mathcal{T}) \rangle$, coupled with a subset $T_\ell$ of $Sit(\mathcal{T})$ that characterizes the local consequence relation $\models_{T_\ell}$,

- a domain of diagram sites $\mathcal{S} = \langle Sit(\mathcal{S}), Soa(\mathcal{S}) \rangle$, coupled with a subset $S_\ell$ of $Sit(\mathcal{S})$ that characterizes the local consequence relation $\models_{S_\ell}$,

---

[15]In Shimojima [1995], we heavily used the notion "geometrical constraints on diagrams" in the sense of the local consequence $\models_{S_\ell}$ on diagram sites, and tried to model free rides (and what I called "half rides") in its terms. The current chapter takes a different path, and uses the local consequence *on operations* to model free rides and overdetermined alternatives.

- a domain of actions $\mathcal{A} = \langle Sit(\mathcal{A}), Soa(\mathcal{A}) \rangle$, coupled with a subset $A_\ell$ of $Sit(\mathcal{A})$ that characterizes the local consequence relation $\models_{A_\ell}$,

- a binary indication relation $\Rightarrow$ holding between $Soa(\mathcal{S})$ and $Soa(\mathcal{T})$,

- a binary signaling relation $\leadsto$ holding between $Sit(\mathcal{S})$ and $Sit(\mathcal{T})$,

- a tertiary input/output relation $\mapsto$ on $Sit(\mathcal{S}) \times Sit(\mathcal{A}) \times Sit(\mathcal{S})$,

- two translation functions *out* and *in* from $Soa(\mathcal{S})$ into $Soa(\mathcal{A})$, and

- a method $\mathcal{M}$ of operations: a binary relation on $Soa(\mathcal{T}) \times Soa(\mathcal{A})$.

We call a combination $\Re = \langle \mathcal{T}, \mathcal{S}, \mathcal{A}, T_\ell, S_\ell, A_\ell, \Rightarrow, \leadsto, \mapsto, out, in, \mathcal{M} \rangle$ of these elements a *diagrammatic representation system*.

## Redefining Free Rides and Overdetermined Alternatives

This framework lets us make our tentative definitions of free ride and overdetermined alternatives more rigorous. We will first present the refined definitions, and use examples in the previous scenarios to illustrate the definitions. All the definitions assume that a particular diagrammatic representation system $\Re = \langle \mathcal{T}, \mathcal{S}, \mathcal{A}, T_\ell, S_\ell, A_\ell, \Rightarrow, \leadsto, \mapsto, out, in, \mathcal{M} \rangle$ is given.

**Definition 4.1 (Free Ride–Refined).** Let $\theta, \ldots, \theta'$ and $\theta^*$ be $\mathcal{T}$-infons. The representation system $\Re$ provides a *free ride from* the information $\theta, \ldots, \theta'$ *to* the information $\theta^*$ iff there are $\mathcal{A}$-infons $\omega, \ldots, \omega'$ and an $\mathcal{S}$-infon $\sigma$ such that:

1. On the assumptions $\{\theta, \ldots, \theta'\}$, the method $\mathcal{M}$ allows an action of the type $\omega \circ \ldots \circ \omega'$.

2. The following operational constraint holds: $\omega \circ \ldots \circ \omega' \models_{A_\ell} out(\sigma)$.

3. For every $\mathcal{A}$-infon $\omega^*$ in $\{\omega, \ldots, \omega'\}$, $\omega^* \not\models out(\sigma)$.

4. The $\mathcal{S}$-infon $\sigma$ indicates the $\mathcal{T}$-infon $\theta^*$ on the semantic convention $\Rightarrow$.

**Definition 4.2 (Correctness of Free Ride–Refined).** A free ride from the information $\theta, \ldots, \theta'$ to the information $\theta^*$ will be called *correct* if $\theta, \ldots, \theta' \models_{T_\ell} \theta^*$. It is *incorrect* otherwise.

**Definition 4.3 (Overdetermined Alternatives–Refined).** Let $\theta, \ldots, \theta'$ be $\mathcal{T}$-infons. The representation system $\Re$ imposes *overdetermined alternatives on the assumptions* $\theta, \ldots, \theta'$ iff there are $\mathcal{A}$-infons $\omega, \ldots, \omega'$ and $\mathcal{S}$-infons $\sigma, \ldots, \sigma'$ such that:

1. On the basis of assumptions $\{\theta, \ldots, \theta'\}$, the method $\mathcal{M}$ allows an action of the type $\omega \circ \ldots \circ \omega'$.

2. The following operational constraint holds:
$$\omega \circ \ldots \circ \omega' \models_{A_\ell} \{out(\sigma), \ldots, out(\sigma')\}.$$

3. On the semantic convention $\Rightarrow$, each of the $\mathcal{S}$-infons $\sigma, \ldots, \sigma'$ indicates at least one $\mathcal{T}$-infon $\theta^*$ such that $\{\theta, \ldots, \theta'\} \not\models_{T_\ell} \theta^*$.

Let us see how these definitions capture free rides and overdetermined alternatives occurring in our previous scenarios.

Scenario 1 is a case in which a representation system associated with Venn diagrams provides a correct free ride from the information $\theta_1, \theta_2$ to the information $\theta_3$. To wit, the method of operations $Venn$ allows a sequence of actions of the type $\omega_1 \circ \omega_2 \circ \omega_3$ on the assumptions $\{\theta_1, \theta_2\}$. While none of the instructions $\omega_1, \omega_2, \omega_3$ entails the realization of the fact $\sigma_1$, this sequence of actions is constrained to realize $\sigma_1$ on the diagram site in which it results. That is, while $\omega^* \not\models out(\sigma_1)$ for every member $\omega^*$ in $\{\omega_1, \omega_2, \omega_3\}$, the operational constraint, $\omega_1 \circ \omega_2 \circ \omega_3 \models_{A_\ell} out(\sigma_1)$ holds. Now the fact $\sigma_1$ indicates an infon $\theta_3$ on the semantic convention $\Rightarrow$ in effect. Fortunately, $\{\theta_1, \theta_2\} \models_{T_\ell} \theta_3$. We thus obtain a correct free ride from the information $\theta_1, \theta_2$ to the information $\theta_3$.

Scenario 2 can be modeled in a similar way, where the relevant operational constraint is: $\omega_4 \circ \omega_5 \models_{A_\ell} out(\sigma_2)$. The operation method $Euler$ allows a sequence of actions of the type $\omega_4 \circ \omega_5$ on the assumptions $\{\theta_1, \theta_2\}$, and in virtue of the above constraint, this sequence of actions realizes a fact $\sigma_2$ on its output site. Although neither $\omega_4 \models out(\sigma_2)$ nor $\omega_5 \models out(\sigma_2)$, the fact $\sigma_2$ indicates a piece of information $\theta_3$ via the semantic convention $\Rightarrow$ in effect. Thus, we get a correct free ride from $\theta_1, \theta_2$ to $\theta_3$ just as in Scenario 1, but in virtue of a different operational constraint.

Scenario 3 involves a case of overdetermined alternatives. The operation method $Euler$ allows a sequence of actions of the type $\omega_4 \circ \omega_5 \circ \omega_6$ on the assumptions $\{\theta_1, \theta_2, \theta_4\}$. However, the operational constraint, $\omega_4 \circ \omega_5 \circ \omega_6 \models_{A_\ell} \{out(\sigma_3), out(\sigma_4)\}$ holds. Thus, this sequence of operations realizes $either$ $\sigma_3$ or $\sigma_4$ on the diagram site in which it results. On the semantic convention $\Rightarrow$ in effect, however, $\sigma_3, \sigma_4$ indicate $\theta_6, \theta_7$ respectively. Unfortunately, neither $\theta_6$ nor $\theta_7$ follows from the initial assumptions $\theta_1, \theta_2, \theta_4$—that is, neither $\{\theta_1, \theta_2, \theta_4\} \models_{A_\ell} \theta_6$ nor $\{\theta_1, \theta_2, \theta_4\} \models_{A_\ell} \theta_7$. Thus, Scenario 3 is a case in which the representation system associated with Euler circles imposes the overdetermined alternatives $\sigma_3, \sigma_4$ on the assumptions $\theta_1, \theta_2, \theta_4$.

The same representation system imposes overdetermined alternatives also on the assumptions $\theta_1, \theta_2, \theta_5$, due to the following operational constraint: $\omega_4 \circ \omega_5 \circ \omega_7 \models_{A_\ell} \{out(\sigma_5), out(\sigma_6), out(\sigma_7)\}$. In Scenario 4, the operation method *Euler* allows a sequence of actions of the type $\omega_4 \circ \omega_5 \circ \omega_7$ on the assumptions $\{\theta_1, \theta_2, \theta_5\}$. However, because of the above operational constraint, this sequence of actions realizes at least one of the facts $\sigma_5, \sigma_6, \sigma_7$. Unfortunately, each of $\sigma_5, \sigma_6, \sigma_7$ indicates an infon that does not follow from the initial assumptions $\{\theta_1, \theta_2, \theta_5\}$—the infons $\sigma_5, \sigma_6, \sigma_7$ respectively indicate $\theta_8, \theta_9, \theta_{10}$ while neither $\{\theta_1, \theta_2, \theta_5\} \models_{T_\ell} \theta_8$ nor $\{\theta_1, \theta_2, \theta_5\} \models_{T_\ell} \theta_9$ nor $\{\theta_1, \theta_2, \theta_5\} \models_{T_\ell} \theta_{10}$.

# 5  Conclusions

Throughout this chapter, we have been trying to identify, as accurately as possible, two ways in which operational constraints over diagrams intervene in the process of reasoning. As a result, we hope, the notions of free ride and overdetermined alternatives have become clear enough to convince the reader that there are such phenomena, and that they are rooted in constraints that govern the constructions of the diagrams to be drawn.

With these two notions at hand, we can now give a partial answer to the question posed in the introduction. Depending upon what representation system is associated with a diagram, there may or may not be free rides and overdetermined alternatives in the process of the diagram's encoding information through operations. The presence or absence of free rides and overdetermined alternatives in this process are two of the important factors that determine the suitedness of the particular type of diagrams to a task of reasoning. More specifically, if a task of reasoning involves an inference from the information $\theta, \ldots, \theta'$ to the information $\theta^*$, then the presence of a free ride from $\theta, \ldots, \theta'$ to $\theta^*$ in this process makes the type of diagrams more suited to the task. On the other hand, if a task of reasoning involves any inference based on the assumptions $\theta, \ldots, \theta'$, then the presence of overdetermined alternatives on the assumptions $\theta, \ldots, \theta'$ makes the type of diagrams less suited to the task.[16]

This is, however, only a beginning of the project. There are at least two directions in which we can further develop our model of diagrammatic reasoning.

First, there are vast arrays of diagrammatic reasoning to be explored, from everyday life to scientific fields such as statistics, geography, and even pure mathematics. It is yet to be seen (i) how our notions of free ride and overdetermined alternatives extend to these real-life examples of reasoning

---

[16]These statements should be read under the proviso that "the other conditions are the same." In particular, the representation system developed in Barwise and Etchemendy [1994] contains an operation rule called "case exhaustives," which allows a reasoner to extract only valid conclusions in the case of finite overdetermined alternatives. Under this rule, the presence of overdetermined alternatives is not necessarily a threat to the utility of the given type of diagrams.

and explain the suitedness and ill-suitedness of the diagrams used in them. The study of wider varieties of diagrammatic reasoning may also yield explicit answers to the following questions: (ii) why a representation system that provides more free rides tends to impose more cases of overdetermined alternatives, and (iii) how different representation systems can be combined to provide a maximal number of correct free rides about a target domain while preventing incorrect free rides and overdetermined alternatives[17].

Second, the focus of this chapter has been entirely upon the processes in which a diagram site comes to encode new information through the operations applied to it. To keep this focus clear, we have made the methodological assumptions that every individual operation is comprehensible and executable with the same ease, no matter what type of operation it is, and that once information is encoded in a diagram, it is retrievable from the diagram with the same ease, no matter how it is encoded in it. However, in order for our model to fully capture the suitedness and ill-suitedness of different types of diagrams to different tasks of reasoning, we should abandon these methodological assumptions, and address the issues of the ease of comprehending and executing individual operations and the ease of retrieving information from diagram sites. Although we do believe that operational constraints over diagrams play a role in these aspects of diagrammatic reasoning, the notions of free ride and overdetermined alternatives, as defined in this particular chapter, have nothing to say about them[18].

---

[17]Furthermore, Barwise and Seligman [1995] are developing a rich mathematical theory around the notions "classification domain," "indication" and "signaling" between classification domains, and "translations" from a classification domain to another. If embedded in such a mathematical framework, our notions of free ride and overdetermined alternatives will obtain more rigor, with their information-theoretic implications fully explicated.

[18]In Shimojima [1995], we tried to analyze the ease of comprehending and executing a certain diagrammatic action, and pointed to another pattern of constraint-intervention under the name of "half ride." Although we still believe that there are such phenomena, we no longer subscribe to that particular definition of half ride.

# Chapter III

# Diagrams and the Concept of Logical System

Jon Barwise and Eric Hammer

In attempting to analyze the notion of a logical system, there are various approaches that could be taken. One would be to look at the things people have called logical systems and try to develop a natural framework which would encompass most or many of these, and then explore the consequences of the framework, seeing what else falls under the framework and what the consequences of the general notion happen to be. This was basically the approach taken, for example, in Barwise [1974], one of the early attempts to develop such a framework.

This approach has much to recommend it, but it also has at least two serious drawbacks. It is too dependent on accidents of history, that is, on what particular systems of logic people happened to have developed. There is at least the theoretical possibility that biases of precedent and fashion have played a significant role in the way things have gone. If so, the abstraction away from practice has the danger of codifying these historically-contingent biases, making them appear like necessary features of a logical system. The flip side of this problem is that there may well be some unnatural logical systems which contort the framework. But how else could one proceed in an attempt to get a principled notion of logical system?

Another approach, the one we take here, is to look at the existing logical systems that people happened to have developed and to try to see what they were up to in more general terms. Our hope is to find some interesting natural phenomenon lurking behind these systems, a "natural kind," if you will. If there is such a natural phenomenon, it could be used to guide the formulation of an abstract notion of logical system.

If a characterization of logical systems could be found using this approach, it would have potentially two significant advantages over the more orthodox approach. First, it would provide a basis from which one could give a principled critique of existing systems claimed to be logical systems. Second, though, it would point out gaps, that is, logical systems which have yet to be developed.

Thus, in this chapter we argue that there is a natural way to understand most logical systems, that this leads to a natural notion of logical system (however, we do not completely spell out the details here), and that there are indeed many logical systems yet to be developed. To be honest, this chapter was motivated in the opposite way, from our conviction that there are many logical systems yet to be developed, logical systems that are quite different in some important respects from most of the logical systems being studied.

# 1    The Standard Story

Let us begin by rehearsing the story one usually tells by way of motivating the study of some particular formal system of logic.

Motivation comes from trying to capture formally certain sorts of instances of logical consequence. For example, from "Ahab is neither tired nor wants to go home," one can infer "It is not the case that Ahab is either tired or wants to go home." And from "Sue is tired and wants to go home" follows "Sue wants to go home."

Any number of different logical systems can model the validity of such inferences. Propositional logic, one of the simplest logical systems, begins with the observation that these inferences do not depend on the particular meanings of "Ahab," "Sue," "is tired," or "wants to go home." Their validity is due solely to the meanings of the words "and," "neither...nor," "or," and "not." Propositional logic looks at these statements in terms of grammatical units built up from atomic sentence letters using "and," "or," and "not," and interprets these sentence letters by truth values, interpreting more complex sentences in such a way as to respect the intuitive meaning of the connectives. The first inference mentioned above would be represented in the system by replacing "Ahab is tired" by some letter "P" and "Ahab wants to go home" by some other letter "Q." The premise would then be represented by "not-P and not-Q" and the conclusion by "not-(P and Q)." The validity of the inference would then be captured in the system by the fact that any assignment of truth values to "P" and "Q" making the premise true is also an assignment which makes the conclusion true.

Such a system may also include syntactic rules for deriving one sentence from another which preserve truth value. So a second way the inference might be modeled in the system is by the existence of a proof in the system of the conclusion from the premise using these syntactic rules.

Beyond such familiar targets of logical analysis, i.e., those concepts traditionally thought of as "logical constants", logical systems can account for the validity of inferences involving *any* well-defined concept. For example, from the premises "There are infinitely many primes" and "Only one prime is even" it follows that "There are infinitely many primes that are not even" in virtue of the meanings of "infinitely many," "only one," and "there are." Just as with inferences depending on the meanings of "and," "or," and "not," there are logical systems which model inferences depending on the meaning of "infinitely many." Similarly, there are logics for dealing with inductive definitions, transitive closures of relations, cardinalities like "uncountably many," and so on.

When we look beyond mathematics we find logical systems which attempt to model inferences involving concepts expressed by words like "necessarily," "possibly," "always," "knows," and the like. There are also logical systems which break away from strictly logical inference, trying to model notions of plausible inference and default inference.

Further, logical systems have attempted to model "natural reasoning". Relevance logics, for example, were originally motivated by the desire to model the difference between using relevant and irrelevant information in the course of carrying out some argument. In another direction, distinctions between natural deduction systems and Hilbert-style deduction systems rest on how they model the process of reasoning. New developments, like linear logic, attempt to model reasoning where resource considerations are vital. For example, if we are attempting to develop automatic proof systems, we may want to restrict the ability to use a given premise more than once.

Logical systems always have either a mathematical semantics or a proof theory; sometimes they have both. A model-theoretic semantics for a logical system, when one is given, is a mathematical model explicating what it is that makes one sentence a logical consequence of another sentence. A proof theory, by contrast, gives a precise answer to the question of how we can go about showing in the system that one sentence is a consequence of others. Based on the observations above, we propose the following informal characterization of logical system:

**Thesis** A *logical system* is a mathematical model of some pretheoretic notion of consequence and an existing (or possible) inferential practice that honors it.

This thesis is intended to be relatively neutral between logical systems based primarily on semantic considerations and those based primarily on proof-theoretic considerations. The difference is seen as a matter of what aspect of inference one is modeling. Some logical systems model both aspects explicitly while others leave one or the other aspect implicit, as not being something the model is trying to capture.

It is not to be thought that everything that has been called a logical system fits perfectly with this thesis, any more than that everything that has been called gold is gold. But we do claim that most of the systems people have called logical systems do fit the thesis, and that it provides a useful way to understand work on logical systems. It allows us to judge them on their own ground; to relate existing systems, and to develop, investigate, and use new logical systems.

## Mathematical models of inference

The thesis can be refined in several ways. For one thing, in this chapter we intend that "inference" be taken to concern relationships among structured representations in some sort of conventional representation system. A broader notion of inference would include non-conventional inference. For example, it could be said that one infers the sentence "There is someone at the door" from certain knocking sounds heard at certain places. While it is of interest to develop mathematical models of inference thus broadly construed, we are not inclined to think of them as *logical* systems, so we restrict attention to the narrower class.

An understanding of the thesis obviously presupposes an understanding of the nature of mathematical modeling more generally. We take mathematical modeling to be the process whereby some natural phenomenon is idealized and represented within the universe of mathematical objects. Consider mathematical models of the weather. Such a model may be a good one or a poor one, depending on how close a fit there is between the model and the actual weather. One of the ways we judge a mathematical model is to see how well its predictions conform to our experience with the phenomenon modeled. A good model has a good fit and can then be used in interesting ways. For example, it might be simulated on a computer to make long-range predictions.

There is much to be said about mathematical modeling, but space restricts us to three points that are most important for our project. The first is that there is a difference between a model and the thing modeled. No one would confuse a mathematical model of the weather with the weather itself. The weather can flood the basement; the model cannot.

The second point is that the same phenomenon (in our case the same inference practice) can be modeled in many different ways. Consider for an example the different sorts of systems of first order logic: Hilbert-style systems, natural deduction systems, resolution systems, analytic tableaux systems, Gentzen systems and so on. In a sense these are all mathematical models of the very same inference practice since they are extensionally equivalent. They all agree with one another on what follows from what, on what is inconsistent, and on what is logically true, etc.

While these systems are all models of the same inference practice, say first-order inference in mathematics, they nonetheless each provide a different perspective on it. Hilbert-style systems, for example, provide a particularly simple and elegant model of what can be shown to follow from what, but they fail to reflect accurately the actual rules of proof employed. Natural deduction systems are much less elegant, yet fairly nicely reflect the structure of the proofs people actually give. Resolution systems again are a perfectly good model of derivability, but similarly fail to reflect the proof structure of actual practice. But resolution systems remain of interest since they are much easier to implement on a computer than natural deduction and Hilbert-style systems. Finally, Gentzen systems are of interest because they are particularly well-suited to metamathematical study of the model itself.

A model of first-order inference must at least capture its most coarse-grained features: it must provide a characterization of logical consequence which is faithful to the informal practice being modeled. For just this purpose a mere non-effective listing would suffice. But one is generally interested in more than just pure extensional adequacy, hence the diversity of systems of first-order logic. Different systems capture some of the more fine-grained features of the inference practice. One may provide an effective procedure for listing all logical truths, another may reflect the structure of the informal proofs given, and so on.

This same point holds for any other phenomenon to be mathematically modeled. Any model of the weather, for example, must satisfy certain minimal conditions, such as providing an accurate description of weather conditions. But just as with modeling inference, there are also more fine-grained features one may also be interested in, such as how current conditions depend on larger weather patterns. For any given phenomenon to be modeled, there simply is no single one mathematical model of interest.

The third point about models has to do with the idealizations necessary for mathematically modeling natural phenomena. The world is typically too complex to model everything that is relevant to some phenomenon. Idealizations must be made even to get the project off the ground; this is just one of the rules of the game.

Part of the evidence for our thesis is that it is fairly easy to see the idealizations being made in typical logical systems. They include such things as the following, though some may be irrelevent in case of logical systems that ignore either the consequence (semantics) or the inference (proof theory):

**Idealization 1.1** Each representational object of the system has an unambiguous syntactic structure.

In other words, for each such representational object it is determinate what its parts are and how they are arranged.

**Idealization 1.2** The well-formed representations are finite and linear in form and so can be modeled by finite sequences of symbols.

This is to say that it is assumed that the well-formed representations resemble the sentences of a written human language, in contrast to something like a picture or a diagram.

**Idealization 1.3** The content of a given well-formed object is unambiguous.

While in actual practice context may be needed to disambiguate a given syntactic object, this assumption presupposes that this context has been adequately captured by the system.

**Idealization 1.4** The consequence relation between meaningful objects of the system is a function of this syntax alone, whether or not there are effective rules for determining this relation.

This idealization arises from the assumptions that the content of representation is completely determined by its syntactic structure, and that the consequence relation is a function of the contents of the representations.

**Idealization 1.5** The grammar and the semantics of the system are finitely specifiable.

**Idealization 1.6** Limitations on the complexity and size of the well-formed objects and of proofs are ignored.

There are certainly examples of logical systems that do not make all of these idealizations. This only points out that they are idealizations, ones that may turn out to be a problem. If a model is based on the assumption that some particular aspect of a phenemona is peripheral, and that aspect is in fact a major aspect, then the model will be flawed. For example, one may be interested in developing a formal system with the property of having a fixed polynomial $P(n)$ such that for every sentence of length $n$ provable in the system, there is a proof of it in the system of length less than $P(n)$, all of the sentences of which are also bounded in length by $P(n)$. For this sort of system, one cannot make Idealization 1.6, since it abstracts away from the very features one is interested in.

Given that these are idealizations, ones which may have to be abandoned, the question arises as to which, if any, should be built into an analysis of the notion of a logical system. We intend our thesis to be silent on this matter. We think that it should be possible to develop interesting models which abandon any of these idealizations, though maybe not all at once.

As a particular type of example of logical systems not meeting all the idealizations above, in this chapter we examine several *diagrammatic* systems and several *heterogeneous* systems, both types of which violate Idealization 1.2. By a "heterogeneous" system we mean one that seeks to model inferences carried out between two or more different types of representations. Of particular interest is inference between sentences and diagrammatic or other non-linguistic representations.

As examples of diagrammatic logics we discuss logics of Venn diagrams, Euler diagrams, existential graphs, and geometry diagrams. As examples of heterogeneous logics we discuss Hyperproof, a logic of charts and sentences, and a logic of first-order sentences and Venn diagrams. These are all examples of inferential practices where Idealization 1.2 is clearly and importantly false.

After presenting these example systems we examine some of the properties of diagrammatic and heterogeneous systems. In particular, we address the following sorts of questions. Can anything useful be said about the general features that make a representation system diagrammatic? Are there, as is usually assumed, special difficulties with having a sound diagrammatic logic? What are the potential advantages of using a diagrammatic system to model a given inference practice? What domains are particularly well-suited for diagrammatic/heterogeneous treatment? And, finally, in light of the various systems examined, what can be said about what a logical system is?

# 2   Examples of Diagrammatic Logics

## Venn diagrams and Euler circles

The following is a sketch of a formalization of a system of Venn diagrams incorporating ideas found in Venn [1971], Peirce [1933], Shin [1991a], and Hammer and Danner [1995]. The well-formed diagrams of the system are built up from the five basic types of primitive objects: rectangles used to represent the universe, closed curves used to represent subsets of it, shading used to assert emptiness of a set, and Xs connected by lines used to assert non-emptiness.

Well-formed diagrams consist of a rectangle within which are drawn any number of closed curves (labeled by names), with the restriction that they overlap one another in an appropriate way. Any area can be shaded and any area can contain a chain of Xs connected by lines. This is all described more fully in Shin [1991a] and Hammer and Danner [1995].

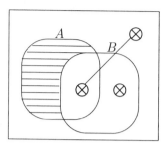

Figure 1: A Venn diagram.

Figure 1 displays a well-formed diagram. The shading or hatching asserts that the set represented by that region is empty, that nothing is $A$ and not $B$. The single X asserts non-emptiness of the set represented, that something is $B$ and not $A$; the chain of two Xs connected by a line asserts that something is either both $A$ and $B$ or else neither.

The semantics for the system is simply a mathematical representation of the intuitive meaning just sketched. Models[1] consist of a set along with an interpretation function mapping the rectangle to the whole set and closed curves to subsets of it, and curves sharing the same label to the same subset. Whether a diagram is true in a model depends on which of its areas are shaded and which of them have a chain of Xs connected by lines. A diagram $D$ is a "logical consequence" of a set $\Delta$ of diagrams if and only if every model of each diagram in $\Delta$ is a model of $D$.

Formal proofs can also be carried out by means of rules of inference including the following:

**Extending Sequences** Any chain of Xs can be extended by additional Xs separated by lines. This rule corresponds to the addition of new disjuncts to a sentence.

**Erasure** The shading occurring in any region can be erased. Any entire X-sequence can be erased. A closed curve can be erased provided that each minimal region having shading that would be unbounded upon erasure of the curve is first erased. This rule is the counterpart of conjunction-elimination.

**Shortening Sequences** A link of an X-sequence can be removed and the two halves reconnected provided that the link falls within shading.

---

[1]Here "model" is being used in its standard model-theoretic sense as opposed to its use above in "mathematical model." It should always be clear from context in what way we are using the term.

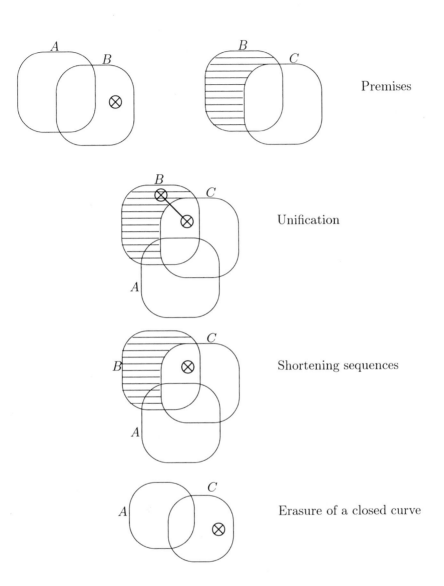

Premises

Unification

Shortening sequences

Erasure of a closed curve

Figure 2: A proof using Venn diagrams.

**Unification** $D_3$ follows from $D_1$ and $D_2$ by unification if the set of labels of $D_3$ is the same as the set of labels occurring in either $D_1$ or $D_2$, and for each shading (X-sequence) occurring in a region of either $D_1$ or $D_2$ there is a corresponding region of $D_3$ also having a shading (X-sequence), and vice versa. This rule is similar to conjunction-introduction, allowing one to combine the information of two diagrams.

An example of a proof is given in Figure 2. Shin [1991a] proved that for finite sets $\Delta$, a diagram is provable from $\Delta$ if and only if it is a logical consequence of $\Delta$; the result is extended to arbitrary sets $\Delta$ in Hammer and Danner [1995].

A variation of the system above utilizes an alternative to shading for asserting the emptiness of a set, namely containment or disjointness of curves. The syntax of this system allows curves to be drawn within a rectangle in any arrangement whatsoever. Shading and X-sequences are allowed to appear in diagrams as before. A well-formed Euler diagram is shown in Figure 3.

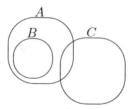

Figure 3: An Euler diagram.

Models are exactly as in the Venn system. Truth of a diagram $D$ in a model is slightly different, though X-sequences and shading are handled as before. An additional clause states that if $A$ and $B$ are sets that partition the set of curves of a diagram $D$ (one of them possibly empty) and if no area of $D$ falls within each curve in $A$ and outside each curve in $B$, then the intersection of the interpretations of all the curves in $A$ is such that subtracting from it each of the interpretations of the curves in $B$ results in the empty set. So the diagram in Figure 3 asserts that no $B$ is $C$, all $B$ are $A$, and, subsequently, that nothing is simultaneously $A$, $B$, and $C$.

Directed edges can also be added to the syntax as a mechanism for representing binary relations diagrammatically as in Harel [1987a] and Hammer [1995a]. An example is shown in Figure 4. Intuitively the diagram asserts that some $P$ bears the relation $R$ to every $Q$, and, by the arrangement of the closed figures, that no $P$ is $Q$. Additional rules of inference for such a system allow one to manipulate edges appropriately; for example, if an end of an edge contacts a closed curve within which occurs an X-sequence, then

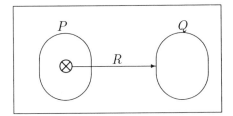

Figure 4: An example of a higraph.

the end can be moved inwards to that X-sequence. This would be similar
to a form of universal instantiation.

## Peirce's Existential Graphs

The Alpha part of Peirce's existential graphsis a diagrammatic system
equivalent in expressive and deductive power to propositional logic. It was
proposed in Peirce [1933] and later studied and modified in Zeman [1964]
and Roberts [1933]. The Beta part, discussed in the following section, is
equivalent to first-order logic. Further extensions of the system studied by
Peirce incorporate higher-order and modal quantification.

Figure 5: An existential graph.

The grammatical resources of the system are minimal. Graphs are
constructed from propositional letters $P, Q, \ldots$ and "cuts" or drawn closed
figures. The syntax is simple: any two cuts of a graph must be such that
one is contained within the other or else is entirely separated from the
other, and any letter must fall either entirely within or entirely outside of
each cut.

Juxtaposition of elements of a graph has the same effect as conjunction.
A cut acts as the negation of the "conjunctive" claim within. Figure 5
displays an Alpha graph. This graph can be read in at least two different
but logically equivalent ways: it can be read as asserting $\neg(P \wedge \neg(Q \wedge P))$;

alternatively, it can be read as a conditional, with what is nested within one cut being the antecedent and what is nested within two cuts the consequent, as $P \to (Q \land P)$.

It is fairly obvious what the semantics of the graphs will be. An "assignment function" assigns truth values to letters. Such an assignment function is then uniquely extendable to an evaluation $v$ assigning truth values to entire graphs according to the following restrictions. A subgraph consisting of the juxtaposition of sentence letters is assigned truth if and only if each sentence letter is. A subgraph consisting of a cut drawn around another subgraph is assigned falsehood if and only if at least one of the enclosed immediate subgraphs is assigned falsehood. Finally, the juxtaposition of several subgraphs is assigned truth if and only if each of the juxtaposed subgraphs is assigned truth. This is explained more explicitly in the references cited.

The rules of inference are very simple. Call a subgraph "evenly enclosed" if it falls within an even number of cuts or else does not fall within a cut. Otherwise it is "oddly enclosed." The following rules are sound and complete with respect to the semantics:

**Double Cut** Two cuts may be drawn around or removed from any subgraph of a graph. This corresponds to double negation.

**Erasure** Any evenly enclosed subgraph may be erased. This corresponds to strengthening an antecedent.

**Insertion** Any graph may be drawn on an existing graph provided it is thereby oddly enclosed. This corresponds to weakening a consequent.

**Iteration** Any subgraph occurring in a graph may be recopied on the graph provided it is enclosed by every cut enclosing the subgraph copied. This is similar to the rule: from $A \to B$, infer $A \to (A \land B)$.

**Deiteration** Any subgraph which could have been drawn by an application of the Iteration rule can be erased. This is analogous to: from $A \to (A \land B)$, infer $A \to B$.

The Beta part of Peirce's Existential Graphs is a diagrammatic logical system equivalent to first-order logic. The propositional letters of the Alpha part are replaced by predicates of each arity. Each $n$-ary predicate symbol has $n$ "hooks" or argument places that can be quantified over. The Beta equivalent of a quantifier is a drawn, heavy "line of identity." A single line of identity can have any number of branches and still be a single line, provided all these branches are connected. Each line corresponds to a distinct quantifier.

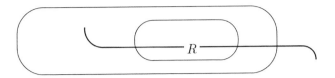

Figure 6: A Beta graph.

The syntax is the same as for the Alpha part, except for the following two conditions. Lines of identity can cross cuts, and each hook of a predicate must be contacted by exactly one line of identity.

Cuts behave just as in the Alpha part. The precedence of one quantifier (line of identity) over another is determined by whether the one has some portion less deeply nested within cuts than the other. First, therefore, those lines having parts enclosed by no cuts are read, then those having parts enclosed by one cut are read, then those whose least enclosed parts are enclosed by two cuts, and so on.

Consider the Beta graph in Figure 6. It has two lines of identity, a one-place predicate $P$ and a two-place predicate $R$. The right-hand line of identity is the one with a least deeply embedded part, so it takes precedence over the other. Unelegantly, translating cuts as negations and lines of identity as existential quantifiers, it would be read as $\exists x \neg (\exists y \neg R(y, x))$. A more sympathetic reading would translate the oddly embedded line of identity universally: $\exists x \forall y R(y, x)$.

Rules for the Beta part extend those of the Alpha part. A full description is rather involved, as can be seen from Zeman [1964], so some examples will have to suffice: the rule of Double Cut is as before, except that lines of identity are allowed to cross both cuts; the rule of Breaking a Line of Identity allows one to erase part of an evenly enclosed line of identity. A proof of the Beta analog of $\exists x(P(x) \wedge Q(x)) \rightarrow \exists x P(x)$ is shown in Figure 7. In actual practice, one would not recopy the original with each step, but rather erase and add to a single graph. To capture the dynamic process on the printed page, however, it is necessary to recopy a graph each time a rule is applied.

## A Logic of Geometry Diagrams

The most notorious fallacies involving the use of diagrams have been in geometry. Nevertheless, by making the syntax and semantic content of the sort of diagrams typically used clear, one can use them in perfectly rigorous proofs. This topic of the formal logic of geometry diagrams in

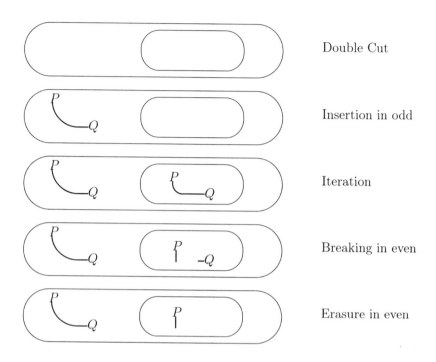

Figure 7: A proof in Beta of $\exists x(P(x) \wedge Q(x)) \rightarrow \exists x P(x)$.

heterogeneous and diagrammatic proofs is currently being studied by Luengo [1995].

Diagrams are taken to be configurations of various syntactic primitives like drawn lines, points, labels, congruence indicators for angles and line segments, and parallel line indicators, all drawn within a rectangle. For example, Figure 8 displays a diagram of such a formal system. Intuitively it asserts that the two lines labeled by "$\int$" refer to parallel lines, and that line $AB$ intersects these lines at point $A$ and point $B$.

There are some particularly interesting issues concerning such geometry diagrams. One involves the construction rules typically employed in their informal use. Geometry diagrams assert something about a structured domain satisfying various constraints, perhaps Hilbert's axioms. These constraints ensure the existence of various objects, such as a point between any two points on a given line or a point not on a given line, a line through any two points, and so on. To be faithful to actual practice, the semantics of a diagrammatic system must legitimate such construction rules.

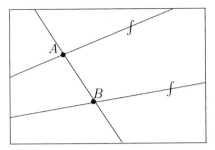

Figure 8: A geometry diagram.

The following is a sketch of such a semantics. A model $M$ for a diagram $D$ consists of disjoint sets of "points" and "lines" and of a "lying on" relation between points and lines, a "between" relation between triples of points, a "parallel" relation between pairs of lines, and a "congruence" relation between pairs of pairs of points (congruence of segments) and between pairs of pairs of lines (congruence of angles). These must satisfy, say, Hilbert's axioms. $M$ also assigns a line to each drawn line in $D$ and a point to each drawn point in $D$. $D$ is true in $M$ provided these interpretations are such that the congruence and parallel assertions made in the diagram by use of the drawn indicators are preserved by the interpretation in the obvious way, and likewise for the diagrammatic assertions of a point being on a particular line.

The notion of logical consequence is then defined in such a way as to allow the application of construction rules to $D$ as well as other rules (such as erasure of a point, a line or an indicator). For example, the fact that it is valid to draw a new point between two points of $D$ falling on some single drawn line follows from the fact that one can extend the interpretation function of $M$ so as to assign a point in the model bearing the appropriate relations to the referents of the two original, drawn points. Logical consequence, then, is defined in terms of being able to extend interpretation functions in appropriate ways.

Such a definition fairly accurately reflects actual usage of diagrams in plane geometry proofs. One typically constructs a diagram step-by-step, perhaps starting with given assumptions, then adding new lines and points to it in accordance with the nature of the space in question. Finally, having manipulated the diagram in useful ways, one is able to read conclusions off the diagram, thereby showing them to be consequences of the original premises. The sort of semantics sketched here validates such inferential practices.

# 3   Examples of Heterogeneous Logics

Heterogeneous logical systems are logics having both linguistic and non-linguistic elements, such as diagrams, charts, tables, etc. They are very important with respect to our main thesis since a great deal of inference involving non-linguistic representations combines the non-linguistic with the linguistic. Sentences are commonly inferred from diagrams, tables, and charts; likewise, sentences are commonly applied to existing diagrams, tables, and charts. Accurate models of such inference will need to take this heterogeneity into account. We now describe some examples of heterogeneous logics.

## Hyperproof

The historically first example of a formal, heterogeneous system is Hyperproof (Barwise and Etchemendy [1991a], Barwise and Etchemendy [1994])[2].

## A logic of charts

We next look at a different sort of heterogeneous logic, one that uses charts as first-class representations. Charts exist because they provide a very convenient way of presenting some kinds of information. They are also very useful in certain sorts of reasoning, especially reasoning involving systematic matching of objects: last names with first names, owner with dog, etc. Typical examples of such reasoning tasks are found in the sort of problems given in the analytic section of the Graduate Record Exam or in logic puzzle books, though charts are obviously of use in many other contexts. Since they are also simple, they serve as a good case study of how one can give a rigorous mathematical model of an existing inferential practice that clearly violates Idealization 1.2.

For problems usefully solved with a chart, one typically chooses a particular sort of chart tailored to the peculiarities of the problem at hand. Making a good choice of representational conventions is always important in solving a problem, but especially true of charts. This sensitivity of type of chart to the particularities of the task at hand makes a very general logic of charts useless. There are as many logics of charts as there are different sorts of charts that can be useful in solving problems. The specific system presented here should be taken to be illustrative rather than exhaustive of the topic. It is merely a system for solving a particular sort of chart problem. For modeling the reasoning involved in other sorts of chart problems,

---

[2]The original version contained a much larger section on Hyperproof. Please refer to chapter I

one would likely want a formal system having entirely different well-formed charts.

The sort of problem dealt with here involves a finite domain of say $n$ elements, each of which can be named in $m$ different ways. The problem is to figure out which names denote the same object. We think of this in terms of the matching names of $m$ different types, where each type has $n$ names of that type, each of which refers to a different object. Since there are $n$ objects, every name of some type refers to the same object as some name from each of the other types. The task, then, is to match each name of each type with those names of each other type that co-refer. For example, one may be given four sorts of names (first names, last names, horse names, and jockey names) and, for each of the four sorts, five names of that sort. The problem may be to determine of five people their first names, their last names, the name of the horse they own, and the name of the jockey of the horse they own.

A chart logic of this sort, then, is relative to a particular selection of sorts and names of that sort:

Sort $\alpha_1$ having names $a_1^1, \ldots a_n^1$
Sort $\alpha_2$ having names $a_1^2, \ldots a_n^2$
. . .
Sort $\alpha_m$ having names $a_1^m, \ldots a_n^m$

Given such a choice, a well-formed chart is of the following form (letting $m$ be four and $n$ three):

| $\alpha_1$ | $\alpha_2$ | $\alpha_3$ | $\alpha_4$ |
|---|---|---|---|
|  |  |  |  |
|  |  |  |  |
|  |  |  |  |

For convenience, if sort "$\alpha_i$" labels a column, it will be referred to as "column $\alpha_i$." For such a chart, any name of sort $\alpha_i$ can be written in a box of column $\alpha_i$ provided that it does not already occur in the chart. These are the only conditions on well-formed charts.

Each sort is treated as a unary predicate symbol, though not every predicate symbol need be a sort. A problem will also involve linguistically-presented assumptions. To model these, we use a standard first-order predicate language with identity. Some of the premises of a problem will typically be non-identities or identities among the names in question, such as $a_3^3 \neq a_3^2$. Other premises may involve other predicates, like $R(a, b) \wedge \neg R(a, c)$ for names $a$, $b$, and $c$ and relation $R$.

A model for such a system consists of an $n$-membered structure $M$ for the language in question satisfying the condition that for each sort $\alpha$, the domain of $M$ is the set $\{a^M \mid a$ is a name of sort $\alpha\}$, where $a^M$ is the element of $M$ assigned to the name $a$. Due to this assumption, we will take as linguistic axioms sentences asserting that every object is named by exactly one of the names of each sort.

We need to say what it means for a chart to be true in a model, but this should be obvious. Whether a chart is true in a model is a function solely of whether pairs of names occurring in the chart occur in the same row or not. If they do, they must be assigned the same object. If the two names occur in different rows, they must be assigned different objects. If these conditions hold for all pairs of names occurring in the chart, the chart is true in the model.

To model the inferential practice of reasoning with charts, we need some rules of inference. In addition to the usual first-order axioms and rules (in any form), we need rules for charts. Here are some examples of how we can use charts in reasoning.

=-**Extract:** If both $a$ and $b$ occur in the same row of the chart, then it is legitimate to infer the sentence $a = b$. This principle is justified by the truth conditions given above.

=-**Apply:**    1. Let $a$ be of sort $\alpha$ and $b$ be of sort $\beta$. From $a = b$ and a chart with $a$ in row $n$, one can write $b$ in column $\beta$ of row $n$. This is again justified by the semantic principles noted in the paragraph above.

2. Suppose one has established the sentence $a = b$ where $a$ is of sort $\alpha$ and $b$ is of sort $\beta$. Suppose neither $a$ nor $b$ occur in the chart, and that only empty rows of the chart are such that both columns $\alpha$ and $\beta$ of a row are empty. Then one can write $a$ in column $\alpha$ and $b$ in column $\beta$ of any such row.

3. Suppose neither $a$ nor $b$ appears in a chart and that there is only one row having both columns $\alpha$ and $\beta$ empty. Then from the sentence $a = b$, one can write $a$ in column $\alpha$ of that row and $b$ in column $\beta$ of that row.

$\neq$-**Extract:** If $a$ and $b$ occur in different rows of the chart, then one can infer $a \neq b$.

$\neq$-**Apply:**    1. Let $a$ be of sort $\alpha$ and $b$ be of sort $\beta$. Suppose $a$ occurs in row $n$ of a chart but $b$ does not occur, and suppose there is only one row of column $\beta$ other than $n$ having no name. Then from $a \neq b$, one is entitled to write $b$ in that row.

2. Let $a$ be of sort $\alpha$ and $b$ be of of sort $\beta$. Suppose $\alpha$ occurs in row $n$ of a chart, and suppose every other row having nothing

in column $\beta$ has no name in any column. Then from $a \neq b$, one is entitled to write $b$ in any such row of column $\beta$.

3. Let $a$ be of sort $\alpha$ and $b$ be of of sort $\beta$. Suppose neither $a$ nor $b$ occurs in a chart, and suppose that every two distinct rows $m$ and $n$ having no names in column $\alpha$ or $\beta$, respectively, are empty rows. Then one can choose any such $m$ and $n$ and put $a$ in row $m$ and $b$ in row $n$.

4. Let $a$ be of sort $\alpha$ and $b$ be of of sort $\beta$. Suppose neither $a$ nor $b$ occur in a chart, and suppose that $m$ and $n$ are the only two distinct rows having no names in column $\alpha$ or $\beta$, respectively. Then one can put $a$ in row $m$ and $b$ in row $n$.

**Column completion:** If exactly $n - 1$ of the names of sort $\alpha$ occur in column $\alpha$ of the chart, then one can write the remaining name of that sort in the blank row of the column.

**Name insertion:** If $a$ is of sort $\alpha$ and each of the rows in which there is no name in column $\alpha$ is completely empty, then one can put $a$ in any such row of column $\alpha$.

**Empty chart:** An empty chart can be asserted without justification.

**Weakening:** Any name can be erased from a chart.

Notice that each of these rules is valid and that each involves charts. Some of them have to do with getting information into charts from sentences. Some have to do with getting information from charts to sentences. Some have to do with inference between charts. Moreover, the rules given, along with the axioms mentioned and some complete set of first-order axioms and rules, form a complete set. In other words, given any set $\Gamma$ of sentences and possibly a chart, if $\phi$ is either a chart or a sentence such that every model in which every member of $\Gamma$ is true is a model in which $\phi$ is true, then $\phi$ can be proved from $\Gamma$ using only the rules and the axiom described above, and the first-order rules.

## A logic of sentences and Venn diagrams

Any of the diagrammatic systems described above can be extended to be heterogeneous by adding appropriate sentences, enriching the syntax of the diagrams if needed, and providing rules of inference allowing inference between the two types of representations. For example, the addition of interpreted first-order sentences built from predicates like $Between(x, y, z)$, $On(x, y)$, etc. to the system of geometry, along with appropriate linguistic axioms and heterogeneous rules, would allow one to carry out rigorous heterogeneous proofs very much like those actually given in plane geometry.

Similarly, one can combine first-order sentences with a version of the system of Venn diagrams presented above, as in Hammer [1995]. We will briefly describe such a system.

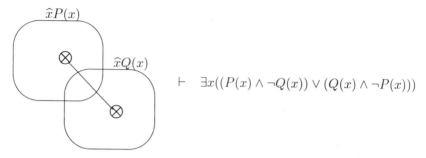

$$\vdash \quad \exists x((P(x) \wedge \neg Q(x)) \vee (Q(x) \wedge \neg P(x)))$$

Figure 9: An instance of the rule of Existential-observe.

Sentences are built up from constant symbols and predicate symbols of each arity. Diagrams are just as in the system above, except that each closed curve is tagged by a "set term" rather than an atomic label as in the system above. These set terms are formed by abstracting over the free variable in an open formula, as with "$\hat{x}P(x)$" and "$\hat{y}(Q(y) \vee \exists z R(y, z))$." Models for the system are extensions of first-order models. The interpretation of a closed curve in a model is as expected: it is assigned the set of objects satisfying the open formula labeling the curve in the model. Truth in a model for sentences is as usual; truth in a model for diagrams is just as in the Venn system above.

The diagram-to-diagram rules are exactly as above; for sentence-to-sentence rules one can take any complete set of first-order rules and axioms. The occurrence of set terms as labels of closed curves obviously enriches the syntax of the diagrams sufficiently to allow one to formulate explicit and effective diagram-to-sentence and sentence-to-diagram rules. One way to do this is to associate regions of a diagram with set terms in a systematic manner based on those occurring as labels in the diagram. The region enclosed by a curve is associated with the set term labeling it. If a region $r$ is associated with some set term $\hat{x}\phi$, then the region within the rectangle but outside of $r$ is associated with $\hat{x}\neg\phi$. Similarly, overlap of regions is associated with conjunction, the combination of two regions is associated with disjunction, and so on. Given this relation, effective rules of inference can be stated. For example, if a diagram has shading in region $r$, and the region within the rectangle but outside $r$ is associated with $\hat{x}\phi$, one can infer $\forall x\phi$. Figure 9 displays an instance of a heterogeneous rule in this system. Completeness of the system is proved in Hammer [1995].

An issue arises with heterogeneous systems of whether a "sentence-elimination theorem" is provable (see Hammer [1995a]). In other words, if a diagram is a logical consequence of another diagram (or a set of diagrams) in a heterogeneous system, can it be proved from the other without using heterogeneous and linguistic rules of inference?

This sort of property is an issue of concern for the logic of charts above, for example. If one chart is a logical consequence of another, it would be very inefficient to have to translate the first into sentences, then manipulate these sentences using first-order rules, and finally translate the resulting information back into chart form. A theorem is clearly needed to show that this sort of roundabout process is always unnecessary for chart-to-chart inference, that in such cases a direct proof can always be given.

The sentence-elimination property does not hold for the heterogeneous Venn system because of the potentially complex logical structure allowed in the labels of the diagrams. However, such a theorem does hold with respect to a weaker, "diagrammatic" notion of logical consequence holding between two diagrams when no analysis of the logical structure of the labels occurring in the diagrams is needed to verify that one is a consequence of the other. This sort of "canceling out" of the linguistic components in heterogeneous reasoning and representation is of potential computational as well as theoretical interest.

# 4 Classifications of Diagrammatic Systems

There are some features that have been invariant among the logics examined here and elsewhere, whether linguistic, diagrammatic, or heterogeneous. Namely, each must have a *grammar*, each must have a class of *structures*, each must have a notion of *logical consequence* holding among well-formed objects defined by means of structures, and each must have some (possibly empty) set of *rules of inference*. These four components can be characterized by the following very provisional conditions. (We certainly do not want to rule out logical systems that cannot be subsumed easily under these specific conditions.)

A *grammar* consists of a classification of external representations into types. First of all, it has finitely many sorts of "primitive grammatical objects." Secondly, it has finitely many "primitive grammatical relations" which can hold among primitive objects. A "well-formed unit" or "well-formed representation" of the grammar consists of finitely many primitive objects standing in various primitive relations. These well-formed units classify external representations according to whether they consist of appropriate tokens of the primitive objects standing in the appropriate primitive relations to one another.

Any logical system of the kind we have in mind has implicit in it the idea that well-formed units contain information about some target domain.

It is typical to model the target domain by a mathematical *structure*. Each such structure models a possible way things could be, consistent with the information given by the representation. Typically, a structure will have the form $M = (U, S_1, \ldots, S_m, I, \ldots)$ consisting of some (possibly empty) set $U$ of objects (possibly organized into sorts), a class of relations $S_i$ holding among the objects, and a function $I$ assigning objects of the structure to some or all of the primitive grammatical objects. A structure may have other features and may put various restrictions on its various components. The class of all *structures* that could model the target domain, consistent with some well-formed units, is then used to classify the content of those units.

A relation of *truth in a structure* is a relation between structures and well-formed units. Whether the relation holds or not between a structure $M = (U, S_1, \ldots, S_m, I, \ldots)$ and a well-formed unit $\phi$ depends on each of the primitive grammatical relations holding among the grammatical primitives of $\phi$. For each such grammatical relation $R$ holding among grammatical primitives $a_1, \ldots, a_n$, a fixed condition among the relations of the structure must be met. In other words, the fact that $R$ holds among grammatical primitives $a_1, \ldots, a_n$ is associated with some condition $\Phi_R(M, a_1, \ldots, a_n)$. If for each such grammatical primitive relation $R$ of $\phi$ the corresponding condition $\Phi_R$ is met by $M$, $\phi$ is true in $M$. Various conditions may be put on the relation of truth in a structure, such as preservation of truth in a structure under isomorphic copies of it for some particular notion of isomorphism.

A relation of *logical consequence* is a relation holding among well-formed units, defined in terms of truth in a structure. Let $\Gamma$ be some set of well-formed object and $\phi$ be a well-formed object. The logical consequence of $\phi$ from $\Gamma$ depends on $\phi$ and the class of all structures $M$ such that every member of $\Gamma$ is true in $M$.

A *rule of inference* is a relation holding between sets of well-formed units and well-formed units. Whether this relation holds is a function purely of the grammatical relations holding among the diagrammatic primitives of the various well-formed units in the set.

This description of the components of a logic should not be too unusual, though the notion of a grammar is slightly more inclusive than usual. Of greater interest are the further, more fine-grained classifications of systems suggested by the diagrammatic and heterogeneous systems presented above, a matter to which we now turn.

Logical systems have traditionally been classified according to considerations along the following lines: whether every class of structures definable in one system is definable in some other system; whether the class of denumerable structures is definable in a given system; whether elementary equivalence of two structures entails isomorphism; whether a certain type of isomorphism entails elementary equivalence; whether the set of valid sentences is effectively enumerable; and whether the Beth property holds for a system.

The systems considered here, however, suggest some very different potential classifications of logical systems. First of all, they focus attention on the representational level of proof in addition to the level of content of proof. Secondly, they display some very unusual relationships between representations and what a system seeks to represent, suggesting the possibility of a mathematical study of representation and how it represents, beyond the usual mathematics of inference and consequence.

For example, where standard analyses are concerned with various notions of isomorphism between structures of a system, some of the systems under examination here suggest investigation of various notions of isomorphism between a structure $M$ of a system and those representations that are true in $M$. One may very well be interested in defining some notion of isomorphism "$\cong$" having the following property: if a representation $R$ is true in $M$, then $R \cong M$, where $R \cong M$ provides more illumination into the connection between representation and structure than "$R$ is true in $M$." As in the case of Hyperproof, these special relationships between representations and structures may allow for non-standard deductive practices, such as allowing one to prove satisfiability of a sentence or non-consequence. One could think of such a study of representation as a formalization of some of the informal semiotics of iconic representation that has been carried out since Peirce.

## Homomorphic systems

In the remainder of the chapter, we briefly examine some of the new criteria with which logics, especially diagrammatic and other non-linguistic ones, can be compared. First, we will provide an explicit definition of a "homomorphic" or "diagrammatic" system for purposes of comparison rather than as a cut-and-dried, definitive definition:

1. Objects in the domain of a structure, "target objects", are represented by tokens of diagrammatic primitive objects, "icon tokens," with different sorts of objects represented by different types of tokens.

2. If $\pi$ is the interpretation function of a structure, then for those representations true in the structure, $\pi$ preserves the grammatical structure holding among the icon tokens constituting such representations in the following ways:

   - If icon tokens of a representation stand in some relevant relationship $R$, i.e. they hold of a primitive grammatical relation, then there is a corresponding "target" relationship $S$ holding among the objects of the domain to which they are assigned by $\pi$.

- The converse holds as well.

- If a grammatical relationship among icon tokens has some structural property (like transitivity, asymmetry, irreflexivity, etc.), then this same property must hold of the objects assigned to the tokens by $\pi$.

- The converse holds as well.

- If a token $t$ of some type $T$ (say closed curve) has some special property $P$ (say being shaded), then $\pi(t)$ is an object of some type $\pi(T)$ having some special property $\pi(P)$ on the domain (say, an empty set rather than just a set).

- The converse holds as well.

3. Every representation is true in some structure.

A system will be called "more diagrammatic/homomorphic" or "less diagrammatic/homomorphic" in virtue of having more or fewer of these features listed above, and also in virtue of having stronger or weaker versions of them.

We illustrate these definitions with some examples. Let us start with a very extreme case of a diagrammatic logic, a logic for reasoning about the relationships of containment of drawn closed figures within other drawn figures. A structure of this logic consists of a number of drawn figures standing in relations of containment or non-containment with one another. Each drawn figure (as a syntactic object) is interpreted in a structure as some drawn closed figure. Truth of a diagram in a structure depends simply on whether the relationships of containment and non-containment among the drawn figures is (literally) preserved under their interpretation in a structure. So the system has a particularly strong version of Condition 1 and also a particularly strong version of the first clause of Condition 2. One reasons about certain relationships among certain types of objects with the objects and relationships themselves; one reasons with the target objects and target relations.

Let us now look at another, slightly less extremely diagrammatic system. The primitives consist of names $a, b, c \ldots$ and a bar $-$. Diagrams consist of finitely many names separated by bars, like $a - b - c - b - a - d$. The only grammatical relation is the left-of relation among names. In this system, unlike the system above, names are not interpreted as names but rather as arbitrary objects, so that it has a weaker version of Condition 1. The only relevant relation among objects of the domain is the left-of relation. For truth in a structure, the left-of relation must be preserved under the interpretation function. Again, it has a very strong version of the first clause of Condition 2. For example, $a - b - d$ is a logical consequence of $a - b - c - d$, and any diagram is a logical consequence of $a - b - c - b$, since this last is unsatisfiable.

Both of the logics above have rather extreme diagrammatic features. In each case, the single primitive grammatical relation is required to be literally preserved under interpretation functions. The first logic is even more extremely diagrammatic than the second since the primitive syntactic components, closed figures, represent objects of the very same sort: closed figures. An even more extreme case could have them representing themselves.

It is clearly far too much to ask of a logic that it have such extremely homomorphic features as the two logics above to qualify as diagrammatic. In most diagrammatic systems, grammatical relations among grammatical objects are not required to be preserved literally under the interpretation function. For example, consider a logic with the same grammar as the drawn-figure logic above, but with figures now interpreted as sets, and containment among figures now corresponding to the subset relationship among the sets they denote. In this system, it is not literally the same relationship required to be preserved from representation to domain for truth in a structure. The grammatical relation is a physical relation between physical objects, the target relation it represents an abstract one among abstract objects.

Other clearly diagrammatic logics enjoy an even less direct connection between grammatical relations and target relations. With most diagrammatic systems there is no one-to-one correspondence between grammatical relations and relations in the domain as with the previous three systems. In other words, with most diagrammatic logics, it is not the case that with each grammatical relation $R$ there is a unique target relation $S$ required to hold of the referents of grammatical objects whenever they hold of $R$ in a diagram and vice versa; it is not generally the case that when a diagram is true in a structure, the structure's interpretation function is a homomorphism from diagram to structure.

This is most obvious with a system like existential graphs, where most of the syntactic objects are not referential and where the syntax is entirely isomorphic to linguistic systems. So in general, the following sort of connection between representation and structure is all that is required for truth in the structure. For each grammatical relation $R$ holding among grammatical primitives, a fixed condition $\Phi_R$ must be met involving the representation's grammatical relations and objects, the target objects and relations, and the interpretation function.

Since this alone is obviously insufficient to distinguish diagrammatic from non-diagrammatic systems, there is a need for further criteria for determining the extent to which such systems are diagrammatic. While this matter demands a much more detailed treatment than can be given here, a temporary solution is simply to call one such logic more diagrammatic than another if the correspondence between grammatical relations and relations on the domain required for truth in a structure in the first logic is more natural than for the other. Obviously the "naturalness" of a diagrammatic system is at least somewhat relative to the capacities of the particular processing system at hand, whether this is a human system or some particular computational system.

To conclude the discussion of the definition above, consider Condition 3, which we illustrate using the system of Venn diagrams described above. The Venn system does not satisfy this condition since the same region can be both shaded and have an X-sequence. Therefore, it is less diagrammatic than a system that enjoys all the features the Venn system has, while having the feature that every representation is satisfiable. However, it does have a weaker version of Condition 3 since there is an effective procedure for determining of any given diagram whether it is satisfiable. So it is more diagrammatic than a system having the same homomorphic features except that the satisfiability of its diagrams is not effectively decidable.

Even linguistic systems can have homomorphic properties. For example, the temporal ordering of spoken English sentences describing a succession of events can have the effect of being an assertion of the same temporal ordering among the events mentioned. Thus, the three sentences "Ahab ate his salad. Then he ate his soup. Then he ate his cheese," describe a different succession of events than does "Ahab ate his salad. Then he ate his cheese. Then he ate his soup," solely in virtue of the three event descriptions occurring in a different order. One can find many other homomorphic features in various languages.

## Heterogeneity and language in inference

What is special about highly homomorphic systems is that they can very closely and naturally mirror objects and properties being represented. We saw that in extreme cases the very objects and properties themselves can be used in the representations reasoned with.

Perhaps unfortunately, the expressive generality of a system is often incompatible with its capacity for being diagrammatic. If a system needs to be able to represent the left-of or subset relation it can do so in a highly diagrammatic manner. However, if it is to represent *arbitrary* binary relations, say, its potential for being homomorphic drops dramatically. It is hopeless to try to have a separate diagrammatic representation for every binary relation: one for father-of, one for owns, one for front-of, one for taller-than, etc. If a combinatorial explosion of notation is to be avoided, the only homomorphic features retainable concern those properties of binary relations common to all of them, such things as having two argument places, having a distinguishable order among the argument places, and being distinguishable from one another. The overt, diagrammatic features characteristic of the systems having only to represent a few particular relations have been necessarily traded for economy of representational resources, elegance, and readability. The problem obviously worsens for a system needing to be able to represent, say, arbitrary $n$-ary relations, arbitrary second-order properties, and so forth.

Despite this trade-off between degree of homomorphism and expressive range, heterogeneous systems can allow one to balance expressive range with homomorphic representation, to have one's cake and eat it too. Since they are essentially combinations of two or more systems, each subsystem of a heterogeneous system can be specially adapted to a particular aspect of the domain to be represented. Representational labor can thereby be divided.

As a real-life example of this sort of division of representational labor, consider the case of circuit design. Here it is typical to appeal simultaneously to timing diagrams, state charts, circuit diagrams, and language in reasoning about a single piece of hardware. The reason these different sorts of representations are used in the same reasoning process is that each one is specially attuned to a different aspect of the type of hardware in question. The state diagrams are attuned to the issue of control, circuit diagrams to the construction from logic gates, timing diagrams to the value of a wire as it changes through time, and language to high-level description. To attempt to combine these various representational tasks into a single type of representation would result in chaos. It is much more useful to keep them separate and to reason back and forth between them.

What is needed in cases of heterogeneous reasoning is usually not a supersystem able to represent everything in some canonical fashion. Rather, what is needed is a semantic underpinning tying the different types of representations together, as illustrated with the heterogeneous systems presented above. By utilizing different sorts of representational systems simultaneously, one is able to exploit the homomorphic power of various formalisms without restricting one's expressive power in the process by their specificity of application.

It may be that dividing representational labor in some cases results in a corresponding increase in complexity in the heterogeneous rules needed to translate between the different components of such systems. We leave this matter to further study.

Besides generality, a second limitation on the degree of homomorphism a system can have concerns the fact that some expressive tasks simply leave very little room for it. Disjunction of assertions, for example, is not ripe with representational possibilities. Infix notation in a language is more-or-less as diagrammatic a mechanism as is possible. One might call the expression of disjunction a "thin" representational task, one which is expressible as well by language as by diagram. Other thin representational tasks include conjunction, negation, universal quantification, and so on.

Diagrammatic systems built around the representation of thin concepts show a marked lack of the representational perspicuity sought in diagrams. Peirce's system of existential graphs, for example, is a diagrammatic system able to represent only thin concepts. This creates its structural isomorphism with certain first-order linguistic systems having the same expressive range (see Zeman [1964]).

On the other hand, representational tasks like the expression of a linear ordering or the inclusion relation among sets are "thick" in allowing for a much greater range in degree of homomorphism among different representations of them. They have more elaborate and specific properties than do thin tasks, thus allowing these specific properties to be closely mirrored in a representation. Diagrams are especially useful for thick representational tasks, and perhaps any other sort of job is best left to other kinds of representation.

## Scalability

Many have expressed the concern that, nice as diagrammatic and heterogeneous formalisms can be in simple cases, they are simply not scalable to more complex cases. By way of addressing this worry, we make three comments. First of all, the same worry might easily be directed towards various first-order formal systems. It is not at all obvious that a few trivial-looking rules and axioms like modus ponens or universal generalization would be useful at all in a real-life, complex domain such as mathematics or computer science. However, the appearance is clearly misleading in this case and perhaps in the case of some diagrammatic and heterogeneous systems as well.

Secondly, heterogeneous systems allow one to do such things as extend standard linguistic systems for the purposes of allowing a more perspicuous expression of common cases or key features, say, in mathematical proofs. So they can increase (or at least not decrease) the power of already quite powerful linguistic systems.

Thirdly, many non-linguistic systems are able to express very large amounts of data in a compact way. Topographical charts are an example of this. Practically an infinite amount of information can be expressed by means of a very few lines with one of these. A linguistic expression of the same information would be much more complex. So at least in some cases, scalability is more of a problem for linguistic systems than for diagrammatic ones. Because of these sorts of considerations we do not feel that the problem of scalability is an unavoidable obstacle, though it may be a problem in certain cases.

## Valid and invalid reasoning with diagrams

There is also a concern that reasoning involving diagrams is essentially non-rigorous. Indeed, despite the fact that have been used for thousands of years in mathematics, diagrams are notorious for having led to fallacies, classic examples of which are found in Euclid. We describe two ways a diagrammatic logic can encourage invalid reasoning and discuss how a good diagrammatic logic can facilitate valid reasoning.

A diagrammatic system invites error when natural interpretations of grammatical relations are superseded in favor of less natural ones. For example, were "$b-c-a$" in the system above reinterpreted as meaning that $a$ is left of $c$ which is left of $b$, error would be avoided only with difficulty. The obvious and natural interpretation would have been superseded.

Similarly, from a diagram having a point labeled "A" falling within a drawn triangle in a system of geometrical diagrams, one would be strongly tempted to infer that the point falls within the triangle. But one's semantics need not assign this meaning to the diagram. Depending on the semantics, the point could be any point, inside or outside the triangle. This pitfall would be all the more dangerous if one's semantics were only vaguely specified as was the case with the diagrams in Euclid's *Elements*. Fallacy is avoidable given carefully specified semantics and easily avoidable given a natural semantics, one in which diagrammatic relations are mapped in a conceptually natural way to target relations. This point has been made in Shimojima [1995].

Ideally, one should rely on natural diagrammatic constraints both in the demarcation and interpretation of the well-formed units whenever possible rather than on purely conventional stipulations. If one wants to reason about some transitive relation and chooses a transitive grammatical relation to represent it (like the left-of ordering), one has wisely exploited physical properties of the grammar; one has allowed part of the inferential burden to be carried by one's representations.

# 5   Conclusion

The thesis underlying this chapter has been that logical systems are meant to serve as mathematical models of informal inference practices and pre-theoretic consequence relations underlying these practices. It was noted that particular systems arise not only from the inference practice being modeled, but also from what idealizations are made about it. We argued that the diversity of logical systems arising from taking both of these variables into consideration is not handled well by means of standard accounts of what constitutes a logical system.

Though any of the idealizations mentioned could be dropped with an increase in coverage, we concentrated on logical systems violating Idealization 1.2. This was the assumption that the external representations of an inference practice can be adequately modeled by means of a linear sequence of symbols. When one drops this assumption, the resulting systems display many logical properties not readily expressible in terms of linguistic systems. For example, the representations of some of these systems display close relationships to structures themselves, sometimes serving as representations of them, allowing one to establish deductively facts usually obtainable only model-theoretically. Other systems allow one to hard-wire part of one's inferential burden into the representations themselves. Others provide a more accurate model of inference practices involving charts, tables, diagrams, etc. For example, heterogeneous systems appear when Idealization 1.2 is dropped, thus allowing one to model many features of actual reasoning not easily capturable by linguistic or strictly diagrammatic systems. As is often done in actual practice, such systems allow one to divide representational labor among different types of representations and to transfer information from one type to another.

Many of these systems also have interesting logical properties, a topic we were able to treat only cursorily. For example, heterogeneous systems suggest the study of how one representational component of such a system can be isolated either proof-theoretically or model-theoretically from the others. Does a restricted completeness theorem hold within a single component of the heterogeneous system or not? How do the various components compare in terms of expressive range?

A great deal of real-life reasoning and representation is heterogeneous, diagrammatic, graphical, and so on. We hope to have pointed out some of the topics of concern that will arise in a logical treatment of this area and to have made it obvious that there are many other such topics not yet discovered. We hope also to have provided motivation for the development of a potentially very fruitful new field.

# Part B

# Case Studies

## Chapter IV

# Situation-Theoretic Account of Valid Reasoning with Venn Diagrams

Sun-Joo Shin

Venn diagrams are widely used to solve problems in set theory and to test the validity of syllogisms in logic. Since elementary school we have been taught how to draw Venn diagrams for a problem, how to manipulate them, how to interpret the resulting diagrams, and so on. However, it is a fact that Venn diagrams are not considered valid proofs, but heuristic tools for finding valid formal proofs. This is just a reflection of a general prejudice against visualization which resides in the mathematical tradition. With this bias for linguistic representation systems, little attempt has been made to analyze any nonlinguistic representation system despite the fact that many forms of visualization are used to help our reasoning.

The purpose of this chapter is to give a semantic analysis for *a* visual representation system—the Venn diagram representation system.[1] We were mainly motivated to undertake this project by the discussion of multiple forms of representation presented in Chapter I More specifically, we will clarify the following passage in that chapter, by presenting Venn diagrams as a formal system of representations equipped with its own syntax and semantics:

> As the preceding demonstration illustrated, Venn diagrams provide us with a formalism that consists of a standardized system of representations, together with rules of manipulating them. ... We think it should be possible to give an information-theoretic analysis of this system, ....

In the following, the formal system of Venn diagrams is named VENN. The analysis of VENN will lead to interesting issues which have their ana-

---

[1]This chapter is limited to the use of Venn diagrams to test the validity of syllogisms from traditional logic.

logues in other deductive systems. An interesting point is that VENN, whose primitive objects are diagrammatic, not linguistic, casts these issues in a different light from linguistic representation systems. Accordingly, this VENN system helps us to realize what we take for granted in other more familiar deductive systems. Through comparison with symbolic logic, we hope the presentation of VENN contributes some support to the idea that valid reasoning should be thought of in terms of manipulation of information, not just in terms of manipulation of linguistic symbols.

To support our claim that this use of Venn diagrams is a standard representation system, we aim to develop the syntax and the semantics of this formal system in the following way:

In §1, the primitive objects are clarified for this system and well-formed diagrams are defined. Several interesing issues arise from the fact that the primitive objects of VENN are diagrammatic. For example, unlike with linguistic representation systems, we need an extra relation among tokens of the same type. Also, we need to specify a relation among diagrams which look very similar to each other.

In §2, the semantics of VENN is developed with the help of situation-theoretic tools. First, a homomorphic relationship is formalized between Venn diagrams drawn, say, on a piece of a paper, and information conveyed in syllogisms. It is this relation which allows us to represent certain facts (about which we aim to reason) in terms of certain diagrams and to tell what a diagram conveys. What it is for one diagram to follow from other diagram(s) is definable by the relation of the contents of the diagrams.

In §3, we define what it is to obtain one diagram from other diagrams in this system, and introduce five ways of manipulating diagrams. This establishes the syntax of this system.

The soundness of this system is proved in §4. That is, whenever diagram $D$ is obtainable (as defined in §3) from a set of diagrams $\Delta$, diagram $D$ follows (as defined in §2) from $\Delta$.

In the last section, §5, this system is proved complete. That is, this system, along with its own transformation rules, allows us to obtain any diagram $D$ from a set of diagrams $\Delta$, if $D$ follows from $\Delta$.

# 1   Syntax

## Preliminary Remarks

Let us assume that any representation system aims to represent information about the situation about which we want to reason. VENN, which we are about to examine, adopts diagrams as its medium to effect this representation. We aim to examine the formalism with which Venn diagrams provide us in the following respects:

1. What are the formation rules of meaningful units in this system?
2. What are the meaningful units of this system about?

These two questions help us to answer whether this Venn diagram system is a standard formal representation system or not. If this system is deductive (which we want to claim), then one more question should be answered:

3. What are the rules for manipulating the objects of this system?

These questions will be discussed in §1, §2 and §3, respectively. In order to address the first point, i.e. what are the formation rules, we need to specify the set of primitive objects of which a meaningful unit in this system consists. Before this syntactic discussion begins, let us consider some of the features we want to incorporate into this representation system.

Let us think of the information which this system aims to convey. The following are examples:

All unicorns are red.
No unicorns are red.
Some unicorns are red.
Some unicorns are not red.

These four pieces of information have something in common. That is, all of these are about some relation between the following sets–the set of unicorns and the set of red things. Each piece of information shows a different relation between these two sets. Therefore, the Venn diagram system needs to represent the following: sets and relations between sets.

A set is represented by a differentiable closed curve which does not self-intersect, as follows:

However, a main question is whether we want to have an infinite number of different closed curve-types *or* only one closed curve-type. An analogy with sentential logic might be helpful in this matter. In sentential logic we are given an infinite sequence of sentence symbols, $A_1$, $A_2$, .... An atomic sentence of English is translated into a sentence symbol. When we translate different atomic sentences of English into the language of sentential logic, we choose different sentence symbols. It does not matter which sentence symbols we use, as long as we use different symbol-types for different English sentence-types. Another important point is that after choosing a sentence symbol (type), say $A_{17}$, for a certain English sentence (type), we have to keep using this sentence symbol, the 17th sentence symbol, for the translation of this English sentence-type.

Therefore, if the first alternative—to have different closed curve-types— is chosen for this system, then we can say, just as in the language of sentential logic, that tokens of the same closed curve-type represent the same set. However, in this system we would have to accept the following counterintuitive aspect: very similar looking (or even identical looking) closed curve-tokens might belong to different closed curve-types. Even though we think it is theoretically possible to have such a system, we decide to choose the other alternative, that is, to have only one closed curve-type.

Now one question is how to represent different sets by closed curves. Of course, we want to say that in VENN different sets are represented by different closed curves. However, these different closed curves are tokens of the same type–the closed curve-type, since we have only one closed curve-type. In the case of sentential logic, we have an infinite number of sentence symbol-types to represent an infinite number of English sentence-types. Therefore, different English sentence-types are represented by different sentence symbol-types. In VENN we have only one closed curve-type to represent an infinite number of sets. A main problem is how to tell whether given closed curves represent different sets or not. Of course, we cannot rely on how these tokens look, since every token of a closed curve belongs to one and the same type. It seems obvious that we need an extra mechanism to keep straight the relation among tokens of a closed curve, unlike in the case of sentential logic. This point will be dicussed after the primitive objects are introduced.

Suppose that the following closed curve represents the set of unicorns:

Accordingly, this closed curve makes a distinction between the set of unicorns and anything else. Strictly speaking, the area enclosed by the closed curve, not the closed curve itself, represents the set of unicorns. It will be good if we can treat anything else as a set as well. However, there is no such set as the set of non-unicorns, unless there is a background set. Therefore, we want to introduce a way to represent the background set in each case. Whatever sets we want to represent by closed curves, we can always come up with a background set which is large enough to include all the members of the sets represented by the drawn closed curves.

A background set is represented by a rectangle, as follows:

As in the case of closed curves, we also need some mechanism in order to make sure whether tokens of a rectangle represent the same background set or not.

For the given example, we will draw two closed curves within a rectangle to represent three sets: the set of unicorns, the set of red things and the background set. However, in order to represent the four pieces of information mentioned above, we should be able to represent the following sets: the set of non-red unicorns and the set of red unicorns.[2] We might need to represent the set of red non-unicorns and the set of non-red non-unicorns as well, depending upon the information we want to convey. The moral is to draw closed curves in such a way that we should be able to represent all of these sets in one diagram:

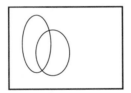

In addition to the background set, the set of unicorns and the set of red things, the overlapping closed curves make a distinction among the set of red unicorns, the set of non-red unicorns, the set of red non-unicorns and the set of non-red non-unicorns. This feature should be incorporated not only into the syntax of this system, that is, into the formation rules, but into the semantics of this system in the following way: Two sets represented by two disjoint areas do not share any element. And a background set, which a rectangle represents, is divided exhaustively by the sets represented by the enclosed areas which are included in the rectangle.[3]

So far, we discussed how this system represents sets. Now what we need is a way to represent relations between sets. For example, the information

---

[2] "All unicorns are red" conveys the information that the set of non-red unicorns is empty, while "Some unicorns are not red" conveys the opposite information, that is, the set of non-red unicorns is not empty. "No unicorn is red" says that the set of red unicorns is empty, while "Some unicorns are red" says the opposite.

[3] After establishing the semantics, we can prove that these two desired features are expressed in this semantics. For more detail, refer to Shin [1990].

that all unicorns are red conveys information about a certain relation between the set of unicorns and the set of red things. That is, every member of the former set is also a member of the latter set. However, this relation can be expressed in terms of the set of non-red unicorns. That is, the set of non-red unicorns is empty. In the previous paragraph, we suggested that this system should represent the set of non-red unicorns. Therefore the problem of representing relations between sets reduces to the problem of representing the emptiness or non-emptiness of sets. For the emptiness of a set, we shade the whole area which represents the set. In order to represent that a set is not empty, we put down $\otimes$ in the area representing the set. If the set is represented by more than one area, we draw $\otimes$ in each area and connect the $\otimes$'s by lines. For this, we adopt the expression $\otimes^n$ ($n \geq 1$) and call it an X-sequence. Each X-sequence consists of a finite number of X's and (possibly) lines. The formation rules deal with each object in detail.

## Primitive Objects

We assume we are given the following sequence of distinct diagrammatic objects to which we give names as follows:

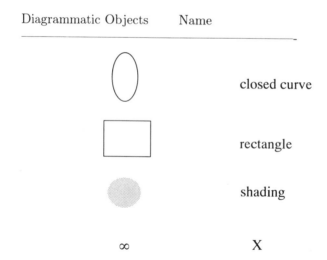

| Diagrammatic Objects | Name |
| --- | --- |
| (closed curve) | closed curve |
| (rectangle) | rectangle |
| (shading) | shading |
| $\infty$ | X |

How can we talk about diagrams or parts of diagrams of this system? In the case of linguistic representation systems, we adopt the convention to use quotation marks. For this visual representation system, we suggest writing down a letter for the name of each diagram and each closed curve and each rectangle. Introducing letters as names (not as part of the language but as a convention for our convenience) solves our problem of how to mention diagrams, rectangles or closed curves. But, how do we mention the rest of our system, i.e., shadings and X's?

First, let me introduce three terms for our further discussion—region, basic region and minimal region. By *region*, we mean any enclosed area in a diagram. By *basic region*, we mean a region enclosed by a rectangle or by a closed curve. By *minimal region*, we mean a region within which no other region is included. The set of regions of a diagram $D$ (let us name it $RG(D)$) is the smallest set satisfying the following clauses:

1. Any basic region of diagram $D$ is in $RG(D)$.

2. If $R_1$ and $R_2$ are in set $RG(D)$, then so are the intersection of $R_1$ and $R_2$, the union of $R_1$ and $R_2$, and the difference between $R_1$ and $R_2$.

For reasons that we will see soon, we need to refer to the regions of a diagram. We can name the regions which are made up of rectangles or closed curves by using the names of the rectangles and closed curves. For example, in the following diagram,

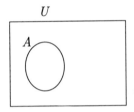

there are three regions—a part enclosed by a rectangle, $U$, a part enclosed by a closed curve, $A$, and a part enclosed by $U$ and and not by $A$. As said above, let us name a region after the name of the closed curve or the rectangle which encloses it. So, the first region is region $U$ and the second is region $A$. Since the third region is the difference between region $U$ and region $A$, we name it region $U - A$. Let us think of the case in which some closed curves overlap with each other, as in the following example:

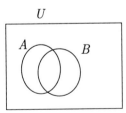

We refer to the region intersected by both region $A$ and region $B$ as region *A-and-B*, and refer to the region which is the union of region A and region B as region $A + B$.

To implement these ideas, we get the following convention of naming the regions:

1. A basic region enclosed by a closed curve, say, $A$, or enclosed by a rectangle, say, $U$, is named region $A$ or region $U$.

   Let $R_1$ and $R_2$ be regions. Then,

2. A region which is the intersection of $R_1$ and $R_2$ is named $R_1$-and-$R_2$.

3. A region which is the union of $R_1$ and $R_2$ is named $R_1 + R_2$.

4. A region which is the difference between $R_1$ and $R_2$ is named $R_1 - R_2$.

Recalling the definition of set $RG(D)$ (the set of regions of diagram $D$) given above, we know that this convention of naming the regions exhausts the cases.

Let us go back to the question of how to talk about shadings and X's. As we will see soon, any shading or any X of any diagram (at least any interesting diagram) is in some region. Now, in order to mention these constituents of our language we can refer to them in terms of the names of the smallest regions. For example, we can refer to a shading or an X which is in region $A$ (where $A$ is the smallest region with these constituents) as the shading in region $A$ or the X in region $A$.

Before moving to the formation rules of this system, we need to discuss one more point mentioned in the preliminary remarks: a relation among closed curve-tokens and a relation among rectangle-tokens. Suppose that the following are given to us:

How can we tell whether these two closed curves represent different sets or not? It depends on whether a user of the Venn diagrams intends to represent the same set or different sets by these two tokens of the closed curve. Accordingly, the relation in which we are interested is the relation that holds among closed curve-tokens or among rectangle-tokens which represent the same set. Let us name this relation a counterpart relation. Then, we can think of the following features for this special relation: First of all, this relation should be an equivalence relation among basic regions of given diagrams. Second, a counterpart relation holds only among tokens of the same type—among closed curves-tokens and among rectangle-tokens. Third, since a user would not draw two closed curves within one diagram

to represent the same set, we want to say that within one diagram a counterpart relation does not hold among distinct basic regions.

Given diagrams $D_1, \ldots, D_n$, let a counterpart relation (let us call it set
$cp$) be an equivalence relation on the set of basic regions of $D_1, \ldots, D_n$
satisfying the following:

1. If $\langle A, B \rangle \in cp$, then both $A$ and $B$ are either closed curves or rectangles.

2. If $\langle A, B \rangle \in cp$, then <u>either</u> $A$ is identical to $B$ <u>or</u> $A$ and $B$ are in
   different diagrams.

Within one diagram, every basic region enclosed by a closed curve or a
rectangle has only one counterpart, that is, itself. Therefore, we have only
one $cp$ set. However, when more than one diagram is given, there would
not be a unique set $cp$. For example, in the following diagrams,

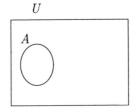
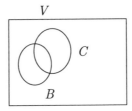

all of the following sets satisfy the conditions of set $cp$:
1. $\{\langle U, U \rangle, \langle V, V \rangle, \langle A, A \rangle, \langle B, B \rangle, \langle C, C \rangle\}$
2. $\{\langle U, U \rangle, \langle V, V \rangle, \langle A, A \rangle, \langle B, B \rangle, \langle C, C \rangle, \langle U, V \rangle, \langle V, U \rangle\}$
3. $\{\langle U, U \rangle, \langle V, V \rangle, \langle A, A \rangle, \langle B, B \rangle, \langle C, C \rangle, \langle A, B \rangle, \langle B, A \rangle\}$
4. $\{\langle U, U \rangle, \langle V, V \rangle, \langle A, A \rangle, \langle B, B \rangle, \langle C, C \rangle, \langle A, C \rangle, \langle C, A \rangle\}$
5. $\{\langle U, U \rangle, \langle V, V \rangle, \langle A, A \rangle, \langle B, B \rangle, \langle C, C \rangle, \langle U, V \rangle, \langle V, U \rangle, \langle A, B \rangle, \langle B, A \rangle\}$
6. $\{\langle U, U \rangle, \langle V, V \rangle, \langle A, A \rangle, \langle B, B \rangle, \langle C, C \rangle, \langle U, V \rangle, \langle V, U \rangle, \langle A, C \rangle, \langle C, A \rangle\}$

Among these equivalence relations, a user chooses set $cp$ for each occasion.
For example, if a user intends to represent the same set with $A$ and $C$ and
the same set with $U$ and $V$, then this user chooses the sixth equivalence
relation as set $cp$. Some user might intend to represent the same set by $A$
and $B$ and the same set by $U$ and $V$. In this case, the fifth relation above
will be the set $cp$ the user chooses. Or, some user might intend to represent
different sets by each closed curve and by each rectangle. In this case, the
user chooses set $cp$ such that all of its elements consist of a basic region
and itself—the first relation above.

## Well-Formed Diagrams

We assumed that any finite combination of diagrammatic objects is a diagram. However, not all of the diagrams are well-formed diagrams, just as not all of the expressions are well-formed formulas in sentential logic or first-order logic. The set of well-formed diagrams, say $\mathcal{D}$, is the smallest set satisfying the following rules:

1. Any rectangle drawn in the plane is in set $\mathcal{D}$.

2. If $D$ is in the set $\mathcal{D}$, then if $D'$ results by adding a closed curve interior to the rectangle of $D$ by the partial-overlapping rule (described below), then $D'$ is in set $\mathcal{D}$.

   Partial-overlapping rule: A new closed curve should overlap *every* existent minimal region, but *only* once and *only* part of each minimal region.

3. If $D$ is in the set $\mathcal{D}$, and if $D'$ results by shading some entire region of $D$, then $D'$ is in set $\mathcal{D}$.

4. If $D$ is in the set $\mathcal{D}$, and if $D'$ results by adding an X to a minimal region of $D$, then $D'$ is in set $\mathcal{D}$.

5. If $D$ is in the set $\mathcal{D}$, and if $D'$ results by connecting existing X's by lines (where each X is in different regions), then $D'$ is in set $\mathcal{D}$.

According to this recursive definition, every well-formed diagram should have one and only one rectangle. It also tells us that if there is any closed curve on a diagram, it should be in the rectangle. Therefore, this definition rules out all the following diagrams as ill-formed:

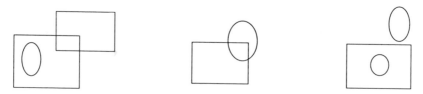

Let me illustrate through examples how the partial-overlapping rule in clause 2 works. By the first clause, for any well-formed diagram there should be a rectangle in it. Let us name it $U$ as follows:

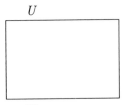

Diagram *a*

First, let us try to draw a new closed curve, $A$. How does this partial-overlapping rule work? In diagram $a$, there is only one minimal region—the region $U$. The new closed curve $A$ should be drawn to overlap a part of this existent region.

Therefore,

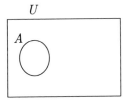

Diagram *b*

Next, we are going to draw another new closed curve, $B$, on this sheet of paper. In diagram $b$, there are two minimal regions—region $A$ and region $U - A$. According to this partial-overlapping rule, the new closed curve $B$ should overlap each of these two regions, but only partially and only once. That is,

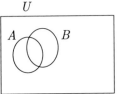

Diagram *c*

Therefore, the following diagrams are ruled out:

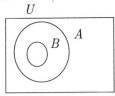

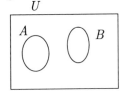

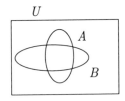

Diagram 1                    Diagram 2                    Diagram 3

In Diagram 1, one minimal region—region $U - A$—is not overlapped by the new closed curve $B$. In Diagram 2, one minimal region—region $A$—is not overlapped by $B$ at all. In Diagram 3, minimal region $U - A$ is overlapped by the new closed curve $B$ twice.

Next, we want to draw one more closed curve, $C$. All the following diagrams are eliminated:

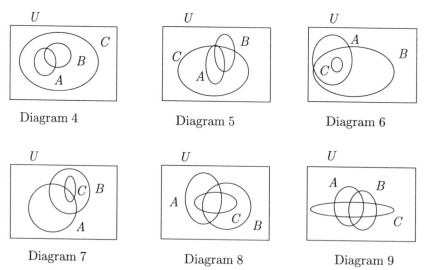

Diagram 4           Diagram 5           Diagram 6

Diagram 7           Diagram 8           Diagram 9

Diagram $c$ on the previous page has four minimal regions: region $U - (A + B)$, region $A - B$, region $A$-and-$B$ and region $B - A$. We have to make sure that the third closed curve, $C$, should overlap every part of these four minimal regions. That is,

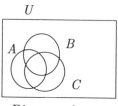

Diagram $d$

Clause 3 says that, a shading, if there is any, should fill up region(s). Therefore, the following is not well-formed:

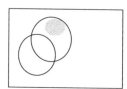

Clause 4 tells us that the following diagram cannot be well-formed, since an X is not in a minimal region. It is in region $B$.

However, region $B$ is not a minimal region:

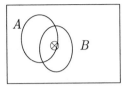

Clause 4 and Clause 5 together tell us that if there is any X-sequence, each X of the sequence should be in a minimal region. Clause 5 also tells us that each X of an X-sequence should be in a different minimal region. The following are well-formed:

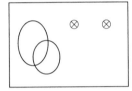
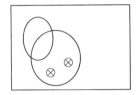

On the other hand, the following cannot be well-formed:

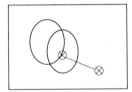
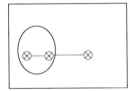
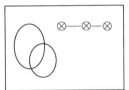

From now on, let us abbreviate "well-formed diagram" by "*wfd.*"

# 2   Semantics

As discussed in the preliminary remarks, this representation system aims to represent sets and certain relations among those sets. We think that two kinds of homomorphisms are needed for this representation system, one for the representation of sets and the other for the representation of relations among sets. Based on these two homomorphisms (which are defined in below), we will formalize what it is for one diagram to follow other diagrams.

## From regions to sets

Each basic region, which is made by a closed curve or a rectangle, represents a set. Since we are concerned with *wfds*, let us define the set BRG to be the set of all basic regions of *wfds*. Let $\mathcal{D}$ be a set of *wfds*. That is,

BRG = {a basic region of $D \mid D \in \mathcal{D}$ }.

Let $U$ be a non-empty domain. Then, for any function $f$ such that

$f$: BRG $\rightarrow \mathcal{P}(U)$, where if $\langle A, B \rangle \in cp$, then $f(A) = f(B)$,

we can extend this function to get the mapping from set RG—the set of all regions of diagrams in set $\mathcal{D}$—to $\mathcal{P}(U)$. This extended relation is a homomorphism between regions and sets. That is, $\overline{f} :$ RG $\rightarrow \mathcal{P}(U)$, where

$$\overline{f} = \begin{cases} f(A) & \text{if } A \in \text{BRG} \\ \overline{f}(A_1) - \overline{f}(A_2) & \text{if } A = A_1 - A_2 \\ \overline{f}(A_1) \cap \overline{f}(A_2) & \text{if } A = A_1\text{-}and\text{-}A_2 \\ \overline{f}(A_1) \cup \overline{f}(A_2) & \text{if } A = A_1 + A_2 \end{cases}$$

## From facts to facts

Among the primitive objects of this system listed in §1, rectangle-tokens and closed curve-tokens make up regions, and these regions represent sets as seen above. The other objects — a shading and an X — represent certain facts about the sets represented by the regions in which these constituents are drawn. The following are important representational relations in this system:

- A shaded region represents the empty set.

- A region with an X-sequence represents a non-empty set.

How do we define this representational relation? We want to define a function between facts about regions of a diagram and facts about sets of a situation. There are many facts about regions of a diagram. However, as said before, not all of them are representing facts. The function we have in mind is concerned only with the representing facts in diagrams. What are the representing facts in this system? The two kinds of representational relations listed above show us what the representing facts are:

1. A region, say $A$, is shaded.
2. An X-sequence is in a region, say $A$.

We need some remark about the second statement. This statement can be ambiguous in the following reason: If an X-sequence is in region $A$, then we can say that the X-sequence is also in region $B$ if region A is a part of region $B$. For example, it is true that the X-sequence, $\otimes^2$, is in region $A$ in the following diagram:

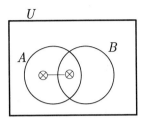

However, it is also true that the X-sequence is in region $A + B$, or in region $U$. In this case, we are concerned with the smallest region with the X-sequence. Since each $\otimes$ of the X-sequence is in a minimal region in a *wfd*, the union of the minimal regions with $\otimes$ is the smallest region with the X-sequence. Now, we can express the representing facts (listed above) by means of situation-theoretic terminology—infons—as follows:

(1) $\langle\!\langle \text{shaded}, A; 1 \rangle\!\rangle$.
(2) $\langle\!\langle \text{In}, \otimes^n, A; 1 \rangle\!\rangle$, where
$\qquad A = A_1 + \cdots + A_n$ and
$\qquad$ for every $1 \leq i \leq n$, $A_i$ is a minimal region with $\otimes$.

What are the facts that these representing facts represent? Based upon the homomorphism $\overline{f}$ defined above, let us express these represented facts by means of situation-theoretic terminology:

(1') $\langle\!\langle \text{Empty}, \overline{f}(A); 1 \rangle\!\rangle$
(2') $\langle\!\langle \text{Empty}, \overline{f}(A); 0 \rangle\!\rangle$

If these were all representing facts, then we would have to say that the following two diagrams contain the same representing facts:

 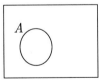

However, we want to say that these two diagrams represent different facts. Intuitively, the diagram on the right represents the set region $A$ represents along with the background set, while the left one does not represent any set, except the background set. Therefore, we want to add one more representing fact:

(3) $\langle\!\langle \text{Region}, A; 1 \rangle\!\rangle$

The following fact is represented by this representing fact:

(3') $\langle\langle\text{Set}, \overline{f}(A); 1\rangle\rangle$

Let $\mathcal{D}$ be a set of *wfds*. Let $\mathcal{D}$-*Facts* be the set of the facts about diagrams in $\mathcal{D}$. That is,

$\mathcal{D}$-*Facts* $= \{\alpha \mid D \models \alpha$ and $D \in \mathcal{D}\}$, where
$\quad\quad D \models \alpha$ iff $\alpha$ is true of the diagram $D$.

Let $\mathcal{S}$-*Facts* be as follows: (Suppose that $U$ is a non-empty domain.)

$\mathcal{S}$-*Facts* $= \{\alpha \mid \alpha = \langle\langle\text{Empty}, a; i\rangle\rangle$ or $\langle\langle\text{Set}, a; 1\rangle\rangle\}$, where
$\quad\quad i \in \{0, 1\}$ and $a \in \mathcal{P}(U)$.

Since not all of the facts about diagrams are representing facts, the homomorphism between $\mathcal{D}$-*Facts* and $\mathcal{S}$-*Facts* must be partial. Define a homomorphism $h$ from facts about diagrams to facts about sets as follows:

$h(\langle\langle\text{Shaded}, A; 1\rangle\rangle) = \langle\langle\text{Empty}, \overline{f}(A); 1\rangle\rangle$,
$h(\langle\langle\text{In}, \otimes^n, A; 1\rangle\rangle) = \langle\langle\text{Empty}, \overline{f}(A); 0\rangle\rangle$.
$h(\langle\langle\text{Region}, A; 1\rangle\rangle) = \langle\langle\text{Set}, \overline{f}(A); 1\rangle\rangle$.

## Content of a diagram

In a deductive system, the semantics of the system allows one to define what it is for a sentence (of the language) to follow from a set of other sentences (of the language). In the case of sentential logic, *wff* $\alpha$ follows from a set $\Gamma$ of *wffs* if and only if every truth assignment which satisfies every member of $\Gamma$ also satisfies $\alpha$. In the case of first-order logic, sentence $\alpha$ follows from a set $\Gamma$ of sentences if and only if every model of $\Gamma$ is also a model of $\alpha$. In either case, a definition for a logical consequence seems to fit our intuition that a conclusion follows from the premises if the truth of the premises guarantees the truth of the conclusion.

What we want is for the semantics of VENN to define a similar kind of inference between a *wfd* and a set of *wfds*. What is it for one *wfd* to follow from a set of other *wfds*, using the analogy of deductive systems? We think that in this representation system, the content of a *wfd* is a counterpart of truth assignment (in sentential logic) or of structure (in first-order logic). As a logical consequence relation between *wffs* is defined in terms of the truth values of *wffs*, we can expect a similar consequence relation between *wfds* to be defined in terms of the contents of *wfds*, as follows:

(1) *Wfd* $D$ follows from a set $\Delta$ of *wfds* ($\Delta \models D$) iff the content of the diagrams in $\Delta$ involves the content of the diagram $D$.

Therefore, we need to formalize the content of a diagram and the involvement relation between the contents of diagrams.

What is the content of a diagram? By the two homomorphisms defined above, we can draw a diagram to represent certain facts of the situations about which we aim to reason. Also, we can talk about what a diagram represents—the content of a diagram. Therefore, the content of a *wfd D*, $Cont(D)$, is defined as the set of the represented facts:

$Cont(D) = \{h(\alpha) \mid D \models \alpha$ and $D \in \mathcal{D}\}$, where
$\qquad\qquad h$ is the homomorphism defined above.

Suppose $\Delta$ is a set of *wfds*. Then, the content of the diagrams in this set (say, $Cont(\Delta)$) is the union of the contents of every diagram in $\Delta$. So,

$$Cont(\Delta) = \bigcup_{D \in \Delta} Cont(D)$$

What does it mean that the content of *wfds* in $\Delta$ involves the content of *wfd* $D$? Let us express this as $Cont(\Delta) \Longrightarrow Cont(D)$. Here, we use Barwise and Etchemendy's infon algebra scheme to define the relation between the contents of diagrams.

Let $U$ be a set such that it is a universe of objects. Let $Sit$ be a subset of $\mathcal{P}(\mathcal{P}(U))$ such that it is closed under $\cup$ and $-$. We define a situation $s$ to be $s \in Sit$—a set of subsets of $U$ closed under $\cup$ and $-$. Let $\sigma$ be a basic infon such that $\sigma = \langle\!\langle R, a; i \rangle\!\rangle$, where $R \in \{\text{Empty, Set}\}$, $a$ is a set and $i \in \{0, 1\}$. We define what it means for a basic infon $\sigma$ to be supported by one of these situations $s$, as follows:

$\qquad s \models \langle\!\langle \text{Empty}, x; 1 \rangle\!\rangle \qquad$ iff $\qquad x \in s$ and $x = \emptyset$.
$\qquad s \models \langle\!\langle \text{Empty}, x; 0 \rangle\!\rangle \qquad$ iff $\qquad x \in s$ and $x \neq \emptyset$.
$\qquad s \models \langle\!\langle \text{Set}, x; 1 \rangle\!\rangle \qquad$ iff $\qquad x \in s$.

Let $\Sigma_1$ and $\Sigma_2$ be sets of infons. We define the involvement relation as follows:

$\qquad$ (2) $\Sigma_1 \Longrightarrow \Sigma_2 \qquad$ iff $\qquad \forall_{s \in Sit}(\forall_{\alpha \in \Sigma_1} s \models \alpha \rightarrow \forall_{\beta \in \Sigma_2} s \models \beta)$

The formal scheme expressed in (2) reshapes our intuitive idea on the inference of a *wfd* from a set of *wfds*, expressed in (1), as follows:

**Definition:** *Wfd D follows* from set of *wfds* $\Delta$ ($\Delta \models D$) iff every situation which supports every member of $Cont(\Delta)$ also supports every member of $Cont(D)$ ($Cont(\Delta) \Longrightarrow Cont(D)$).

Recall that our definition of the content of a *wfd* tells us the information that the diagram conveys. The content of the diagrams in $\Delta$ involves the content of the diagram $D$ if and only if the information of diagram $D$ is extractable from the information of the diagrams in $\Delta$. Therefore, the above definition for $\Delta \models D$ reflects our intuition that a valid inference is a process of extracting certain information from given information.

# 3  Rules of Transformation

In this section, we define what it means to obtain a diagram from other diagrams.

**Definition**: Let $\Delta$ be a set of *wfds* and $D$ be a *wfd*. *Wfd* $D$ is *obtainable* from a set $\Delta$ of *wfds* ($\Delta \vdash D$) iff there is a sequence of *wfds* $< D_1, \ldots, D_n >$ such that $D_n \equiv D^4$ and for each $1 \le k \le n$ *either*
(a) there is some $D'$ such that $D' \in \Delta$ and $D' \equiv D_k$, *or*
(b) there is some $D'$ such that for some $i, j < k$, a rule of transformation allows us to get $D'$ from either $D_i$ or $D_j$ (or both) and $D' \equiv D_k$.

We are concerned with transformations only from *wfds* to *wfds*. Therefore, let us assume that given diagrams are always well-formed. Also, it is assumed that we should not get an ill-formed diagram and should apply each rule within this limit so as to get only *wfds*.[5]

R1: *The rule of erasure of a diagrammatic object*
    We may copy[6] a *wfd* omitting a diagrammatic object, that is, a closed curve or a shading or a whole X-sequence. Let us go through examples for erasing each object.

(i) When we erase a closed curve, certain regions disappear. Shadings drawn in these regions are erased as well so that the resulting diagram is a *wfd*. In the following cases, the transformation from the left figure into the right one is done by the application of this rule.

(Case 1)

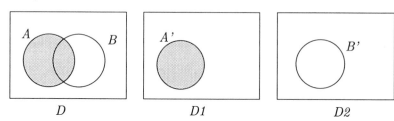

| $D$ | $D1$ | $D2$ |

---

[4] $D_1$ is equivalent to $D_2$ if and only if (i) every basic region of $D_1$ has a counterpart region in $D_2$ and vice versa, (ii) every shading of $D_1$ has a counterpart shading in $D_2$ and vice versa, (iii) every X-sequence of $D_1$ has a counterpart X-sequence in $D_2$ and vice versa. For a more rigorous definition, refer to §2.3.2 of Shin [1990].
    [5] Another alternative: We could formulate each rule in such a way as to prevent us from getting any ill-formed diagrams.
    [6] If diagram $D_1$ is a *copy* of diagram $D_2$, then two diagrams are equivalent to each other. For more detail, refer to Shin [1990].

(Case 2)

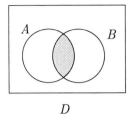
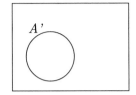
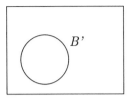

D

(ii) When we omit the shading in some region, we should erase the entire shading in a minimal region. Otherwise, we get an ill-formed diagram. In the following case, this rule allows us to transform the diagram on the left to the diagram on the right.

(Case 3)

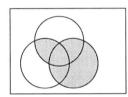
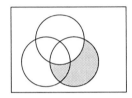

(iii) The erasure of a whole X-sequence allows the transformation from the left figure to the right one.

(Case 4)

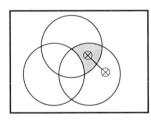
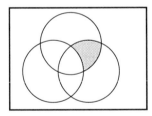

R2: *The rule of erasure of the part of an X-sequence*

We may copy a *wfd* omitting any part of an X-sequence only if that part is in a shaded region. That is, we may erase ⊗- or -⊗, only if the ⊗ in ⊗- or -⊗ is in a shaded region. Let us compare the following two cases:

(Case 5)

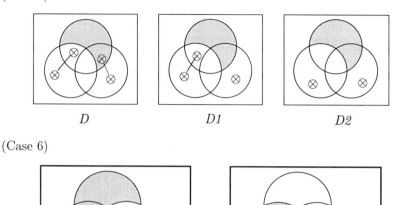

D                    D1                    D2

(Case 6)

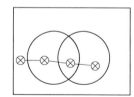

The transformation in Case 5 is legitimate by this rule. However, we do not have any rule to allow the transformation in Case 6. The part of the X-sequence which is erased in the diagram on the right, that is, -⊗, is not in the shaded part of the diagram on the left. Therefore, Rule 2 does not allow this partial erasure. Rule 1 is concerned only with the erasure of a whole X-sequence, not with a proper sub-part of an X-sequence.

R3: *The rule of spreading X's*

If *wfd D* has an X-sequence, then we may copy *D* with ⊗ drawn in some other region and connected to the existing X-sequence. For example,

(Case 7)

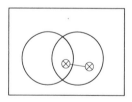
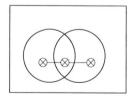
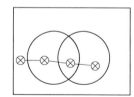

(Case 8)

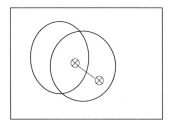  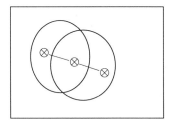

**R4:** *The rule of conflicting information*

If a diagram has a region with both a shading and an X-sequence, then we may transform this diagram to any diagram. This rule allows us to transform the diagram on the left to the diagram on the right.

(Case 9)

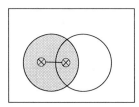  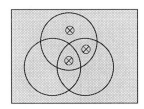

**R5:** *The rule of unification of diagrams*

We may unify two diagrams, $D_1$ and $D_2$, into one diagram, call it $D$, if the given $cp$ relation contains the ordered pair of the rectangle of $D_1$ and the rectangle of $D_2$.

$D$ is the *unification* of $D_1$ and $D_2$ if the following conditions are satisfied:

1. The rectangle and the closed curves of $D_1$ are copied[7] in $D$.

2. The closed curves of $D_2$ which do not stand in the given $cp$ relation to any of the closed curves of $D_1$ are copied in $D$. (Note: Since $D$ is a *wfd*, the partial overlapping rule should be observed.)

3. For any region $A$ shaded in $D_1$ or $D_2$, the $\overline{cp}$-related region[8] to $A$ of $D$ should be shaded.

---

[7]Let $A$ and $B$ be closed curves. If $A$ is a *copy* of $B$, then $\langle region A, region \rangle \in cp$.

[8]Given set $cp$, set $\overline{cp}$ is a binary relation on RG such that $\overline{cp}$ is the smallest set satisfying the following:

1. If $\langle A, B \rangle \in cp$, then $\langle A, B \rangle \in \overline{cp}$.

Suppose that $\langle A, B \rangle \in \overline{cp}$ and $\langle C, D \rangle \in \overline{cp}$.

2. If $A + C \in$ RG and $B + D \in$ RG, then $\langle A + C, B + D \rangle \in \overline{cp}$, $\langle A\text{-and-}C, B\text{-and-}D \rangle \in \overline{cp}$, $\langle A - C, B - D \rangle \in \overline{cp}$ and $\langle C - A, D - B \rangle \in \overline{cp}$.

4. For any region $A$ with an X-sequence in $D_1$ or $D_2$, an X-sequence should be drawn in the $\overline{cp}$-related regions to $A$ of $D$.

Let me illustrate this rule through several examples.

(Case 10) Two diagrams, $D_1$ and $D_2$, are given, where $\langle U_1, U_2 \rangle$, $\langle A_1, A_2 \rangle \in cp$:

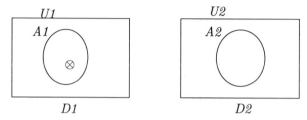

Since the given $cp$ relation holds between the rectangle of $D_1$ and the rectangle of $D_2$, we can unify two diagrams. First, we copy the rectangle and the closed curve of $D_1$ and name them $U_3$ and $A_3$ respectively. Accordingly, $\langle U_1, U_3 \rangle$, $\langle A_1, A_3 \rangle \in cp$. Since the closed curve of $D_2$, i.e. $A_2$, is $cp$-related to the closed curve of $D_1$, i.e. $A_1$, we do not add any closed curve. An X in region $A_1$ of $D_1$ should be drawn in region $A_3$ of $D$, since $A_1$ and $A_3$ are $\overline{cp}$-related and $A_3$ is a minimal region. Therefore, we obtain diagram $D$:

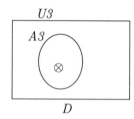

(Case 11) Let $\langle U_1, U_2 \rangle \in cp$, and $\langle A_1, A_2 \rangle \notin cp$. Since $A_2$ is not $cp$-related to any closed curve in $D_1$, we draw the $cp$-related closed curve, i.e. $A_4$, in $D$, to get diagram $D$ as follows (notice that the partial overlapping rule is observed):

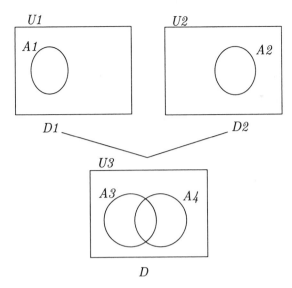

(Case 12) Let $\langle U_1, U_2 \rangle \in cp$, $\langle A_1, A_4 \rangle \in cp$, $\langle A_2, A_3 \rangle \notin cp$. By definition of set $cp$, $\langle A_1, A_2 \rangle \notin cp$, $\langle A_3, A_4 \rangle \notin cp$. Accordingly, $\langle A_1, A_3 \rangle \notin cp$ (since $cp$ is an equivalence relation). After copying the rectangle and the closed curves of $D_1$, we need to copy closed curve $A_3$. Therefore, the following holds: $\langle U_1, U_3 \rangle, \langle U_2, U_3 \rangle, \langle A_1, A_5 \rangle, \langle A_4, A_5 \rangle, \langle A_2, A_6 \rangle, \langle A_3, A_7 \rangle \in cp$.

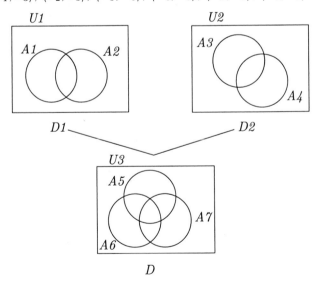

Now, we will see how this rule transforms diagrams with shadings or X-sequences into one diagram:

(Case 13) Let $\langle U_1, U_2 \rangle \in cp$ and $\langle A_1, A_3 \rangle, \langle A_2, A_3 \rangle \notin cp$.

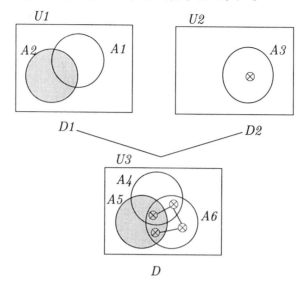

Suppose that closed curve $A_4$ is the copy of $A_1$, $A_5$ is of $A_2$ and $A_6$ is of $A_3$. Accordingly, $\langle A_1, A_4 \rangle, \langle A_2, A_5 \rangle, \langle A_3, A_6 \rangle \in cp$. Clause 3 of the unification rule tells us that the shading in region $A_2$ of $D_1$ should be copied in the $\overline{cp}$-related region, i.e. region $A_5$, in diagram $D$. Our syntactic rule prevents us from copying the X in region $A_3$ into the $\overline{cp}$-related region, i.e. region $A_6$, in the unified diagram, since region $A_6$ is not a minimal region any more. Clause 4 of the unification rule guides us to draw $\otimes^4$ in the $\overline{cp}$-related region, i.e. $A_6$, to get a well-formed unified diagram $D$.

## 4  Soundness

We defined what it is for one diagram to follow from other diagrams ($\Delta \models D$). We also defined what it is for one diagram to be obtained from other diagrams ($\Delta \vdash D$). Now, we raise the question about the soundness of this representation system. Whenever one *wfd* $D$ is obtainable from a set $\Delta$ of *wfds* (i.e., $\Delta \vdash D$), is it the case that the content of diagrams in $\Delta$ involves the content of $D$ (i.e., $\Delta \models D$)? That is, we want to prove that if $\Delta \vdash D$, then $\Delta \models D$.

**Proof:** Suppose that $\Delta \vdash D$. By definition, there is a sequence of *wfds* $< D_1, \ldots, D_n >$ such that $D_n \equiv D$ and for each $1 \leq k \leq n$ *either* (a) there is some $D'$ such that $D' \in \Delta$ and $D' \equiv D_k$, *or* (b) there is some $D'$ such that for some $i, j < k$, a rule of transformation allows us to get $D'$ from either $D_1$ or $D_2$ (or both) and $D' \equiv D_k$. We show by induction on the length of a sequence of *wfds* that for any diagram $D$ obtainable from $\Delta$, the content of the diagrams in $\Delta$ involves the content of $D$.

(Basis Case) This is when the length of the sequence is 1. That is, $D_1 \equiv D$. Since there is no previous diagram in this sequence, it should be the case that there is some $D'$ such that $D' \in \Delta$ and $D' \equiv D_1$. Since $D_1 \equiv D$ and $D' \equiv D_1$,

1. $D' \equiv D$ (since $\equiv$ is symmetric and transitive)
2. $Cont(D') = Cont(D)$ (by 1 and corollary 8.2 of Appendix B)
3. $Cont(D') \subseteq Cont(\Delta)$ (since $D' \in \Delta$, by the definition of $Cont(\Delta)$)
4. $Cont(D) \subseteq Cont(\Delta)$ (by 2 and 3)
5. $Cont(\Delta) \Longrightarrow Cont(D)$ (by 4 and the definition of $\Longrightarrow$)
Therefore, $\Delta \models D$.

(Inductive Step) Suppose that for any *wfd* $D$ if $D$ has a length of a sequence less than $n$, then $\Delta \models D$. We want to show that if *wfd* $D$ has a length of a sequence $n$ then $\Delta \models D$. That is, $D_n \equiv D$. If there is some $D'$ such that $D' \in \Delta$ and $D' \equiv D_n$, then as we proved in the basis case, $\Delta \models D$. Otherwise, it must be the case that there is some $D'$ such that for some $i, j < n$, a rule of transformation allows us to get $D'$ from either $D_1$ or $D_2$ (or both) and $D' \equiv D_n$. By our inductive hypothesis, $\Delta \models D_i$ and $\Delta \models D_j$. That is, $Cont(\Delta) \Longrightarrow Cont(D_i)$ and $Cont(\Delta) \Longrightarrow Cont(D_j)$. Therefore, $Cont(\Delta) \Longrightarrow (Cont(D_i) \cup Cont(D_j))$. Since each rule of transformation is valid,[9] if $D'$ is obtained by either $D_i$ or $D_j$, then $(Cont(D_i) \cup Cont(D_j)) \Longrightarrow Cont(D')$. By the transitivity of the involvement relation, it is the case that $Cont(\Delta) \Longrightarrow Cont(D')$. Since $D' \equiv D_n$ and $D_n \equiv D$, $D' \equiv D$. Hence, $Cont(D') = Cont(D)$. Accordingly, $Cont(\Delta) \Longrightarrow Cont(D)$. Therefore, $\Delta \models D$. □

# 5   Completeness

In this section, we raise the question about the completeness of this representation system. Whenever the content of diagrams in $\Delta$ involves the content of D (i.e., $\Delta \models D$), is it the case that one *wfd* $D$ is obtainable from a set $\Delta$ of *wfds* (i.e., $\Delta \vdash D$) in this system?

## Closure Content

According to the definition of the content of a diagram in §2, given a homomorphism, the representing facts of a diagram determine the content of the diagram. However, according to the definition of the involvement in

---

[9]For the proof, refer to Shin [1990].

§2, the content of a diagram might involve more than its content itself. For example, the following diagram supports only two infons—$\langle\langle \text{In}, \otimes^2, A; 1\rangle\rangle$ and $\langle\langle \text{Shaded}, A\text{-}and\text{-}B; 1\rangle\rangle$:

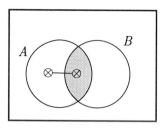

Hence, $Cont(D) = \{\langle\langle \text{Empty}, \overline{f}(A); 0\rangle\rangle, \langle\langle \text{Empty}, \overline{f}(A\text{-}and\text{-}B); 1\rangle\rangle\}$. However, the content of this diagram involves other sets of infons as well. For example, $\{\langle\langle \text{Empty}, \overline{f}(A - B); 0\rangle\rangle, \langle\langle \text{Empty}, \overline{f}(A + B); 0\rangle\rangle\}$ is involved by the content of this diagram. That is, the content of the diagram above involves the content of the following diagram:

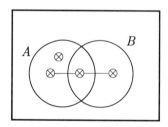

If we unify these two diagrams by the unification rule, then the content of the unified diagram is involved by the content of these two diagrams. Here, we are interested in the maximal content involved by the content of a given diagram. Let $Closure\text{-}Cont(D)$ be a set such that it is the maximal content involved by the content of diagram $D$. That is,

$$Closure\text{-}Cont(D) = \{\alpha \mid Cont(D) \Longrightarrow \{\alpha\}\ \}.$$

By the definition of $Closure\text{-}Cont(D)$, we have $Cont(D) \Longrightarrow Closure\text{-}Cont(D)$. We also know that $Cont(D)$ is a subset of $Closure\text{-}Cont(D)$. Therefore, by the definition of involvement relation, $Closure\text{-}Cont(D) \Longrightarrow Cont(D)$. We can prove[10] that for any diagram $D$ which does not convey conflicting information[11] VENN allows us to obtain a diagram whose content is the maximal content of $D$.

---

[10] Refer to Theorem 9 of Appendix C of Shin [1990].

[11] That is, $D$ does not have a region both with a shading and an X-sequence. If $D$ has a region both a shading and an X-sequence, then by rule of confliction information we can get any diagram. It is also uninteresting.

## Maximal Representation

Let us extend this idea to a set of diagrams. In §2.3 we defined the content of diagrams in $\Delta$ (i.e., $Cont(\Delta)$) as the union of the contents of diagrams in $\Delta$. Here we define the closure content of diagrams in $\Delta$ as the set of the maximal content involved by $Cont(\Delta)$. That is,

$$Closure\text{-}Cont(\Delta) = \{\alpha \mid Cont(\Delta) \Longrightarrow \{\alpha\}\}$$

We know that $Cont(\Delta) \Longrightarrow Closure\text{-}Cont(\Delta)$ and $Closure\text{-}Cont(\Delta) \Longrightarrow Cont(\Delta)$. By the induction of the cardinality of set $Cont(\Delta)$, we can prove the following interesting theorem[12]:

### Maximal Representation Theorem
*Given set $\Delta$ of diagrams, there is a diagram $D$ such that $\Delta \vdash D$, where $Cont(D) = Closure\text{-}Cont(\Delta)$.*

## Completeness

Now, we want to prove that if $\Delta \models D$ then $\Delta \vdash D$.

Proof: Suppose that $\Delta \models D$. That is, $Cont(D)$ is involved by $Cont(\Delta)$. Hence, $Cont(D) \subseteq (Closure\text{-}Cont(\Delta))$. The Maximal Representation Theorem tells us that diagram $D'$ whose content is $Closure\text{-}Cont(\Delta)$ is obtainable from $\Delta$. Therefore, $Cont(D) \subseteq Cont(D')$. It suffices to show that $\{D'\} \vdash D$.

If $Cont(D) = Cont(D')$, then $D'$ is what we want.

If $Cont(D) \subset Cont(D')$, check what $Cont(D') - Cont(D)$ is. What could be a difference in content between two diagrams? In other words, what kind of diffferent representing facts can two diagrams support? We can think of three kinds of representing facts which can make a difference in content between two diagrams: Whether one region is shaded or not, whether one region has an X-sequence or not, and whether one closed curve exists or not.[13] In each case, we apply the following procedure:

(i) If $\langle\!\langle Empty, a; 1 \rangle\!\rangle \in (Cont(D') - Cont(D))$, then apply the rule of erasure of a primitive object to $D'$ to erase a shading.

(ii) If $\langle\!\langle Empty, a; 0 \rangle\!\rangle \in (Cont(D') - Cont(D))$, then apply the rule of erasure of a primitive object to $D'$ and erase an X-sequence.

(iii) If $\langle\!\langle Set, a; 1 \rangle\!\rangle \in (Cont(D') - Cont(D))$ (where there is a basic region $A$ such that $f(A) = a$), then apply the rule of erasure of a primitive object to erase closed curve $A$ from $D'$.

---

[12]For the proof, refer to Appendix C of Shin [1990].

[13]Since both diagrams are well-formed, it is impossible that two diagrams have the equivalent basic regions but not the equivalent regions.

We removed (from diagram $D'$) the representing facts which make a difference in these two sets. Hence, we get diagram $D$ such that $\{D'\} \vdash D$ where $Cont(D') - Cont(D)$, that is, $Cont(D) \subseteq (Closure\text{-}Cont(\Delta))$. (Completeness)                                              $\square$

# Chapter V

# Towards a Model Theory of Venn Diagrams

Eric Hammer and Norman Danner

One of the goals of logical analysis is to construct mathematical models of various practices of deductive inference. Traditionally, this is done by means of giving semantics and rules of inference for carefully specified formal languages. While this has proved to be an extremely fruitful line of analysis, some facets of actual inference are not accurately modeled by these techniques. The example we have in mind concerns the diversity of types of external representations employed in actual deductive reasoning. Besides language, these include diagrams, charts, tables, graphs, and so on. When the semantic content of such non-linguistic representations is made clear, they can be used in perfectly rigorous proofs.

A simple example of this is the use of Venn diagrams in deductive reasoning. If used correctly, valid inferences can be made with these diagrams, and if used incorrectly, they can be the source of invalid inferences; there are standards for their correct use. To analyze such standards, one might construct a formal system of Venn diagrams where the syntax, rules of inference, and notion of logical consequence have all been made precise and explicit, as is done in the case of first-order logic. In this chapter, we will study such a system of Venn diagrams, a variation of Shin's system VENN formulated and studied in Shin [1991] and Shin [1991a] (see Chapter IV of this book). Shin proves a soundness theorem and a finite completeness theorem (if $\Delta$ is a finite set of diagrams, $D$ is a diagram, and $D$ is a logical consequence of $\Delta$, then $D$ is provable from $\Delta$). We extend Shin's completeness theorem to the general case: if $\Delta$ is any set of diagrams, $D$ is a diagram, and $D$ is a logical consequence of $\Delta$, then $D$ is provable from $\Delta$.

We hope that the fairly simple diagrammatic system discussed here will help motivate closer study of the use of more complicated diagrams in actual inference. Formal models of inference involving diagrams may lead to new issues, such as a richer account of the syntax of formal systems able to accomodate diagrams, an account of the formal relationships between syntactic mechanisms and their semantic content suitable for visual representations, shorter or more perspicuous diagrammatic proofs than corresponding purely linguistic proofs, and insight into the nature of the interaction between diagrams and language in inference.

# 1  Syntax

The "primitive diagrammatic objects" of the system consist of the objects displayed in Figure 1. From left to right they are called, respectively, the "rectangle," "closed curve," "shading," "⊗," and "line."

Figure 1: Primitive diagrammatic objects.

The rectangle is used to represent the domain of discourse, differentiable closed curves which do not self-intersect are used to represent subsets of the domain, shading is used to assert the emptiness of a represented set, and ⊗'s connected by lines are used to assert the non-emptiness of a represented set.

In addition to the diagrammatic primitives, the system also has countably many "labels" or "tags," $A, B, C, \ldots$, used to tag closed curves. These serve to determine when two closed curves are intentionally being used to represent the same set.

Diagrams, defined below, will consist of a rectangle drawn on a two-dimensional plane within which are drawn various closed curves as well as shading, ⊗'s, labels, and lines. Before defining the well-formed diagrams, it is helpful to develop some terminology to facilitate the discussion of the syntax of diagrams. We define the basic syntactic objects that will represent sets, "regions," as follows.

A "basic region" of a diagram $D$ is the area enclosed by the rectangle of $D$ or any closed curve of $D$.

The "regions" of a diagram $D$ are defined inductively: Any basic region is a region, and if $r$ and $s$ are regions of $D$, then so are:

1. The combined area consisting of $r$ together with $s$, denoted by "$r \cup s$."

2. The area of overlap of $r$ and $s$ if there is such an area, denoted by "$r \cap s$."

3. The area included in $r$ but not in $s$, if there is such an area, denoted by "$r \setminus s$."

We will be using the same operation symbols, "$\cap$," "$\cup$," and "$\setminus$," both for syntactic operations on regions as just defined and also with their usual set-theoretic meaning. It will always be clear from context which operation is intended: if used between names of regions, the symbol is being used as a syntactic operation, and if used between names of sets, it is being used with its usual set-theoretic meaning. The reason for this double-usage is that we will want to give a semantics linking each such syntactic operation with the corresponding set-theoretic operation. We use lower case letters such as $r$, $s$, and $t$ to refer to regions.

For notational convenience, call a region $r$ of a diagram $D$ a "subregion" of a region $s$ of $D$ just in case every region that is a part of $r$ is also part of $s$. To put it another way, $r$ is a subregion of $s$ if and only if either $r = s$ or there is some region $t$ such that $(r \cup t) = s$.

A region $r$ of a diagram $D$ is a "minimal region" if and only if for all regions $s$, if $s$ is a subregion of $r$, then $s = r$. So minimal regions are those regions which have no other regions as proper parts.

To illustrate the definition of regions, consider the diagram in Figure 2.

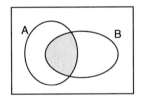

Figure 2: A diagram illustrating regions.

It has three basic regions: the basic region enclosed by the rectangle, the basic region enclosed by the left-hand curve, "$s$," and the basic region enclosed by the right-hand curve, "$t$." It contains four minimal regions. The area enclosed by the left curve but not the right curve is a minimal region. The area enclosed by the right curve but not the left is also a minimal region. The area consisting of both these minimal regions is also a region, but neither minimal nor basic. (So a region does not need to be spatially continuous.) The area of overlap of the two closed curves, $s \cap t$, is a minimal region, and so is $t \setminus s$. In all, the diagram contains fifteen different regions, since it contains fifteen different non-empty combinations of its four minimal regions. Similarly, a diagram consisting of a single closed curve within a rectangle will have two basic regions (the region within the rectangle and the region within the curve), two minimal regions (the region within the rectangle but outside the curve and the region within the curve), and three regions (the two minimal regions and the basic region within the rectangle).

We now define the well-formed diagrams of the system and give some examples. The informal notions needed to state the syntax are quite modest: whether a label tags a particular closed curve; whether there is an area within some particular closed curves but outside of others; whether or not an ⊗ or some shading falls within particular closed curves; and whether lines connect ⊗'s into a chain. An adequate formalization of the syntax of diagrams would merely need to be rich enough to capture these sorts of relationships among primitive diagrammatic objects formally.

**Definition** The "well-formed diagrams" are defined in the following way:

1. Any single, drawn rectangle is a well-formed diagram.

2. If $D$ is a well-formed diagram and $D'$ results from $D$ by adding a closed curve tagged by some label not occurring in $D$ and added according to the "partial overlapping rule" described below, then $D'$ is a well-formed diagram. The partial overlapping rule demands that the new curve overlaps a proper part of every minimal region of $D$ once and only once. (Equivalently, the minimal regions of the resulting diagram must be connected and non-empty.) This rule is illustrated in Figures 3 and 4 below.

3. If $D$ is a well-formed diagram and $D'$ is obtained from $D$ by shading some entire minimal region of $D$, then $D'$ is a well-formed diagram.

4. If $D$ is a well-formed diagram and $D'$ is obtained from $D$ by adding a chain of one or more ⊗ connected by lines (an "⊗-sequence") to $D$ such that each ⊗ of the chain falls within a distinct minimal region and no other chain of ⊗'s in $D$ has its ⊗'s fall in exactly those minimal regions, then $D'$ is a well-formed diagram.

5. Nothing else is a well-formed diagram.

To illustrate the definition, consider the two diagrams in Figure 3.

The one on the left is well-formed. However, the one on the right is not well-formed. It violates the partial overlapping rule. Also, it violates the restriction that any shading in a minimal region must entirely fill it, and also the restriction that the same label can only occur once in a diagram. Consider the three ill-formed diagrams in Figure 4.

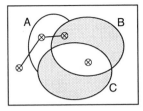
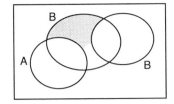

Figure 3:

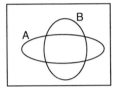
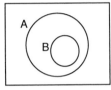
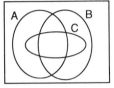

Figure 4:

None of them satisfy the partial overlapping rule. To construct the one on the left one would have to first add one of the curves, but then to add the second one would be forced to overlap one of the minimal regions twice: the minimal region within the rectangle but outside the first curve. Likewise, neither of the other two diagrams can be constructed in accordance with the partial overlapping rule.

For notational convenience, when we refer to an $\otimes$-sequence "occurring in a region" $r$ or of $r$ "having an $\otimes$-sequence," it is understood that $r$ is the smallest region such that every link occurs in some minimal region that is a subregion of $r$. Two distinct $\otimes$-sequence can cross one another.

We will say that regions $r$ and $s$ are "counterparts" if they are built up in the same way (via the syntactic operations $\cup$, $\cap$, and $\backslash$) from basic regions having the same labels. For example, if $r$ is the area of overlap of two curves tagged by $A$ and $B$, respectively, and $s$ is the region of overlap of two curves from a different diagram also tagged by $A$ and $B$, then $r$ and $s$ are counterparts. Intuitively, the counterpart relation holding between two regions means that they are explicitly intended to represent the same set. This equivalence relation is defined more precisely as follows:

**Definition** The "counterpart relation" between regions is an equivalence relation on regions (reflexive, transitive, and symmetric) defined in the following way:

1. If $r$ and $s$ are basic regions enclosed by closed curves tagged by the same label, then $r$ and $s$ are counterparts.

2. If $r$ and $s$ are basic regions enclosed by rectangles, then $r$ and $s$ are counterparts.

3. If $r_1$ and $s_1$ are counterparts and $r_2$ and $s_2$ are counterparts where $r_1$ and $r_2$ are regions of the same diagram and $s_1$ and $s_2$ are regions of the same diagram, then so are $r_1 \cup r_2$ and $s_1 \cup s_2$, $r_1 \cap r_2$ and $s_1 \cap s_2$, and $r_1 \setminus r_2$ and $s_1 \setminus s_2$.

4. No regions are counterparts except in virtue of the above clauses.

We now turn to the following issues: (1) whether we consider diagrams to be drawn tokens or types of drawn tokens, (2) whether we consider regions to be tokens or types, and (3) the conditions under which two tokens of a diagram (respectively, two tokens of a region) are tokens of the same type. We take the route that seems the simplest for studying the mathematical properties of the formal system: we take diagrams to be types, of which there can be any number of drawn tokens. Furthermore, since regions are essentially parts of diagrams, we will also take regions to be types, of which there can be as many tokens as there are tokens of the diagrams of which they are a part.

As for the conditions under which two diagram tokens are tokens of the same type or tokens of the same diagram, we consider this to be entirely analogous to the question of when two sentence tokens are tokens of the same sentence. In that case, what is important is not incidental properties of the shapes and sizes of the various symbol-tokens constituting the sentence token. All that is relevant is the type of symbol of each symbol-token, and in what order the various symbol-tokens occur. Similarly, the relevant features of a diagram are not the particular shapes and sizes of the closed curves, rectangle, $\otimes$, etc. of the diagram token. What is relevant are the various topological relationships among the rectangle, curves, labels, $\otimes$'s, lines, and shading. We give the following definition to capture this idea.

**Definition**  Two tokens of diagrams are "instances of the same diagram" or "tokens of the same diagram" if and only if the set of tags of the two diagrams are identical, and whenever two regions $r$ and $s$ of the two tokens are counterparts, then:

1. Region $r$ is shaded if and only if $s$ is shaded, and

2. Region $r$ has an $\otimes$-sequence if and only if $s$ has an $\otimes$-sequence.

Similarly, two regions of two diagram tokens (i.e. two region tokens) are "regions of the same type" if and only if they are counterparts and the two drawn diagrams are tokens of the same diagram type. Figure 5 shows two instances of the same diagram. Being tokens of the same diagram, they also display tokens of the same regions. For example, the two region-tokens contained within the two curve-tokens labeled "A" are tokens of the same region, as are the two regions enclosed by all three curves of the two diagram-tokens.

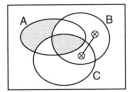 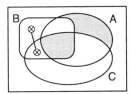

Figure 5:

Because we want to study mathematical properties of the system, it is helpful to be able to collect diagrams and regions together into sets. Our decision to treat diagrams and regions as types makes this possible. For the same reason, when studying the properties of a system of first-order logic, one takes sentences to be types rather than tokens. Had we taken diagrams to be tokens rather than types, it would not have been clear how many of them there were or whether they could be collected together into a set. As types, the matter is easier. Since a diagram consists of a combination of a finite collection of curves, tags, $\otimes$'s, etc., and since there are only finitely many ways to arrange such a collection to get distinct diagrams, there are a denumerable number of diagrams. For the same reason, there are a denumerable number of regions.

**Proposition 1.1** *There are denumerably many well-formed diagrams and denumerably many regions.*

# 2   Semantics

We now define the class of "models" for the system. A model will consist of a set along with an interpretation function assigning subsets of the set to regions of diagrams in a way that respects the intuitive meaning of the overlap of two regions, the region within one region but outside of another, etc. We define models in two stages.

First of all, if $U$ is a set, call a function $v$ assigning subsets of $U$ to basic regions an "assignment function on $U$" if and only if:

1. Every basic region consisting of the area inside a rectangle is assigned the set $U$, and

2. If $r$ is a region enclosed by a closed curve, then $v(r) \subseteq U$, with the restriction that if $r$ and $s$ are any two regions enclosed by closed curves tagged by the same label, then $v(r) = v(s)$.

An assignment function on a set $U$ is analogous to an assignment of truth-values to propositional letters in a propositional logic. Just as these are then extended so to interpret more complex sentences, so assignment functions on a set are now extended to assign sets to arbitrary regions. Before we can do this, however, we need to know that each assignment function on a set $U$ can be uniquely extended to a function assigning subsets of $U$ to all regions in an intuitively appropriate way, i.e., in a way that associates the overlap of two regions with the intersection of the two sets they represent, etc. This information is provided by the following proposition:

**Proposition 2.1** *Let $v$ be an assignment function on a set $U$. Then there is exactly one function $I$ assigning subsets to regions such that for all basic regions $r$, $I(r) = v(r)$, and for all regions $r$ and $s$ of a diagram $D$:*

1. *$I(r \cup s) = I(r) \cup I(s)$,*

2. *If there is a region $r \cap s$, $I(r \cap s) = I(r) \cap I(s)$, and*

3. *If there is a region $r \setminus s$, $I(r \setminus s) = I(r) \setminus I(s)$.*

A "model" is defined to be a pair $M = (U, I)$ consisting of a set $U$ and an interpretation function $I$ such that $I$ is the unique extension of some assignment function $v$ on the set $U$, as warranted by the above proposition.

From the definition of model, we have that for each model $(U, I)$ and diagram $D$: if $r$ and $s$ are regions of $D$ that do not overlap, then $I(r) \cap I(s) = \emptyset$; if $r$ is a subregion of $s$, then $I(r) \subseteq I(s)$; if $t$ is the region of overlap of $r$ and $s$, then $I(t) = I(r) \cap I(s)$; and so on. In short, the definition adequately captures the intuitive correlation of composition of regions with union of sets represented, overlap of regions with intersection of sets represented, disjointness of regions with disjointness of sets represented, subregion with subset, and so forth.

The following proposition observes that regions that are counterparts must be interpreted to represent the same set:

**Proposition 2.2** *If regions $r$ and $s$ are counterparts and $(U, I)$ is a model, then $I(r) = I(s)$.*

Having defined the models of the system, we can now define what it means for a diagram to be "true in a model $M$." For this, there are only two relevant sorts of facts: whether a region is shaded, thereby asserting that the set represented by that region is empty; and whether a region contains an $\otimes$-sequence, thereby asserting that the set represented by that region is not empty.

**Definition** Let $M = (U, I)$ be a model and $D$ be a diagram. Then $D$ is "true in $M$" or "$M$ models $D$" (in symbols $M \models D$) if and only if for each region $r$ of $D$:

1. If $r$ is shaded, then $I(r) = \emptyset$, and

2. If an $\otimes$-sequence occurs in $r$, then $I(r) \neq \emptyset$.

Having the notion of truth in a model at hand, we can now define "logical consequence" between a set of diagrams and a diagram. This is done just as usual. In particular, let $\Delta$ be a set of diagrams and $D$ be a diagram. Then $D$ is a "logical consequence" of $\Delta$ (in symbols $\Delta \models D$) if and only if $D$ is true in every model $M$ which is such that every member of $\Delta$ is true in $M$. A diagram $D$ is "valid" just in case it is true in every model, and "unsatisfiable" just in case it is not true in every model.

# 3   Rules of Inference

We now present the rules of inference for the system, which contain inessential variations on those given by Shin. A sample proof is given following the statement of the rules.

**Erasure of part of an $\otimes$-sequence.** $D'$ is obtainable from $D$ by this rule if and only if $D'$ results from $D$ by the erasure of some link of an $\otimes$-sequence that falls in a shaded region of $D$, provided the two halves of the sequence are reconnected by a line.

**Spreading $\otimes$'s.** $D'$ is obtainable from $D$ by this rule if and only if $D'$ results from the addition of a new link to any sequence of $D$.

**Erasure of a diagrammatic object.** A diagram $D'$ is obtainable from $D$ by this rule if and only if $D'$ results from the erasure of any entire $\otimes$-sequence, or from the erasure of the shading of any region, or by the erasure of any closed curve in accordance with the following condition: the shading of any minimal region of $D$ that would fail to cover an entire minimal region upon erasure of the curve must also be erased, and if the erasure of the curve would result in some $\otimes$-sequence having two links in some minimal region of $D'$, then one of those links must be erased (and the two halves rejoined).

**Introduction of new basic regions.** $D$ can be asserted at any line if $D$ consists of a rectangle within which is a single closed curve but no shading or sequences, or else $D$ consists of a single rectangle.

**Conflicting information.** $D'$ is obtainable from $D$ by this rule if $D'$ is any diagram and $D$ has a region that is both shaded and has an $\otimes$-sequence.

**Unification of two diagrams.** Diagram $D$ is obtainable from $D_1$ and $D_2$ by unification if and only if the following hold:

1. The set of labels of $D$ is the union of the set of labels of $D_1$ and the set of labels of $D_2$.

2. If a region $r$ of either $D_1$ or $D_2$ is shaded, then there is a counterpart of it in $D$ which is also shaded. Likewise, if any region $r$ of $D$ is shaded, then there is a counterpart of it in either $D_1$ or $D_2$ which is also shaded.

3. If $r$ is a region having an $\otimes$-sequence in either $D_1$ or $D_2$, then there is a counterpart of it in $D$ which also has an $\otimes$-sequence. Similarly, if any region $r$ of $D$ has an $\otimes$-sequence, then there is a counterpart of it in either $D_1$ or $D_2$ which also has an $\otimes$-sequence.

By the results of Polythress and Sun [1972] and More [1959] showing that for any number $n$ there is a diagram satisfying the partial-overlapping rule having $n$ closed curves, such a unification is always possible.

The rule allowing the erasure of shading or $\otimes$-sequences is similar to conjunction elimination, permitting one to throw away information. The rule of erasure of part of a sequence is valid because the sequence asserts that there is an object in at least one of the sets represented by the various minimal regions containing links of the sequence, while the shading asserts of some such minimal region that no object falls in the set represented by it. Therefore, it is legitimate to erase the link of the sequence falling in that region. The rule allowing the addition of extra links to a sequence is similar to a rule allowing the addition of extra disjuncts to a disjunction. Unification allows one to combine the assertions made by two diagrams; it is analogous to conjunction introduction.

A diagram $D$ is "provable" from a set of diagrams $\Delta$ (in symbols $\Delta \vdash D$) if and only if there is a sequence of diagrams $D_0, \ldots, D_n$ such that each diagram is a member of $\Delta$ or else is obtainable from earlier diagrams in the sequence by one of the rules of inference. A set of diagrams, $\Delta$, is "consistent" if and only if there is no diagram $D$ such that $\Delta \vdash D$ and

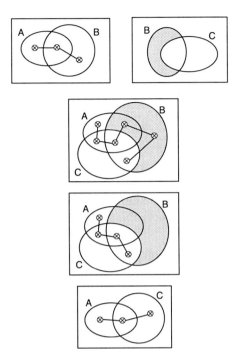

Figure 6: An example of a proof.

for some region $r$ of $D$, $r$ contains an $\otimes$-sequence and is shaded. Figure 6 shows an example of a proof in the system. First, the two premises are unified, then the rule of erasure of part of a sequence is applied, and finally the rule of erasure of a closed curve is applied.

# 4   Soundness and Completeness

**Theorem 4.1** (Soundness) *Let* $\Delta$ *be a collection of diagrams,* $D$ *a diagram. Then if* $\Delta \vdash D$, $\Delta \models D$.

   **Proof:** The proof is a straightforward induction and can be found in Shin [1991a]. $\qquad\qquad\square$

   We now prove that $\Delta \models D$ implies $\Delta \vdash D$ for arbitrary $\Delta$ (finite or infinite), extending the following result of Shin, proved in Shin [1991a]. Since the proof involves unifying together all the diagrams in $\Delta$, it cannot be generalized to handle the infinite case.

**Theorem 4.2** (Finite Completeness) [Shin] *Let $\Delta$ be a finite set of diagrams, $D$ a diagram. Then if $\Delta \models D$ then $\Delta \vdash D$.*

**Proof Sketch:** Assuming $\Delta \models D$, the following provides a procedure for constructing a proof of $D$ from $\Delta$. First, unify all the diagrams of $\Delta$ together. Then, if there are any labels occurring in $D$ that do not occur in the unification, use the rule of introduction of a new basic region and unification to add closed curves with these labels to the unification; call this diagram $U$. Next, apply the rule of erasure of part of an $\otimes$-sequence to $U$ as many times as possible to get a set of diagrams, none of which contain $\otimes$'s in shaded regions. Unify all of these together to get a diagram $U^+$. Then close the set $\{U^+\}$ under the rule of spreading $\otimes$'s. The resulting set is finite. Unify the set together to get another diagram $U^{++}$. Shin has proved that one can then simply apply the rule of erasure of curves, sequences, and shading to $U^{++}$ as needed to get $D$.     □

The key step in our proof of the general completeness theorem will be showing that whenever $\Delta$ is a "maximally consistent" set of diagrams, it has a model $M$:

**Definition** Let $\Delta$ be a consistent set of diagrams. $\Delta$ is "maximally consistent" if and only if for any diagram $D \notin \Delta$, $\Delta \cup \{D\}$ is inconsistent.

Negation typically plays a crucial role in completeness theorems for linguistic systems. Unfortunately, most of the diagrams of the system are not negatable. Since we will nevertheless want to use facts about the negations of certain diagrams in our proof, it is necessary to specify a class of diagrams which do have negations:

**Definition** A "positive diagram" is a diagram that contains exactly one $\otimes$-sequence but no shaded regions. A "negative diagram" is a diagram that contains a shaded region but no $\otimes$-sequences.

The "negation" of a positive or negative diagram is defined as follows:

**Definition** Let $D$ be a positive diagram where region $r$ is the region with the $\otimes$-sequence. Then the "negation" of D, in symbols $\neg D$, is defined to be the diagram just like D except without the $\otimes$-sequence and with region $r$ shaded. Similarly, let $D$ be a negative diagram where region $r$ is the shaded region. Then $\neg D$ is defined to be the diagram just like D except having an $\otimes$-sequence in region $r$ and no shading.

For example, each of the two diagrams in Figure 7 is the negation of the other.

In showing that every maximally consistent set has a model, we will need to know various closure properties of such sets. In particular, we will need analogs of the corresponding closure conditions needed for Henkin-style completeness theorems for linguistic systems. To give an example, in

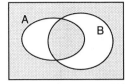 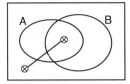

Figure 7: Positive and negative diagrams that are negations of one another.

a linguistic system such as first-order logic one typically would verify such conditions as:

- A conjunction is a member of a maximally consistent set if and only if both conjuncts are;

- A disjunction is a member of such a set if and only if at least one disjunct is.

We will want to establish similar sorts of conditions for maximally consistent sets of diagrams. The following definition gives the diagrammatic analog of the conjuncts of a sentence:

**Definition** Let $D$ be any diagram. An "immediate subdiagram" of $D$ is any diagram $D'$ that is obtained from $D$ by erasing either:

1. All of the shading and all but one of the $\otimes$-sequences, or

2. All of the $\otimes$-sequences (but leaving the shading).

Notice that any immediate subdiagram of a diagram $D$ is either a positive or a negative diagram.

To illustrate, in Figure 8 the two lower diagrams are the immediate subdiagrams of the upper diagram.

The following proposition reveals the relationship between a diagram and its immediate subdiagrams:

**Proposition 4.3** Let $D$ be a diagram and $\{D_1, \ldots, D_n\}$ be its immediate subdiagrams. Then $D$ is provable from $\{D_1, \ldots, D_n\}$ using only the rule of unification, and each of $D_1, \ldots, D_n$ is provable from $D$ using only the rule of erasure.

In virtue of this proposition we have that a diagram is a member of a maximally consistent set if and only if all of its immediate subdiagrams are. Moreover, a diagram is true in a model if and only if each of its immediate subdiagrams is true in the model, since the definition of truth in a model requires the model to satisfy each sequence of the diagram and the shading

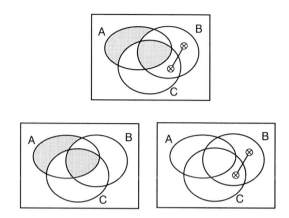

Figure 8: A diagram and its two immediate subdiagrams.

of the diagram. So to show that a maximally consistent set has a model we need only show that there is a model of all of its positive and negative diagrams. This fact gives the desired conjunctive closure condition.

We would also like to have a diagrammatic counterpart of the usual closure condition for disjunction: that a disjunction is a member of a maximally consistent set if and only if a disjunct is. The diagrammatic counterparts of disjunctions will be the positive diagrams since they assert that some object falls in at least one of the sets represented by minimal regions containing a link. The following result yields the desired closure condition for maximally consistent sets concerning these "diagrammatic disjunctions." Shin's finite completeness theorem is used here and in the proof of the more general completeness theorem proved later.

**Lemma 4.4** (Lemma on Links) *Let $D$ be a diagram with a single $\otimes$-sequence and no shading. Let $r_1, \ldots, r_n$ be the minimal regions of $D$ that contain links of the $\otimes$-sequence. If $\Delta \cup \{D\}$ is consistent, then so is $\Delta \cup \{D_i\}$ for some $1 \leq i \leq n$, where $D_i$ is obtained from $D$ by erasing the $\otimes$-sequence and drawing in a single $\otimes$ in region $r_i$.*

**Proof:** Suppose that $\Delta \cup \{D_i\}$ is inconsistent for each $1 \leq i \leq n$. Then for some finite subset $\Delta_0$ of $\Delta$, $\Delta_0 \cup \{D_i\}$ is inconsistent for each $i$. By Soundness, $\Delta_0 \cup \{D_i\}$ is unsatisfiable for each $i$. Therefore, $\Delta_0 \models \neg D_i$ for each $i$. This means that $\Delta_0 \models \neg D$ since $D$ consists of the unification of the $\neg D_i$s for $1 \leq i \leq n$. So by Finite Completeness we have that $\Delta_0 \vdash \neg D$, and so $\Delta \vdash \neg D$. Therefore $\Delta \cup \{D\}$ is inconsistent. □

The following consequence of the Lemma on Links will be needed in the completeness proof:

**Lemma 4.5** *Let $D$ be a diagram having an $\otimes$-sequence $S$ with links in minimal regions $r_1, \ldots, r_n$. If $\Delta \cup \{D\}$ is consistent, then so is $\Delta \cup \{D_i\}$ for some $1 \leq i \leq n$, where $D_i$ is obtained from $D$ by erasing the $\otimes$-sequence and drawing in a single $\otimes$ in region $r_i$.*

**Proof:** Let $D', D_1', \ldots, D_m'$ be the immediate subdiagrams of $D$, where $D'$ is the subdiagram resulting from erasing all shading and all sequences except $S$. Because of the rule of erasure $\Delta \cup \{D', D_1', \ldots, D_m'\}$ is consistent. Let $s_1, \ldots, s_n$ be the minimal regions of $D'$ having links of its sequence. For each $1 \leq i \leq n$, let $D_i''$ follow from $D'$ by erasing the $\otimes$-sequence from $D'$ and drawing in a single $\otimes$ in region $s_i$. Then by the Lemma on Links $\Delta \cup \{D_i'', D_1', \ldots, D_m'\}$ is consistent for some $1 \leq i \leq n$. Hence $\Delta \cup \{D''\}$ is consistent, where $D''$ is the result of unifying together all of $\{D_i'', D_1', \ldots, D_m'\}$. But $D''$ is exactly $D_i$ for some $1 \leq i \leq n$, as needed. $\square$

An immediate consequence of the Lemma on Links is that a positive diagram is a member of a maximally consistent set if and only if one of its diagrammatic "disjuncts" is. Moreover, a positive diagram is true in a model if and only if at least one of its "disjuncts" is.

We have already established that we need only show all positive and negative diagrams in a maximally consistent set have a model. But the Lemma on Links makes the job even easier, since a positive diagram is a member of a maximally consistent set if and only if one of its "disjuncts" is. So to show a maximally consistent set has a model we need only show that all negative diagrams and positive diagrams having a single $\otimes$ in the set have a model. For notational convenience, we will call such positive diagrams "positive atomic" diagrams:

**Definition** An "atomic diagram" is any diagram having either:

1. Exactly one $\otimes$ (i.e. an $\otimes$-sequence of length one) and no shading (a "positive atomic diagram"), or else

2. Exactly one minimal region shaded and no $\otimes$-sequences (a "negative atomic diagram").

We can summarize the above discussion in the following proposition:

**Proposition 4.6** *Let $\Delta$ be a maximal consistent set of diagrams, $M$ a model. Then $M \models \Delta$ if and only if $M \models D$ for all atomic diagrams $D \in \Delta$.*

We can now turn to the task of constructing a model of all the atomic diagrams in a maximally consistent set. As in the proof of the corresponding result for first-order logic, we construct this model $M$ from syntactic objects taken from the maximally consistent set $\Delta$ itself. In particular, the domain of our desired model $M$ will be taken simply to be the set of all

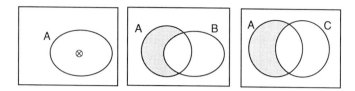

Figure 9: Three possible members of $\Delta$.

the positive atomic diagrams $D_1, D_2, \ldots$ in $\Delta$ (of which there are at most denumerably many).

The model $M$ will have to account for each positive atomic diagram $D_n$ in $\Delta$ by assigning some object, a "witness," to the region having the $\otimes$. $M$ will simply assign $D_n$ itself to the region of $D_n$ with the $\otimes$. However, we cannot determine to which basic regions $D_n$ is to be assigned on the basis of $D_n$ alone. We need to make the assignment so that the witness is not inadvertently assigned to some shaded region of a negative atomic diagram occurring in $\Delta$. For example, suppose $D_n$ is the left-hand diagram in Figure 9. To decide how to satisfy $D_n$ we can't look at $D_n$ alone, say putting some object in the basic region labeled by "A" and no other basic regions. This is because there may be negative diagrams like the middle diagram of Figure 9 in $\Delta$ as well, which would then be false in the model constructed. So, in this case, the witness assigned to the region with the $\otimes$ in $D_n$ would also have to be assigned to the region of the middle diagram labeled by "$B$" in order not to accidentally make it false. Likewise, there may be many other negative diagrams that will need to be considered in deciding how to assign the witness making $D_n$ true, such as the right-hand diagram in Figure 9. To avoid accidentally making this diagram false, $D_n$ would also have to be assigned to the basic region labeled "C." In short, in determining to which regions a witness will be assigned, we will have to look at all the negative diagrams of our set $\Delta$ as well.

We construct a sequence of models $M_1, M_2, \ldots$ which all have domain $\{D_1, D_2, \ldots\}$ such that $I_n(r) \subseteq I_{n+1}(r)$ for all basic regions $r$, and such that each $M_i$ models $D_1, D_2, \ldots, D_i$ and every negative atomic diagram occurring in $\Delta$. Stage $n$ of the construction determines how the witness of the $\otimes$ of $D_n$ is to be assigned to regions. To construct $I_n$ we construct a sequence $I_n^0, I_n^1, \ldots$ each of which is a better approximation of $I_n$ in the sense of satisfying more and more negative diagrams as well as $D_n$. Finally, we define our model to have domain $\{D_1, D_2, \ldots\}$ and define the interpretation of a region to be the union of the interpretations of that region by each of the $I_n$'s. We then show that each atomic diagram in $\Delta$ is true in the model.

**Theorem 4.7** *If* $\Delta$ *is a maximal consistent set of diagrams, then* $\Delta$ *is satisfiable.*

**Proof:** Let $D_1, D_2, \ldots$ enumerate the positive atomic diagrams of $\Delta$ and $E_1, E_2, \ldots$ enumerate the negative atomic diagrams of $\Delta$. And we also let $V = \{D_1, D_2, \ldots\}$. Define the functions $I_n$ inductively as follows. $I_0(r) = \emptyset$. Suppose that $I_{n-1}$ has been defined. In order to define $I_n$, we will first define a sequence of functions $I_n^0, I_n^1, \ldots$ and, simultaneously, a sequence of diagrams $X^0, X^1, \ldots$ as follows. Let $X^0$ be the diagram $D_n$. So $X^0$ contains a single $\otimes$ in some minimal region. Set $I_n^0(r) = I_{n-1}(r) \cup \{D_n\}$ for each basic region $r$ of $X^0$ such that the $\otimes$ of $X^0$ falls within $r$, and $I_n^0(s) = I_{n-1}(s)$ for all other basic regions $s$. So we have assigned the object $D_n$ to regions in such a way as to satisfy $D_n$. Assume that $I_n^{m-1}$ and $X^{m-1}$ have been defined. Unify $X^{m-1}$ and $E_m$, and replace the $\otimes$-sequence in the unification by a single $\otimes$ in accordance with Lemma 4.5; call this diagram $X^m$. Observe that $X^m \in \Delta$. $X^m$ consists, essentially, of unifying $D_n$ with the first $m$ negative atomic diagrams, then shortening the $\otimes$-sequence derived from the $\otimes$ in $D_n$ to a single link. Set $I_n^m(r) = I_n^{m-1}(r) \cup \{D_n\}$ for each basic region $r$ of $X^m$ such that the $\otimes$ of $X^m$ is contained in $r$, and, for *all other* basic regions $s$, $I_n^m(s) = I_n^{m-1}(s)$. $I_n^m$ has now assigned the witness $D_n$ in such a way as to satisfy the diagram $D_n$ along with the first $m$ negative diagrams. Observe that $I_n^m(r) \subseteq I_n^{m+1}(r)$ for all basic regions $r$. Now define $I_n(r) = \bigcup_{m \in \omega} I_n^m(r)$ for all basic regions $r$. By Proposition 2.1, we can assume that $I_n$ has been extended to *all* regions. Finally, define $I(r) = \bigcup_{n \in \omega} I_n(r)$ for all basic regions $r$. Again, by Proposition 2.1, we can assume that $I$ has been extended to all regions. This completes the construction of the desired interpretation function $I$. We now just need to verify that each of $D_1, D_2, \ldots$ and $E_1, E_2, \ldots$ is true in $(V, I)$.

We first show that for each $n$, $(V, I_n) \models E_i$ for each $E_i$. This is the most difficult part of the proof. Suppose for induction that $(V, I_{n-1}) \models E_i$ for all $i$. Pick some arbitrary $E_m$; we will show that $(V, I_n) \models E_m$. By the induction hypothesis, the only way we could have $(V, I_n) \not\models E_m$ would be if $D_n \in I_n(r_m)$ where $r_m$ is the shaded minimal region of $E_m$ (because $I_n$ agrees with $I_{n-1}$ on which regions every object in the domain gets assigned to except possibly the object $D_n$). So we only have to worry about how $D_n$ gets assigned to regions. Suppose, then, that $(V, I_n) \not\models E_m$. Then if $b_1, \ldots, b_i$ are the basic regions of $E_m$ its shading falls within and $c_1, \ldots, c_j$ are the basic regions of $E_m$ its shading falls outside of, we must have that $D_n \in I_n(b_1)$ and $\ldots$ and $D_n \in I_n(b_i)$ and $D_n \notin I_n(c_1)$ and $\ldots$ and $D_n \notin I_n(c_j)$. Consider now the diagram $X^m$; $X^m$ results from first unifying all of $D_n, E_1, \ldots, E_m$ together, then applying Lemma 4.5 to shorten the one $\otimes$-sequence in the unification down to a single link. It was noted above that $X^m$ must be a member of $\Delta$. Since $E_m$ was part of the unification, $X^m$ has basic regions which are counterparts of each of $E_m$'s basic regions $b_1, \ldots, b_i, c_1, \ldots, c_j$; call these $b_1^{cp}, \ldots b_i^{cp}, c_1^{cp}, \ldots c_j^{cp}$. Therefore, $X_m$ has a region which is a counterpart of $r_m$; call this region $r_m^{cp}$. We will now argue that the $\otimes$ of $X^m$ must fall within region $r_m^{cp}$.

Each of the diagrams $X^0, X^1, X^2, \ldots$ in the construction, say $X^k$, contains a single $\otimes$ in some minimal region $r_k$. To construct the next diagram $X^{k+1}$, $X^k$ is unified with $E_{k+1}$ which results in the $\otimes$ of $X^k$ being extended into an $\otimes$-sequence in some counterpart of region $r_k$; this sequence is then shortened down to a single link by the Lemma on Links to get $X^{k+1}$. So the $\otimes$ of $X^{k+1}$ occurs in some subregion of a counterpart of $r_k$. Moreover, the same is true of all the later diagrams $X^{k+2}, X^{k+3}, \ldots$; they all contain a single $\otimes$ in some subregion of a counterpart of $r_k$. So, essentially, the $\otimes$ keeps getting put into smaller and smaller subregions. From these observations it follows that the $\otimes$ of $X^m$ must fall in region $r_m^{cp}$: First, since $D_n$ is eventually assigned to each of $b_1^{cp}, \ldots b_i^{cp}$, and since the $\otimes$'s keep getting put into smaller regions, the $\otimes$ of $X^m$ must already occur within each of $b_1^{cp}, \ldots b_i^{cp}$ (if it did not fall within one of these regions in diagram $X^m$, it would never fall within the region's counterparts at later stages, and so $D_n$ would not be assigned to that region by $I_n$). Likewise, since $D_n$ does not ever get assigned to any of $c_1^{cp}, \ldots c_j^{cp}$ by any of $I_n^0, I_n^1, \ldots$, the $\otimes$ of $X^m$ cannot fall within any of these regions of $X^m$ (otherwise one of $D_n \notin I_n(c_1), \ldots, D_n \notin I_n(c_j)$ would be false). We have established that $X^m$'s $\otimes$ falls within each of $b_1^{cp}, \ldots b_i^{cp}$ and outside of each of $c_1^{cp}, \ldots c_j^{cp}$, that is, within $r_{cp}$. However, $X^m$ consists of unifying $E_m$ with $D_n$ and $E_1, \ldots, E_{m-1}$, and since region $r$ is shaded in $E_m$, region $r_{cp}$ is shaded in $X^m$. Region $r_{cp}$ is both shaded and contains a $\otimes$, contradicting the consistency of $\Delta$. So we have that $(V, I_n) \models E_m$, as needed.

Now suppose that $(V, I) \not\models E_m$ for some negative atomic diagram $E_m$ in $\Delta$, and let $r$ be the shaded minimal region of $E_m$. Then there is a $D_n$ such that $D_n \in I(r)$. Therefore $D_n \in I_n(r)$ since which regions $D_n$ is assigned to by $I$ is determined by which regions it is assigned to by $I_n$. Hence $(V, I_n) \not\models E_m$, a contradiction. Therefore every negative atomic diagram in $\Delta$ is true in $(V, I)$.

We next show that $(V, I)$ models $D_1, D_2, \ldots$. Suppose $r$ is the minimal region of $D_n$ that contains the $\otimes$. Let $b_1, \ldots, b_i$ be the basic regions of $D_n$ its $\otimes$ falls within and $c_1, \ldots, c_j$ be the basic regions of $D_n$ its $\otimes$ falls outside of. So the $\otimes$ of $X^0$ falls within each of $b_1, \ldots, b_i$ and outside each of $c_1, \ldots, c_j$ (since $X^0$ is just $D_n$). Moreover, as argued above, the $\otimes$'s occurring in the diagrams $X_1, X_2, \ldots$ of later stages occur in subregions of counterparts of $r$; that is, they occur within counterparts of each of $b_1, \ldots, b_i$ and outside of counterparts of each of $c_1, \ldots, c_j$. Therefore, we have that $D_n \in I_n(b_1), \ldots, D_n \in I_n(b_i), D_n \notin I_n(c_1), \ldots, D_n \notin I_n(c_j)$, that is, $D_n \in I_n(r)$. Therefore $D_n \in I(b_1), \ldots, D_n \in I(b_i), D_n \notin I(c_1), \ldots, D_n \notin I(c_j)$, that is, $D_n \in I(r)$. So each positive atomic diagram is true in $(V, I)$.

Since every atomic diagram of $\Delta$ is true in $(V, I)$, and since $\Delta$ is maximal, by 4.6 we have that $(V, I) \models \Delta$, as needed. □

By the fact that every consistent set can be extended to a maximally consistent one, established in the usual way, we get the following corollary:

**Corollary 4.8** (Model Existence Theorem) *Every consistent set of diagrams has a model.*

The completeness theorem does not fall out as easily as in systems having negation. The argument one would like to give would be: "Suppose $\Delta \nvdash D$. Then $\Delta \cup \{\neg D\}$ is consistent, so has a model, by the above corollary, and therefore $\Delta \nvDash D$." Unfortunately there need be no such diagram $\neg D$. So, instead, we must appeal to diagrams' immediate subdiagrams and Shin's finite completeness theorem. The lack of negation in the system seems to make everything more difficult to prove, though perhaps as a result more interesting.

**Corollary 4.9** (Completeness) *Let $\Delta$ be a set of diagrams, $D$ a diagram. Then if $\Delta \models D$, $\Delta \vdash D$.*

**Proof:** Suppose that $\Delta \nvdash D$. Let $D_1, \ldots, D_n$ be the immediate subdiagrams of $D$. Then it must be the case that $\Delta \cup \{\neg D_i\}$ is consistent for some $1 \leq i \leq n$. Suppose otherwise. Then there would be a finite subset $\Delta_0$ of $\Delta$ such that $\Delta_0 \cup \neg\{D_i\}$ is inconsistent for each $1 \leq i \leq n$. By Soundness, $\Delta_0 \cup \neg\{D_i\}$ would be unsatisfiable. So $\Delta_0 \models D_i$ for each $i$ and hence $\Delta_0 \models D$. Thus $\Delta_0 \vdash D$ (by 4.2) and thus $\Delta \vdash D$, a contradiction. So, for some $i$, $\Delta \cup \{\neg D_i\}$ is consistent, and therefore satisfiable by the Model Existence Theorem. Let $M \models \Delta \cup \{\neg D_i\}$. Then $M$ is a model of $\Delta$ but not of $D_i$. Thus $M$ does not model $D$. Hence $\Delta \nvDash D$, a contradiction. □

# Chapter VI

# Peircean Graphs for Propositional Logic

ERIC HAMMER

The contributions of C.S. Peirce to the early history of propositional and predicate logic are well known. Much less well known, however, is Peirce's subsequent work (for more than ten years) on diagrammatic versions of propositional and predicate logic. This work was considered by Peirce himself to be his most important contribution to logic.

From his experience with chemistry and other parts of science, Peirce had become convinced that logic needed a more visually perspicuous notation, a notation that displayed the compound structure of propositions the way chemical diagrams displayed the compound structure of molecules. Peirce's graphs for propositional sentences are built up from sentence letters by the operations of enclosing a graph within a closed figure (interpreted as its negation) and juxtaposing two or more graphs on separate parts of the page (interpreted as their conjunction). For example, a graph like

would be interpreted as "If $A$ and $B$, then $C$" or "It is false that $A$ and $B$ and not–$C$." A graph such as

would be read as "If $A$ then $B$, but not $C$."

This chapter gives a modern analysis of Peirce's diagrammatic version of the propositional calculus from the ground up. In particular, it is an investigation of just what is involved in formulating precisely the syntax, semantics, and proof theory of Peirce's graphical approach to propositional logic.

The project is interesting for several reasons. First, given Peirce's importance in the history of logic and his own opinion of the value of his work on graphs, it seems of historical interest to see to what his suggestions amounted. Second, Peirce's work has gained a following in the computer science community, due especially to the work of Sowa [1984], whose system of conceptual graphs is modeled after Peirce's work on diagrammatic approaches to propositional and predicate logic.

Third, in reconstructing Peirce's graphical system we will confront a number of features characteristic of "visual" or "diagrammatic" inference, that is, inference that employs various forms of graphical representations in addition to, or in place of, sentences.[1] Given the ever-increasing importance of computer-generated graphical representations, it is important to get a handle on their logical characteristics. Peirce's work gives us a place to start as it deals with a number of such features. For example, in contrast to a more standard notion of provability is a notion of "provability" of a graph from a set of graphs. This notion of provability does not allow one to refer back to previous stages of a proof, say to use a version of conjunction introduction. Rather, one is restricted to making incremental changes to a single diagram. Thus, as is often done in actual reasoning with diagrams, one successively modifies a single diagram. Another feature of Peirce's system characteristic of visual inference is that additional care must be taken in specifying when two drawn graphs are tokens of the same graph. This question is by now routine in the linguistic case where well-formed representations are modeled as sequences of symbols, but this question typically requires different answers for each graphical logic.

A few previous logical studies of Peirce's system have been given, though often without adequate attention to the unique features of both the semantics and the syntax. Roberts [1933] and Zeman [1964] give a method for translating between the graphs and standard systems of propositional logic. Using this they establish the consistency and weak completeness of the system. White [1984] also proves a version of weak completeness for the system. Sowa [1984] briefly discusses the logic of a system of conceptual graphs based on Peirce's system.

The present chapter is intended to provide a more detailed and direct analysis of the syntax, semantics, and proof theory of Peirce's system than has been provided so far, and also to address a number of logical features of the system (such as strong completeness) that have not yet been examined. It will become clear that in following Peirce's approach to the propositional calculus some aspects of the development are similar to tradional approaches while others are quite different. Most of the space will

---

[1]See Barwise [1993a], Barwise and Etchemendy [1991a], Shin [1994].

be devoted to the novel aspects of Peirce's system.

Peirce actually had three different graphical logics, alpha, beta, and gamma. Alpha is a graphical version of propositional logic, beta of predicate logic, and gamma of a kind of modal logic. In this chapter, we restrict attention to the simplest of these, his alpha logic.[2]

# 1  Graphical Syntax

As with propositional formulas in traditional treatments, alpha graphs are built recursively from a stock of sentence letters: $A, B, C, \ldots$. Graphs are constructed from (1) these letters and (2) a closed figure enclosing nothing (which will be interpreted as bottom or falsehood) by applying two simple operations:

1. drawing a non-self-intersecting closed curve (or "cut" as Peirce calls it) around a graph (which has the effect of negating the enclosed graph), and

2. juxtaposing two or more graphs on separate areas of the page (which has the effect of asserting them conjunctively).

For example,

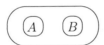

is a graph constructed by enclosing each of $A$ and $B$ within a cut, juxtaposing these two graphs, and then enclosing the result within a cut. When semantics are given this will be interpreted as meaning the same as $\neg(\neg A \wedge \neg B)$. Likewise,

is a graph constructed by juxtaposing $A$ and $B$, enclosing them within a cut, juxtaposing it with $C$, enclosing this graph within a cut, and then juxtaposing it with $A$. Thus, it will be interpreted below as $A \wedge \neg(C \wedge \neg(A \wedge B))$.

---

[2]Compared to the alpha system, the syntax, semantics, and rules of inference of Peirce's beta system are extremely complex. While some of the logic of beta is studied in Roberts [1933], Sowa [1984], and Zeman [1964], further investigation of its logic would certainly be worthwhile.

Just as it is convenient to talk about subformulas of a propositional formula, it is convenient to have a precise notion of subgraph. Thus, if $G$ is a graph of a cut enclosing some graph $G'$, then $G'$ is the only *subgraph* of $G$. If $G$ is a graph consisting of the juxtaposition of graphs $G_1, \ldots, G_n$ where each of these is either a sentence letter or a graph consisting of a cut enclosing some other graph, then $G_1, \ldots, G_n$ are the *immediate subgraphs* of $G$. Nothing else is an immediate subgraph. For example, the graph

$$\boxed{A}\ \boxed{B}\ C$$

has the following three immediate subgraphs:

Subgraph 1    Subgraph 2    Subgraph 3
$$\boxed{A}\qquad\qquad \boxed{B}\qquad\qquad C$$

However, the graph

$$\boxed{\boxed{A}\ \boxed{B}\ C}$$

has only one immediate subgraph:

$$\boxed{A}\ \boxed{B}\ C$$

The *subgraphs* of a graph are defined in the following way. If $G$ is a sentence letter, then the only subgraph of $G$ is $G$ itself. If $G$ consists of the enclosure of some graph $G'$ within a cut, then the subgraphs of $G$ consists of $G$ together with the subgraphs of $G'$. If $G$ consists of the juxtaposition of $G_1, \ldots, G_n$, its immediate subgraphs, then the subgraphs of $G$ consist of $G$ together with the subgraphs of any juxtaposition of any of $G_1, \ldots, G_n$. For example, the subgraphs of

$$\boxed{A}\ \boxed{B}\ C$$

consist of the following nine graphs:

Subgraph 1: $\boxed{A}\ \boxed{B}\ C$         Subgraph 6:     $\boxed{B}$

Subgraph 2: $\boxed{A}\ \boxed{B}$            Subgraph 7: $\boxed{A}$

Subgraph 3: $\boxed{A}\qquad C$              Subgraph 8:  $A$

Subgraph 4: $\qquad\boxed{B}\ C$             Subgraph 9:     $B$

Subgraph 5: $\qquad\qquad C$

## Identity Conditions among Drawn Graphs

Because sentences can be modeled as sequences of symbols, it is very clear when one has written two tokens of the same sentence. However, since graphs are two–dimensional rather than linear, it is not obvious how one determines whether one has two drawn tokens of two different graphs or two drawn tokens of the same graph.

The conditions under which two graph tokens are of the same graph type are defined by the construction history of graphs, i.e., in terms of how they can be built up from sentence letters by the operations of juxtaposition and enclosure within a cut. Thus, two drawn graphs are just two different *instances of the same graph* if and only if they can be constructed from sentence letters by applying the same operations of juxtaposition and cut in the same order. For example, the following are three different drawn tokens of the same graph:

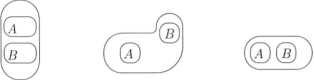

They are all tokens of the same graph because each of them can be constructed by first enclosing $A$ and $B$ within cuts, then juxtaposing them, then enclosing the result within a cut. On the other hand, the graph

is a token of a different graph. It is constructed by enclosing $B$ within a cut, juxtaposing it with $A$, then enclosing the result within a cut. None of the above tokens can be constructed in this way.

## Linear Notation

Peirce occasionally employs a linear notation for his graphs, that is, a notation that is convenient for typesetting and space considerations though not as visually perspicuous as his two-dimensional notation. Cuts are represented by a pair of matching parentheses while juxtaposition is represented by linear juxtaposition, that is, by concatenation. (So the two–dimensional juxtaposition is just a generalization of the familiar operation of linear concatenation.) As an example of this linear notation, the two sequences

$$((A)(B))$$

and

$$((B)(A))$$

are both linear representations of the following graph:

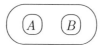

On the other hand, the graph

is represented by any of the following eight sequences:

$$((AB)C)A \qquad A((AB)C)$$
$$((BA)C)A \qquad A((BA)C)$$
$$(C(AB))A \qquad A(C(AB))$$
$$(C(BA))A \qquad A(C(BA))$$

For typographic reasons, this linear notation will be used frequently in the remainder of this chapter.

## Linear Juxtaposition as a Binary Operation

It is possible to conceptualize the syntax of Peirce's graphs in linear notation in a somewhat more standard manner. For the purposes of this subsection, let "¬" be a unary operation symbol taking the place of Peirce's cut, let parentheses serve as the usual grouping symbols rather than as cuts, and let "∗" be a binary operation symbol used to represent the juxtaposition of graphs. Thus, we want ∗ to be interpreted as the commutative and associative operation of juxtaposition, so the expressions $(A * (B * C))$, $(A * (C * B))$, $((B * C) * A)$, $((C * B) * A)$, $(B * (A * C))$, $(B * (C * A))$, $((A * C) * B)$, $((C * A) * B)$, $(C * (B * A))$, $(C * (A * B))$, $((B * A) * C)$, and $((A * B) * C)$ all refer to the same graph. One can therefore simply drop parentheses and ignore order, writing any of $ABC$ or $ACB$ or $BAC$ or $BCA$ or $CAB$ or $CBA$ for any of the above twelve sentences. In fact, one might as well adopt a more coarse-grained approach to the syntax, treating all of these six permutations of the three letters as alternative ways of writing the same sentence. Thus, under this approach, different sequences represent the same sentence. Order is being ignored, but scope of negation symbols is preserved. So a sentence like $A\neg(BAB\neg(CB))$ could be expressed by other tokens, tokens consisting of different sequences of symbols, such as $A\neg(ABB\neg(BC))$, $\neg(\neg(CB)BBA)A$, etc. However, a sequence like $\neg(ABAB\neg(CB))$ represents a different sentence from these because, for example, it lacks an $A$ not enclosed by any negation symbols.

Thus, in a sense, the difference between the syntax of Peirce's graphical notation and this linear notation is captured by the commutativity and associativity of the operation $*$.

## 2   The Interpretation of Peircean Graphs

The semantics for Peirce's system is similar to that for propositional logic.

**Definition 2.1 (Valuation).** A *valuation* is a function $v$ assigning a truth value to each graph such that: (1) $v$ assigns false to the graph (), (2) for every graph $G$, $(G)$ is assigned true if and only if $G$ is assigned false, and (3) for every graph $G$ consisting of the juxtaposition of some graphs $G_1, \ldots, G_n$, $G$ is true if and only if each $G_i$ is true for $1 \leq i \leq n$.

**Notation:**   Where $v$ is a valuation, we write "$v \models G$" to mean that $v$ assigns truth to $G$, and "$v \not\models G$" to mean that $v$ assigns falsehood to $G$.

It is now necessary to prove that any function assigning truth or falsehood to each letter and falsehood to () can be extended uniquely to a valuation assigning truth or falsity to all graphs. What makes the existence part of this unusual, and slightly tricky, is that the operation of juxtaposition is such that graphs lack the property of unique readability. In other words, most graphs fail to have a unique construction history under the operations of enclosure within a cut and juxtaposition. For example, the graph $A(BAC)$ can be constructed by juxtaposing $A$ with $B$, juxtaposing this with $C$, enclosing it within a cut and then juxtaposing it with $C$. Alternatively, it can be constructed by first juxtaposing $A$ with $C$, then juxtaposing this with $B$, and so on as before. Or it can be constructed by simultaneously juxtaposing $A$, $B$ and $C$, and so on as before. What this means is that if some property of graphs is defined inductively in terms of subgraphs, it will not be obvious that the property is well-defined.

Therefore, to prove the needed theorem, we will proceed indirectly by first defining a notion of "strict valuation" which does allow for straightforward induction in terms of immediate subgraphs rather than just subgraphs:

**Definition 2.2 (Strict Valuation).** A *strict valuation* is a function $v$ assigning a truth value to each graph such that: (1) $v$ assigns false to the graph (), (2) for every graph $G$, $(G)$ is assigned true if and only if $G$ is assigned false, and (3) for every graph $G$ consisting of the juxtaposition of graphs $G_1, \ldots, G_n$ where these are its immediate subgraphs, $G$ is true if and only if each $G_i$ is true for $1 \leq i \leq n$.

Since a graph is uniquely decomposable into *immediate* subgraphs, by a standard argument one can prove that every function assigning truth or falsehood to letters and falsehood to () can be extended to a strict valuation:

**Lemma 2.3** *If $f$ is a function assigning a truth value to each sentence letter, then there is a unique strict valuation $v$ extending $f$.*

The next lemma shows that strict valuations have the desired homomorphic properties:

**Lemma 2.4** *Let $v$ be a strict valuation and $G$ be a graph consisting of the juxtaposition of graphs $G_1, \ldots, G_n$. Then $v \models G$ if and only if $v \models G_i$ for each $1 \leq i \leq n$.*

**Proof:** Let $\gamma_1, \ldots, \gamma_m$ be the immediate subgraphs of $G$. Then each of $G_1, \ldots, G_n$ consists of the juxtaposition of one or more of $\gamma_1, \ldots, \gamma_m$. Thus, for each $1 \leq i \leq n$, let $G_i$ consist of the juxtaposition of $\gamma_{i_1}, \ldots, \gamma_{i_{k_i}}$. Thus, $v \models G_i$ if and only if $v \models \gamma_{i_1}$ and $\ldots$ and $v \models \gamma_{i_{k_i}}$. Then we have:

$$
\begin{aligned}
v \models G \quad &\text{iff} \quad v \models \gamma_1 \text{ and } \ldots \text{ and } v \models \gamma_m \\
&\text{iff} \quad \text{for each } 1 \leq i \leq n, \, v \models \gamma_{i_1} \text{ and } \ldots \text{ and } v \models \gamma_{i_{k_i}} \\
&\text{iff} \quad \text{for each } 1 \leq i \leq n, \, v \models G_i
\end{aligned}
$$

$\square$

Using the two above lemmas, the needed theorem can now be easily proved:

**Theorem 2.5** *If $f$ is a function assigning a truth value to each sentence letter, then there is a unique valuation $v$ extending $f$.*

**Proof:** For existence, define a function $v$ as in Lemma 2.3. $v$ is a valuation by Lemma 2.4. Uniqueness is proved by a standard argument. $\square$

What it means for a graph to be a logical consequence of a set of graphs can now be defined as follows:

**Definition 2.6 (Logical Consequence).** Let $\Gamma \cup \{G\}$ be a set of alpha graphs. Then $G$ is a *logical consequence* of $\Gamma$ (written $\Gamma \models G$) if and only if every valuation that assigns true to every graph in $\Gamma$ assigns true to $G$.

The equivalence of two graphs is defined as follows:

**Definition 2.7 (Logical Equivalence).** Let $G$ and $G'$ be graphs. Then $G$ is *logically equivalent* to $G'$, in symbols $G \equiv G'$, if and only if for every valuation $v$, $v \models G$ iff $v \models G'$.

**Definition 2.8 (Satisfiability).** A set of graphs $\Gamma$ is *satisfiable* just in case there is a valuation $v$ that assigns true to all of its members.

# 3   Rules of Inference

Peirce's rules of inference allow one to work with (possibly deeply nested) subgraphs of a graph.

**Insertion in Odd**   Suppose $X$ is a subgraph of $G'$ falling within an odd number of cuts, and suppose $G$ is a graph that results from $G'$ by erasing that occurrence of $X$. Then one can obtain $G'$ from $G$ by Insertion in Odd.

Here are some examples, by the rule of insertion in odd one can infer $A(BC)$ from $A(C)$ by inserting $B$ within one cut, $(B(A(C)((D)A))C)$ from $(B(A(C)(A)))$ by inserting $(D)$ within three cuts, $(A(B))$ from $()$ by inserting $A(B)$, $(((A((B)))))$ from $((((( B)))))$, and $(A(B)(C))$ from $(A(C))$.

**Erasure in Even**   Suppose $X$ is a subgraph of $G$ falling within an even number of cuts (or else no cuts), and suppose $G'$ is a graph that results from $G$ by erasing that occurrence of $X$. Then one can obtain $G'$ from $G$ by Erasure in Even.

For example, by the rule of erasure in even one can infer $(())$ from $((B))$, $(A(C))$ from $(A(BCB))$ by erasing $BB$, $((((( B)))))$ from $(((()))) $ by erasing $(B)$, and $(A())B$ from $(A(()))B$ by erasing $()$.

**Double Cut**   This rule has three different parts.

1. Let $X$ be a subgraph of $G$ where $G = x_1 \ldots x_m X x_{m+1} \ldots x_n$. Then one can obtain $x_1 \ldots x_m((X))x_{m+1} \ldots x_n$ from $G$ by double cut, and one can obtain $G$ from $x_1 \ldots x_m((X))x_{m+1} \ldots x_n$ by double cut.

2. Similarly, if $G = x_1 \ldots x_m x_{m+1} \ldots x_n$, then one can obtain from $G$ $x_1 \ldots x_m(())x_{m+1} \ldots x_n$ or vice versa by this rule.

3. Finally, the graph $(())$ consisting of two cuts is an axiom.

For example by the rule of double cut one can obtain $A(B)$ from $((A))(B)$ (and vice versa), one can obtain $A(((B)))$ from $A(B)$ (and vice versa), $(B)((C))(ABC)$ from $(B)((C)(()))(ABC)$ (and vice versa), $(())$ from nothing, and $(())A(B)$ from $A(B)$ (and vice versa).

**Iteration**   $G'$ is obtainable from $G$ by Iteration if and only if (1) there is a subgraph $X$ of $G'$ falling within cuts $C_1, \ldots, C_n$, (2) there is another instance of $X$ in $G'$ that occurs within at least the cuts $C_1, \ldots, C_n$ (and possibly others) of $G'$, and (3) $G$ results from $G'$ by erasing this second, more deeply enclosed instance of $X$.

For example, $(A)A$ follows from $()A$ by this rule (by iterating $A$), $(((BC))B)$ follows from $(((C))B)$ (by iterating $B$), $(A)(C(B)(A))$ follows from $(A)(C(B))$ (by iterating $(A)$), $ABA$ follows from $AB$ (by iterating $A$), etc.

**Deiteration**   $G'$ is obtainable from $G$ by Deiteration if and only if $G$ is obtainable from $G'$ by the rule of iteration.

For example, $()A$ follows from $(A)A$ (by deiterating $A$), $(((C))B)$ follows from $(((BC))B)$ (by deiterating $B$), $(A)(C(B))$ follows from $(A)(C(B)(A))$ (by deiterating $(A)$), $AB$ follows from $ABA$ (by deiterating $A$), etc.

**Juxtaposition**   One can infer the juxtaposition of $G_1, \ldots, G_n$ from $G_1, \ldots, G_n$. Conversely, one can infer any $G_i$, $1 \leq i \leq n$, from the juxtaposition of $G_1, \ldots, G_n$.

For example, one can infer $(A)(A)B(C(D))$ from the three graphs $(A)B$, $(A)$, and $(C(D))$.

The definition of a graph being provable from a set of graphs is then defined as follows:

**Definition 3.1 (Provability).** Let $\Gamma \cup \{G\}$ be a set of graphs. Then $G$ is *provable* from $\Gamma$ (written $\Gamma \vdash G$) if and only if there is a sequence of graphs $G_1, \ldots, G_n, G$ such that each of $G_1, \ldots, G_n, G$ is either a member of $\Gamma$, the graph $(())$, or else follows from previous graphs by one of the rules of inference.

The following is an example of a proof of $(A)$ from the set $\Gamma = \{(A(B)), (B(C)), (C)\}$:

| | |
|---|---|
| $(C)$ | a member of $\Gamma$ |
| $(B(C))$ | a member of $\Gamma$ |
| $(C)(B(C))$ | by juxtaposition |
| $(C)(B)$ | by deiteration |
| $(B)$ | by erasure |
| $(A(B))$ | a member of $\Gamma$ |
| $(A(B))(B)$ | by juxtaposition |
| $(A)(B)$ | by deiteration |
| $(A)$ | by erasure |

A set of graphs is defined to be consistent if and only if the graph () is not provable from it:

**Definition 3.2 (Consistent).** Let $\Gamma$ be a set of graphs. Then $\Gamma$ is *consistent* if and only $\Gamma \nvdash ()$.

## Provability vs. Peircean Provability

Peirce has a somewhat different notion of provability than that defined above. In particular, he does not have the rule of juxtaposition, instead compensating in other ways. For Peirce, a graph $G$ is provable from a set $\Gamma$ of graphs if and only if one can juxtapose a number of graphs in $\Gamma$, then apply the above rules of inference, excluding juxtaposition, successively to this graph, arriving eventually at $G$. One is not ever allowed to recopy a graph. A proof starts with the juxtaposition of members of $\Gamma$. This graph is modified with a rule of inference to get a new graph, this new graph is modified to get another new graph, and so on until $G$ is reached. One never has the opportunity to go back to earlier graphs and collect together information about them. Any needed information must be carried along as one proceeds. Thus, Peircean provability is defined as follows:

**Definition 3.3 (Peircean Provability).** Let $\Gamma \cup \{G\}$ be a set of graphs. Then $G$ is *Peircean provable* from $\Gamma$ (written $\Gamma \vdash_{Peirce} G$) if and only if there is a sequence of graphs $G_1, \ldots, G_n, G$ such that $G_1$ is either the graph $(())$ or consists of the juxtaposition of one or more members of $\Gamma$, and each of $G_2, \ldots, G_n, G$ follows from the immediately preceding graph by one of the rules of inference with the exception of the rule of juxtaposition.[3]

Despite the apparent differences between the two notions, the following theorem shows that they are in fact equivalent. The difficult direction is showing that $\Gamma \vdash \gamma$ implies $\Gamma \vdash_{Peirce} \gamma$, in essence showing that the juxtaposition rule adds no extra inferential power. Intuitively, the reason the rule is not needed is that previous lines can be carried along, and that one can obtain as many copies as are needed at any time by the rule of iteration. Thus, suppose the following is a standard proof from $\Gamma = \{(A), B\}$.

---

[3]Peirce does not actually define a notion of provability from a set, but he does speak of writing down a number of graphs known to be true and of transforming one graph into another. Since only the weak completeness of Peirce's system has been discussed by other commentators, this aspect of his system has not yet been studied.

$$(A) \qquad\qquad \text{a member of } \Gamma$$
$$B \qquad\qquad\quad \text{a member of } \Gamma$$
$$((B)) \qquad\qquad \text{by double cut}$$
$$(C(B)) \qquad\quad\; \text{by insertion in odd}$$
$$B(C(B))(A) \quad\; \text{by juxtaposition}$$

A Peircean proof from $\Gamma$ of the same graph could be constructed as follows:

| | |
|---|---|
| $(A)B$ | the juxtaposition of members of $\Gamma$ |
| $(A)B\,B$ | by iteration of $B$ |
| $(A)B\,((B))$ | by double cut |
| $(A)B\,((B))\,((B))$ | by iteration of $((B))$ |
| $(A)B\,((B))\,(C(B))$ | by insertion in odd |
| $B(C(B))(A)$ | by erasure in even |

The theorem requires the following lemma stating that the application of a rule to a graph is unaffected by the graph being juxtaposed with another graph. It is easily proved by simply inspecting each of the rules of inference:

**Lemma 3.4** *Let $G$, $G'$ and $\gamma$ be any three graphs. If $G'$ is obtainable from $G$ by any of double cut, insertion, erasure, iteration, or deiteration, then $\gamma G'$, the juxtaposition of $\gamma$ and $G'$, is obtainable from $\gamma G$, the juxtaposition of $\gamma$ and $G$, by the same rule.*

**Theorem 3.5 (Equivalence of Provability and Peircean Provability).** *Let $\Gamma \cup \{\gamma\}$ be a set of graphs. Then $\Gamma \vdash \gamma$ if and only if $\Gamma \vdash_{Peirce} \gamma$.*

**Proof:** Right-to-left is easy. For left-to-right, suppose that $\gamma_1, \ldots, \gamma_n, \gamma$ is a standard proof of $\gamma$ from $\Gamma$. We show by induction that each $\gamma_i$, and hence $\gamma$, is Peircean provable from $\Gamma$. For the base case, $\gamma_1$ is itself a one-line Peircean proof from $\Gamma$. For the induction step, suppose there is a Peircean proof from $\Gamma$, the last line of which consists of the juxtaposition of each of the previous lines: $\gamma_1, \ldots, \gamma_i$. We show there is a Peircean proof from $\Gamma$, the last line of which consists of the juxtaposition of at least one copy of each of $\gamma_1, \ldots, \gamma_i, \gamma_{i+1}$. From this it will follow that there is a Peircean proof of the juxtaposition of $\gamma_1, \ldots, \gamma_n, \gamma$ from $\Gamma$, so that by erasure we will have $\Gamma \vdash_{Peirce} \gamma$. Let $G_1, \ldots, G_m$ be the Peircean proof, the last line of which consists of the juxtaposition of $\gamma_1, \ldots, \gamma_i$. There are four cases:

(Case 1) Suppose $\gamma_{i+1} = (())$. Then $G_1, \ldots, G_m, (())G_m$ is a Peircean proof, the last line of which consists of the juxtaposition of $\gamma_1, \ldots, \gamma_{i+1}$. The last line is obtained from the previous one by the rule of double cut.

(Case 2) Suppose $\gamma_{i+1} \in \Gamma$. If $G_1$ consists of the juxtaposition of members of $\Gamma$, then (by Lemma 3.4)

$$G_1 \gamma_{i+1}, G_2 \gamma_{i+1}, \ldots, G_m \gamma_{i+1}$$

is a Peircean proof of the desired form. Otherwise $G_1$ is the graph $(())$, in which case

$$\gamma_{i+1}, \gamma_{i+1}G_1, \ldots, \gamma_{i+1}G_m$$

is the desired Peircean proof. The first inference is by double cut and the rest are as before, justified by Lemma 3.4.

(Case 3) Suppose $\gamma_{i+1}$ follows from earlier lines by juxtaposition, say lines $\gamma_{i_1}, \ldots, \gamma_{i_m}$. Since $G_m$ consists of the juxtaposition of each of $\gamma_1, \ldots, \gamma_i$, one can apply iteration to $G_m$ to obtain a graph consisting of the juxtaposition of each of $\gamma_1, \ldots, \gamma_i, \gamma_{i+1}$. Thus,

$$G_1, \ldots, G_m, G_m\gamma_{i+1}$$

is a Peircean proof of the needed form.

(Case 4) Suppose $\gamma_{i+1}$ follows from an earlier line by one of the rules other than juxtaposition. Since $G_m$ consists of the juxtaposition of graphs including this one, by Lemma 3.4 one can simply apply the same rule to $G_m$ to get the juxtaposition of $\gamma_1, \ldots, \gamma_i, \gamma_{i+1}$, which completes the proof of the theorem. $\qquad\qquad\square$

# 4  Soundness

The proof of the soundness of the rules requires a replacement theorem, which is obtained as a corollary of the following theorem. The notation $F_G$ is used to refer to a graph having $G$ as a subgraph. $F_{G'}$ then refers to the result of replacing that copy of $G$ with the graph $G'$. The theorem is proved by a routine induction:

**Theorem 4.1** *Suppose $F_G$, $X$, and $Y$ are graphs and $v$ is a valuation. If $v \models X$ if and only if $v \models Y$, then $v \models F_X$ if and only if $v \models F_Y$.*

**Corollary 4.2 (Replacement Theorem).** *Suppose $F_G$, $X$, and $Y$ are graphs. If $X \equiv Y$, then $F_X \equiv F_Y$.*

Using the replacement theorem, the soundness of the system can now be extracted from the following lemmas which show that each of the rules of inference is valid. Proofs that are routine are omitted.

**Lemma 4.3** *If $\gamma$ is obtainable from $\gamma'$ by the rule of double cut, then $\{\gamma'\} \models \gamma$.*

**Lemma 4.4** *If $\gamma$ is obtainable from $\gamma'$ by the rule of juxtaposition, then $\{\gamma'\} \models \gamma$.*

**Lemma 4.5** *If $\gamma$ is obtainable from $\gamma'$ by the rule of iteration or deiteration, then $\{\gamma'\} \models \gamma$.*

**Proof:** There are two cases. One is where for some subgraph of $\gamma'$ consisting of the juxtaposition of graphs $G$ and $H$, $G$ is iterated/deiterated within one or more of the cuts of $H$. The other case is where for some subgraph $G$ of $\gamma'$, $G$ is iterated/deiterated within one or more of its own cuts. Since the two cases are established by very similar arguments, only the first will be examined. We first show that it is valid to iterate a graph enclosed by no cuts into a single cut, and to deiterate a graph inside a single cut. Thus, where $\alpha$, $\beta$, $\gamma$, and $\delta$ are arbitrary graphs, let

$$\phi = \alpha G \beta (\gamma G' \delta)$$

(i.e., the juxtaposition of $\alpha$, $G$, $\beta$, and the graph consisting of a cut enclosing the juxtaposition of $\gamma$, $G'$, and $\delta$) and

$$\psi = \alpha G \beta (\gamma G G' \delta).$$

So $\psi$ results from $\phi$ by iterating $G$ within one cut, and $\phi$ results from $\psi$ by deiterating $G$. Let $v$ be a valuation. Then:

$$
\begin{array}{rl}
v \models \phi \quad \text{iff} & v \models \alpha \text{ and } v \models G \text{ and } v \models \beta \text{ and } v \models (\gamma G' \delta) \\
\text{iff} & v \models \alpha \text{ and } v \models G \text{ and } v \models \beta \text{ and} \\
& [v \not\models \gamma \text{ or } v \not\models G' \text{ or } v \not\models \delta] \\
\text{iff} & v \models \alpha \text{ and } v \models G \text{ and } v \models \beta \text{ and} \\
& [v \not\models \gamma \text{ or } v \not\models G \text{ or } v \not\models G' \text{ or } v \not\models \delta] \\
\text{iff} & v \models \alpha \text{ and } v \models G \text{ and } v \models \beta \text{ and } v \models (\gamma G G' \delta) \\
\text{iff} & v \models \psi
\end{array}
$$

Call this fact just proved (**): if $\phi = \alpha G \beta (\gamma G' \delta)$ and $\psi = \alpha G \beta (\gamma G G' \delta)$, then $\phi \equiv \psi$.

Now suppose $F_{G'}$ is obtainable from $F_G$ by iteration (and so, likewise, $F_G$ is obtainable from $F_{G'}$ by deiteration), where $G = G_1 G''$ and $G_1$ is iterated within additional cuts of $G''$, say $n - 1$ of them. Thus, we have that for some graphs $G_2, \ldots, G_n$:

$$G = G_1 (_1 G_2 (_2 G_3 (_3 \ldots (_{n-1} G_n (_{n-1} \ldots )_1.$$

By (**), iterating $G_1$ into the first cut:

$$G \equiv G_1 (_1 G_1 G_2 (_2 G_3 (_3 \ldots (_{n-1} G_n )_{n-1} \ldots )_1.$$

Again by (**):

$$G_1 G_2 (_2 G_3 (_3 \ldots (_{n-1} G_n (_{n-1} \ldots )_2 \equiv G_1 G_2 (_2 C_2 G_1 G_3 (_3 \ldots (_{n-1} G_n )_{n-1} \ldots )_2$$

and so by the replacement theorem:

$$G \equiv G_1(_1G_1G_2(_2G_1G_3(_3\ldots(_{n-1}G_n)_{n-1}\ldots)_1.$$

By repeating this process $n - 1$ times, using (**) and the replacement theorem, we have:

$$G \equiv G_1(_1G_1G_2(_2G_1G_3(_3\ldots(_{n-1}G_1G_n)_{n-1}\ldots)_1.$$

We now carry out a similar process in reverse to erase all the occurrences of $G_1$ between the outermost and innermost occurrences. By (**) we have:

$$G_1G_{n-2}(G_1G_{n-1}(G_1G_n)\ldots) \equiv G_1G_{n-2}(G_{n-1}(G_1G_n)\ldots)$$

and so by replacement:

$$G \equiv G_1(G_1G_2(\ldots(G_1G_{n-2}(G_{n-1}(G_1G_n)\ldots).$$

Likewise, by (**)

$$G_1G_{n-3}(G_1G_{n-2}(G_{n-1}(G_1G_n)\ldots) \equiv G_1G_{n-3}(G_{n-2}(G_{n-1}(G_1G_n)\ldots)$$

and so by replacement:

$$G \equiv G_1(G_1G_2(\ldots(G_1G_{n-3}(G_{n-2}(G_{n-1}(G_1G_n)\ldots).$$

Repeating this procedure we have:

$$G \equiv G_1(G_2(\ldots(G_{n-1}(G_1G_n)\ldots),$$

or, in other words, $G \equiv G'$. By the replacement theorem we therefore have $F_G \equiv F_{G'}$, and so an application of either iteration or deiteration results in a logically equivalent graph. □

**Lemma 4.6** *If $\gamma$ is obtainable from $\gamma'$ by the rule of insertion or erasure, then $\{\gamma'\} \models \gamma$.*

**Theorem 4.7 (Soundness Theorem).** *Let $\Gamma \cup \{G\}$ be a set of closed graphs. If $\Gamma \models G$, then $\Gamma \vdash G$*

**Proof:** This follows immediately from the previous four lemmas by induction on the length of proofs. □

# 5   Completeness

The proof of the completeness theorem requires the following deduction theorem. The proof is similar in strategy to the familiar result from propositional logic, but the details are quite different.

**Lemma 5.1 (Deduction Theorem).** *Let $\Gamma \cup \{G, G'\}$ be a set of graphs. If $\Gamma \cup \{G\} \vdash G'$, then $\Gamma \vdash (G(G'))$.*

**Proof:** Let $\gamma_1, \ldots, \gamma_n$ be a proof of $G'$ from $\Gamma \cup \{G\}$. We will prove that for each $1 \leq i \leq n$ we have $\Gamma \vdash (G(\gamma_i))$ and so, in particular, $\Gamma \vdash (G(G'))$.

The base case is fairly routine. As an induction hypothesis, suppose that $\Gamma \vdash (G(\gamma_k))$ for all $k < i$. We show that $\Gamma \vdash (G(\gamma_i))$. There are several cases: $\gamma_i \in \Gamma$, $\gamma_i = (())$, $\gamma_i = G$, or $\gamma_i$ is obtained from previous lines by one of insertion in odd, erasure in even, double cut, iteration, deiteration, or juxtaposition. The three cases where $\gamma_i \in \Gamma$, $\gamma_i = (())$, and $\gamma_i = G$ are handled exactly as in the base case. For the other cases:

1. Suppose $\gamma_i$ is obtained from some $\gamma_k$ by insertion in odd. Then $(G(\gamma_i))$ is obtainable from $(G(\gamma_k))$ by insertion in odd as well because of the fact that an oddly enclosed area of $\gamma_k$ is also oddly enclosed in $(G(\gamma_k))$. Thus, since we are assuming $\Gamma \vdash (G(\gamma_k))$ we have that $\Gamma \vdash (G(\gamma_k))$ as well.

2. The cases where $\gamma_i$ is obtained from some $\gamma_k$ by one of erasure in even, double cut, iteration, or deiteration are established by a similar argument.

3. Suppose $\gamma_i$ is obtained from $\gamma_{k_1}, \ldots, \gamma_{k_j}$ by the rule of juxtaposition. We are assuming that

$$\Gamma \vdash (G(\gamma_{k_1})), \ldots, \Gamma \vdash (G(\gamma_{k_j})).$$

Hence, by juxtaposition we have that

$$\Gamma \vdash (G(\gamma_{k_1}))(G(\gamma_{k_2})) \ldots (G(\gamma_{k_j})).$$

By iteration of each $(G(\gamma_{k_i}))$ into $(G(\gamma_{k_1}))$ we have

$$\Gamma \vdash (G(\gamma_{k_1}(G(\gamma_{k_2})) \ldots (G(\gamma_{k_j}))))(G(\gamma_{k_2})) \ldots (G(\gamma_{k_j})).$$

By erasure in even we have

$$\Gamma \vdash (G(\gamma_{k_1}(G(\gamma_{k_2})) \ldots (G(\gamma_{k_j})))).$$

By deiteration of the interior copies of $G$ we have

$$\Gamma \vdash (G(\gamma_{k_1}((\gamma_{k_2})) \ldots ((\gamma_{k_j})))).$$

By double cut we have

$$\Gamma \vdash (G(\gamma_{k_1} \gamma_{k_2} \ldots \gamma_{k_j})),$$

or, in other words, $\Gamma \vdash (G(\gamma_i))$. □

**Notation:** For readability in the following proof, the notation $\bot$ is used for the graph (). Likewise, where $G$ is a graph, the notation $\neg G$ is used to represent the graph $(G)$.

**Theorem 5.2** *Every consistent set of graphs is satisfiable.*

**Proof:** Let $\Gamma_0$ be a consistent set of graphs. Let $G_1, G_2, G_3, \ldots$ be an enumeration of all graphs. We build an increasing sequence $\Delta_1 \subseteq \Delta_2 \subseteq \Delta_3 \subseteq \ldots$ of consistent extensions of $\Gamma_0$ as follows. Let $\Delta_1 = \Gamma_0$. Given $\Delta_n$, we build $\Delta_{n+1}$ by adding one or more graphs. If $\Delta_n \cup \{G_n\}$ is consistent, add $G_n$; otherwise add $\neg G_n$. Furthermore, if a graph $\neg\neg G$ is added, also add $G$. If a graph is added consisting of the juxtaposition of two or more graphs and $G_1, \ldots, G_n$ are its immediate subgraphs, also add each of $G_1, \ldots, G_n$. Finally, let $\Delta$ be the union of all of $\Delta_0, \Delta_1, \ldots$.

We first show that $\Delta$ is consistent. By assumption $\Delta_0$ is consistent. It suffices to show that for any consistent set $\Gamma$ and any graph $G$, either $\Gamma \cup \{G\}$ is consistent or $\Gamma \cup \{\neg G\}$ is consistent. Suppose, for contradiction, that $\Gamma$ is a consistent set, $G$ is a graph, but that both $\Gamma \cup \{G\}$ and $\Gamma \cup \{\neg G\}$ are inconsistent. By double cut, insertion in odd, and iteration, the graph

is provable from $\Gamma$. Hence, by the deduction theorem and juxtaposition, the graph

is provable from $\Gamma$. Using the rule of iteration we can drive the two left-hand graphs into the right-hand graph (and then erase the two left-hand graphs) to get:

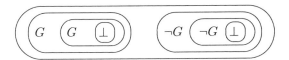

By deiteration we can erase the inner instances of $G$ and $\neg G$ to get:

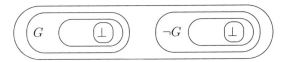

The rule of erasure in even gives:

By deiteration we get:

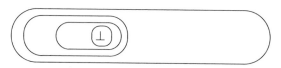

Finally, two applications of double cut show that ⊥ is provable from Γ, contradicting its consistency.

Since $\Delta_1$ is consistent, either $\Delta_1 \cup \{G_1\}$ is consistent or $\Delta_1 \cup \{\neg G_1\}$ is consistent. So $\Delta_2$ is consistent. Likewise, each $\Delta_n$ is consistent, and so their union, $\Delta$, is consistent. Next, let $v$ be the valuation that assigns true to every sentence letter in $\Delta$, false to every other sentence letter, and false to the graph (). By a standard inductive argument we can show that for all graphs $H$, $v \models H$ if and only if $H \in \Delta$, and hence that $\Gamma_0$ is satisfiable. □

**Corollary 5.3 (Completeness).** *If* $\Gamma \models G$, *then* $\Gamma \vdash G$

**Proof:** Suppose $\Gamma \nvdash G$. $\Delta$ must be consistent, since otherwise we can prove

from $\Delta$. By insertion in odd, inserting $(G)$, we can prove

and then by double cut we get $G$. Moreover, we know that $\Gamma \cup \{\neg G\}$ is consistent. Otherwise by the deduction rule we can prove

Therefore by iteration we have

By double cut, then, we have

and so by deiteration we get

Finally, by double cut, we obtain $G$, contradicting that $\Gamma \nvdash G$. Since $\Gamma \cup \{\neg G\}$ is consistent, it is also satisfiable by the previous theorem, so $\Gamma \nvDash G$. $\square$

*Chapter VII*

# A Diagrammatic Subsystem of Hilbert's Geometry

Isabel Luengo

## 1 Introduction

In the last few years there has been an increasing interest in the visual representation of mathematical concepts. The fact that computers can help us perform graphical tasks very easily has been translated into an increasing interest in diagrammatic representations in general. Several experiments have shown that diagrammatic reasoning plays a main role in the way in which experts in several areas solve problems (Gobert and Freferiksen [1992] and Kindfield [1992]). Two kinds of explanations have been given for the advantages of visual representations over linguistic ones. The first kind of explanation is *psychological*. It has been argued that visual representations are easier to use because they resemble the mental models humans build to solve problems Stenning and Oberlander [1991], Johnson-Laird and Byrne [1991], and Tverski [1991]. The second kind of explanation is related to *computational efficiency*. Larkin and Simon [1987] have argued that diagrammatic representations are computationally more efficient than sentential representations because the location of each element in the diagram corresponds to the spatial or topological properties of the objects they represent.

However, the efficiency of the use of diagrams is not enough justification for their use in analytical areas of knowledge. Mathematical discoveries often have been made using visual reasoning, but those very same discoveries were not justified by the visual reasoning. Diagrams are associated with intuitions and illustrations, not with rigorous proofs. Visual representations are allowed in the context of discovery, not in the context of justification. Many authors have considered diagrams in opposition to deductive systems. Lindsay [1988], for instance, has claimed that the main feature of visual representations is that they correspond to a non-deductive kind of inference system. Koedinger and Anderson [1991] have related diagrammatic reasoning in geometry to informal, inductive strategies to solve problems.

Thus, though we have an empirical justification for the use of diagrams in mathematics (people use them and they work!) we do not usually have an analytical justification. In fact, the history of mathematics, and especially the history of geometry, is full of mistakes related to the use of diagrams. Euclidean geometry, as the Greeks developed it, is commonly considered as a defective mathematical system that was not corrected until Hilbert axiomatized it. It has been claimed that Euclid's presentation of plane geometry was flawed on various accounts, one of them being the reliance on diagrams to guide the logic in the construction of proofs (Wallace and West [1992]). This criticism implies that the use of pictures is a flaw in a formal system.

In this chapter, we want to show that the problem is not with diagrams, but with having bad semantics and syntax. We take a small portion of Euclidean geometry (points, lines and segments) and show that a diagrammatic system can be built for it, with formal semantics, syntax and rules of inference, and that it is a sound system, meaning that no fallacies can be derived from it. Fallacies in geometry arise from the fact that we take accidental features of the diagram to be representing features. That is why a system with clear syntax and semantics will make fallacies impossible.

**A word about notation.** Traditional geometry proofs use the variables $A$, $B$, ... for the points in the diagram with no clear distinction made between syntactic verses semantic objects. The fact that by $A$, Hilbert means a mathematical point whereas we mean a diagrammatic point can be confusing for the reader. We are going to respect Hilbert's original notation because we are going to use his axioms and theorems in many of the proofs of this chapter, and we want to make it clear that they have not been modified in any way. Table 1 summarizes the notation.

|          | *Our syntax* | *Our semantics* | *Hilbert's* |
|----------|-------------|-----------------|-------------|
| points   | $A, B, C, \ldots$ | $a, b, c, \ldots$ | $A, B, C, \ldots$ |
| lines    | $l, m, n, \ldots$ | $L, M, N, \ldots$ | $a, b, c, \ldots$ |
| segments | $\overline{AB}, \ldots$ | $\overline{ab}, \ldots$ | $\overline{AB}, \ldots$ |

Table 1: Notation

# 2   Syntax

## Diagrammatic Objects and Relations

It is important to make a clear distinction between diagrammatic objects and the things that they aim to represent, for many of the geometry fallacies associated with diagrams arise from a confusion between the two kinds of entities. We will use a star (*) to distinguish diagrammatic objects and relations from their geometric counterparts. Diagrammatic objects are not mathematical, abstract entities, but very concrete, physical objects. In this section we are going to be careful to point out what diagrammatic objects are and what combinations of them are syntactically well-formed, since those are the only ones that will be given a semantic interpretation in the following section.

In Diagrammatic System 1 (DS1), there are two different classes of diagrammatic objects: primitive and derived. The primitive objects are not defined. The derived objects are defined in terms of the primitive objects.

## Primitive Objects

1. Boxes

   A box is a rectangle with dashed edges.

2. Points*

   A point* is a small dot.

   We will use $A$, $B$, $C$,... with superscripts and subscripts as variables over points*.

3. Lines*

   A line* is a straight edge.

We will use $l$, $m$, $n$,... with superscripts and subscripts as variables over lines*.

4. Indicators

There are two ways of representing Indicators:

(a) a sequence of $n \geq 1$ bars

(b) an arc with $n \geq 1$ transversal bars on it

Figure 1

Indicators will be used to represent segment congruence. There are infinitely many types of indicators. Two indicators are of the same type if and only if they have the same number of bars, regardless of the presence or absence of the arc. Therefore the two indicators in Figure 1 are of the same type.

If two indicators are of the same type we will just say that they are the same indicator. In other words, we are only concerned with indicators at the type level, not at the token level.

We use $\alpha$, $\beta$, $\gamma$, ... for indicators.

## Diagrammatic Relations

There are four relations among diagrammatic objects that are relevant in the system.

1. *In* $\subseteq$ diagrammatic objects $\times$ boxes
   A diagrammatic object is *in* a box iff none of the parts of the object extends outside the box.

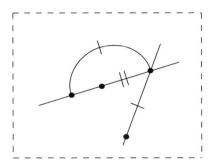

Figure 2: Diagrammatic objects in a box.

2. *On*\* ⊆ points\* × lines\*
   A point\* is on\* a line\* iff they intersect.

Figure 3: A point\* is on\* a line\*.

We will also say that a line\* *l goes through* a point\* *A* if *A* is on\* *l*.

3. *Between*\* ⊆ points\* × (points\* × points\*)
   Point\* *A* is between\* *B* and *C* iff there is a line\* that goes through\*
   *A*, *B* and *C*, and *A* is between *B* and *C* on that line\*.

Figure 4: Point\* A is between\* B and C.

If there is a line\* *l* such that three distinct points\* *A*, *B* and *C* are
on\* *l* and *A* is not between\* *B* and *C* we will say that *B* and *C* are
on the *same side* of *l* with respect to *A*.

4. *Indicates* ⊆ indicators × (points\* × points\*)
   Indicator α *indicates* ⟨A, B⟩ if and only if *A* and *B* are distinct points\*
   on\* some line\* *l*, and

   (a) if α is represented as an arc then one of the end points of the
       arc intersects with *A* and the other end intersects with *B*,

(b) if $\alpha$ is a sequence of bars then all the bars of $\alpha$ intersect with $l$ and $\alpha$ is between $A$ and $B$ and there is no point* between* $A$ and $B$.

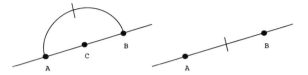

Figure 5: In these examples the indicator is on* $\langle A, B \rangle$.

### Derived Objects

There is only one class of derived objects:

1. Segments*
   A segment* consists of two distinct points* on a line* $l$ and the part of $l$ that lies between them.

   The segment* defined by points* $A$ and $B$ is called $\overline{AB}$ or $\overline{BA}$.

We will say that an indicator indicates a segment* $\overline{AB}$ if and only if it indicates $\langle A, B \rangle$.

## Well-Formed Diagrams

Every *finite* combination of diagrammatic objects is a diagram, but not all diagrams are well-formed diagrams($wfd$).

### Definition 2.1

A diagram is *well-formed* if and only if:

1. it has one and only one box and all the other diagrammatic objects are in* the box,

2. for any two distinct points* there is at most one line* that goes through* them,

3. every indicator indicates a segment*.

For instance, Figure 2 depicts a well-formed diagram. As we will see later boxes do not have a semantic interpretation; their only use is to set the boundaries of the diagram. We are going to use indicators to represent the congruence relation among segments. That is why we need Condition 3 in our definition.

## Diagrams as Equivalence Classes

**Definition 2.2** Diagram $E$ is an extension of diagram $D$ ($D \subseteq E$) if and only if there is a total 1-1 function $\mathcal{C}$ from the set of points* and lines* of $D$ into the set of points* and lines* of $E$ such that:

1. diagrammatic object $x$ is a point* if and only if $\mathcal{C}(x)$ is a point* [1]

2. point* $A$ is on* line* $l$ if and only if $\mathcal{C}(A)$ is on* $\mathcal{C}(l)$

3. point* $A$ is between* $B$ and $C$ if and only if $\mathcal{C}(A)$ is between* $\mathcal{C}(B)$ and $\mathcal{C}(C)$, and

4. if an indicator indicates $\langle A, B \rangle$ then it also indicates $\langle \mathcal{C}(A), \mathcal{C}(B) \rangle$.

Such a function is called an *embedding* of $D$ into $E$.

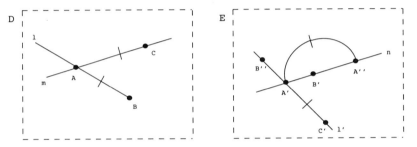

Figure 6: Diagram $E$ is an extension of diagram $D$.

We can define an embedding function $\mathcal{C}_1$ for the diagrams depicted in Figure 6 as follows

$$\mathcal{C}_1 = \{\langle A, A' \rangle, \langle B, C' \rangle, \langle C, A'' \rangle, \langle l, l' \rangle, \langle m, n \rangle, \}.$$

Notice that $\mathcal{C}_1$ is not the only function that meets all the requirements. The following function $\mathcal{C}_2$ also does:

$$\mathcal{C}_2 = \{\langle A, A' \rangle, \langle B, A'' \rangle, \langle C, C' \rangle, \langle l, n \rangle, \langle m, l' \rangle\}.$$

**Definition 2.3** Diagram $D$ is a *copy* of diagram $E$ if and only if $D \subseteq E$ and $E \subseteq D$.

**Proposition 2.4** For every diagram $D$ all the copies of $D$ form an equivalence class.

**Proof:** We need to prove that the relation of being a copy of $D$ is an equivalence relation. It is obvious that it is reflexive and symmetric, by

---

[1] This implies that $x$ is a line* if and only if $\mathcal{C}(x)$ is a line*.

Definition 2.3. In order to prove that it is also transitive we need to prove that relation $\subseteq$ is also transitive. Suppose $D \subseteq E$ and $E \subseteq E'$. That means that there are two relations $C_1 : D \to E$ and $C_2 : E \to E'$ that meet the conditions listed in Definition 2.2. Let us define $C_3$ as $C_1 \circ C_2$. Notice that $C_3$ is a function from $D$ into $E'$ that also meets the conditions of Definition 2.2. Therefore, $D \subseteq E$. $\square$

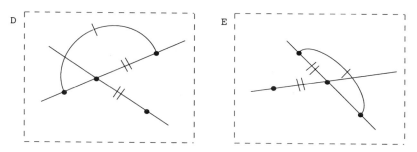

Figure 7: Diagram $E$ is a copy of diagram $D$.

From now on by $D$ we will mean the equivalence class of all the diagrams that are copies of $D$.

# 3 Semantics

## Interpretation Functions and Premodels

**Definition 3.1** $\mathcal{I}$ is an *interpretation function* for $D$ if and only if $\mathcal{I}$ is a total function whose domain is the set of points* and lines* of $D$ and whose range is included in the set of points and lines on a Euclidean plane[2] such that:

1. if $A$ is a point* then $\mathcal{I}(A)$ is a point;

2. if $l$ is a line* then $\mathcal{I}(l)$ is a line;

3. $l$ is a line* and $A$ is a point* then $A$ is on* $l$ if and only if $\mathcal{I}(l)$ goes through $\mathcal{I}(A)$; and

4. if $A$, $B$ and $C$ are points* then $A$ is between* $B$ and $C$ if and only if $\mathcal{I}(A)$ is between $\mathcal{I}(B)$ and $\mathcal{I}(C)$.

We can extend $\mathcal{I}$ to give an interpretation to segments* in the following way:

---

[2]A Euclidean plane is a set of points and lines as described in Hilbert's axioms for geometry.

5. if $\overline{AB}$ is a segment* then $\mathcal{I}(\overline{AB})$ is the segment defined by $\mathcal{I}(A)$ and $\mathcal{I}(B)$.

**Definition 3.2** Let $\mathcal{M}$ be an interpretation function for $D$. $\mathcal{M}$ is a *pre-model* of $D$ (written $\mathcal{M} \models_{pre} D$) if and only if the following condition is satisfied.

1. if indicator $\alpha$ indicates $\overline{AB}$ and $\overline{A'B'}$ then $\mathcal{M}(\overline{AB})$ and $\mathcal{M}(\overline{A'B'})$ are congruent,

2. if $A$ and $B$ are on the same side of line* $l$ with respect to point* $C$, then $\mathcal{M}(A)$ and $\mathcal{M}(B)$ are on the same side of $\mathcal{M}(l)$ with respect to $\mathcal{M}(C)$.

## Deduction Principles

Besides these descriptive conventions, we also want to insure that our diagrams agree with standard usage of diagrams in informal proofs in geometry. While there is no single standard of use, there are certain uses that seem so common in geometry practice that we want to build them into our system. In particular, we want to ensure that the following three deduction principles are valid:

**Principle 3.3** (Line* Introduction)

> **P1** Assume $D$ is a *wfd* that has two distinct points* $A$ and $B$ which are not both on* a single line* of $D$. Let $E$ be an extension of $D$ that is just like $D$ except for the fact there is a new line* and $A$ and $B$ are on* it. Then $E$ is obtainable from $D$.

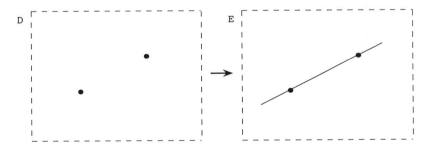

Figure 8: Diagram $E$ is obtainable from diagram $D$ by P1.

## Principle 3.4 (Point* Introduction)

> **P2** Assume $wfd$ $D$ has a line* $l$. Let $E$ be an extension of $D$
> just like $l$ except for the fact that there is a new point* on $l$
> that is not on* any other line*. Then $E$ is obtainable from $D$.

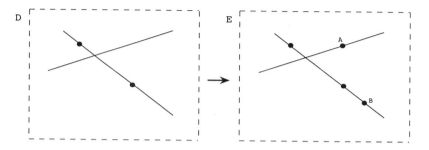

Figure 9: Diagram $E$ is obtainable from diagram $D$ by two succesive applications of P2.

## Principle 3.5 (Existence of Segments*)

We need a principle to correspond with Axiom III.1:

> "If $A, B$ are two points on a line $a$, and $A'$ is a point on the
> same or on another line $a'$ then it is always possible to find a
> point on a given side of the line $a'$ through $A'$ such that the
> segment $AB$ is congruent or equal to the segment $A'B'$."

It can be proven that there is only one such segment[3].

> **P3** Let $D$ be a $wfd$ that has a segment* $\overline{AB}$ and a point* $C$
> on* a line* $l$, and $\alpha$ is an indicator not in $D$. If we call $n$ the
> number of points* on a given side of $l$ with respect to $C$ then
> we can define a sequence of points* $\langle p_1, ..., p_n \rangle$ such that:
>
> 1. $p_1 = C$, and
>
> 2. if $n > 2$ then for each $p_m$, such that $1 < m < n$, $p_m$ is
>    between* $p_{m-1}$ and $p_{m+1}$

To define what diagrams can be obtained from $D$ for each side
of $l$ with respect to $C$ we have to consider two possibilities:
either $n = 1$ or $n > 1$.

---

[3]Uniqueness of Segment Existence in Hilbert [1971], p.13.

1. If $n = 1$ then the extension of $D$ that is just like $D$ but for the fact that a new point* $C'$ is on* $l$ and $\alpha$ indicates $\overline{AB}$ and $\overline{CC'}$ is obtainable from $D$.

2. If $n > 1$ then there is one and only one extension of $D$ that is obtainable from $D$ and that is just like $D$ but for the fact that $\alpha$ indicates $\overline{AB}$ and:

   (a) for some $p_m (m < n)$ there is a new point* $C'$ such that $C'$ is between* $p_m$ and $p_{m+1}$ and $\alpha$ indicates $\overline{CC'}$;

   (b) for some $p_m (m > 1)$ $\alpha$ indicates $\overline{Cp_m}$; or

   (c) for all $p_m (m > 1)$ there is a new point $C'$ such that $p_m$ is between* $C$ and $C'$ and $\alpha$ indicates $\overline{CC'}$.

## Models

### Definition 3.6

An interpretation function $\mathcal{M}$ is a *model* of $D$ if and only if $M \models_{pre} D$, and for each deduction principle $P1$, $P2$ and $P3$, if $S$ is obtainable from $D$ by $P$ then, for some $E$ in $S$, $M$ can be extended to a pre-model of $E$.

If $D$ is a diagram and $\mathcal{M}$ is a model of $D$ then $\mathcal{M}(Lines^*)$ is the set of lines $\{\mathcal{M}(l) \mid l \text{ is a line* of } D\}$.

In order to prove that every 1-1 pre-model is a model we need Proposition 3.7. We use $\mathcal{M}(Lines^*) - \mathcal{M}(l)$ for the set $\mathcal{M}(Lines^*)$ minus $\mathcal{M}(l)$.

**Proposition 3.7** *If $l$ is a line in a diagram $D$ and $\mathcal{M}$ is a 1-1 premodel of $D$ then for any two points $a, b$ on $\mathcal{M}(l)$ there is an infinite number of points between $a$ and $b$ that are not on any line in $\mathcal{M}(Lines^*) - \mathcal{M}(l)$.*

**Proof:** Suppose $a$ and $b$ are two points on $\mathcal{M}(l)$. In that case there is an infinite number of points between them (Hilbert's Theorem 7). However, there is only a finite number of lines* in $D$, and therefore there is only a finite number of lines in $\mathcal{M}(Lines^*)$. We also know that for each line $L$ in $\mathcal{M}(Lines^*)$ that is not equal to $\mathcal{M}(l)$ there is at most one point of $\mathcal{M}(l)$ that is on $L$ (by Axiom I,2). Therefore there is only a finite number of points between $a$ and $b$ that are also on another line in $\mathcal{M}(Lines^*)$, and that means that there is an infinite number of points between $a$ and $b$ that are not on any line in $\mathcal{M}(Lines^*)$ that is not equal to $\mathcal{M}(l)$. $\qquad\square$

**Proposition 3.8** *A pre-model $\mathcal{M}$ is a model if and only if it is 1-1.*

**Proof:** ($\Longleftarrow$) We need to prove that for each deduction principle $P$, if $\mathcal{M} \models_{pre} D$, $\mathcal{M}$ is 1-1, and $D \rightsquigarrow E$ by $P$, then there is an extension $\mathcal{N}$ of $\mathcal{M}$ such that $\mathcal{N} \models_{pre} E$.

Suppose $\mathcal{M} \models_{pre} D$, $\mathcal{M}$ is 1-1 and $D \rightsquigarrow E$ by $P$. We consider the three possible principles $P$ below.

1. (Line* Introduction) In this case $E$ results from $D$ by Line* Intro, so there are two distinct points* $A$ and $B$ not on* the same line* in $D$. Since $\mathcal{M}$ is 1-1, $\mathcal{M}(A) \neq \mathcal{M}(B)$. By Axiom I,1 there is a line $x$ that contains both $\mathcal{M}(A)$ and $\mathcal{M}(B)$. Since $E$ is obtained from $D$ by Line* Introduction then $E$ is just like $D$ but for the fact that there is a new line* $l$ that goes through* $A$ and $B$. Let $\mathcal{N}$ be $\mathcal{M} \cup \{\langle l, x \rangle\}$. In that case $\mathcal{N}$ is an extension of $\mathcal{M}$ that is a premodel of $E$.

2. (Point* Introduction) In this case $E$ results from $D$ Point* Introduction to $D$, so there is a line* $l$ in $D$. Let $C$ be the new point* in $E$. We need to distinguish three possible cases.

   Suppose there are no points* on* $l$. By Axiom I,3 we know that there are two points $a$ and $b$ on $\mathcal{M}(l)$. Let $\mathcal{N} = \mathcal{M} \cup \{\langle C, c \rangle\}$, where $c$ is a point between $a$ and $b$ that is not on any line in $\mathcal{M}(Lines^*)$ not equal to $\mathcal{M}(l)$ (we know there is such a point by Proposition 3.7). In that case $\mathcal{N}$ is an extension of $\mathcal{M}$ that is a premodel of $E$.

   Suppose there is only one point* $A$ on* $l$. By Axiom I,3 we know that there is at least another point $b$ on $\mathcal{M}(l)$. Let $\mathcal{N} = \mathcal{M} \cup \{\langle C, c \rangle\}$, where $c$ is a point between $\mathcal{M}(A)$ and $b$ that is not on any line in $\mathcal{M}(Lines^*)$ not equal to $\mathcal{M}(l)$ (we know there is such a point by Proposition 3.7). In that case $\mathcal{N}$ is an extension of $\mathcal{M}$ that is a premodel of $E$.

   Suppose there is more than one point* on* $l$. That means that either (i) $C$ between* two points* $A, B$ on* $l$ in $E$, or (ii) that there are two points $A', B'$ on* $l$ such that $C$ is between* $A'$ and $B'$ and there are no points* between* $A'$ and $C$.

   If (i), then we know that there is an infinite number of points between $\mathcal{M}(A)$ and $\mathcal{M}(B)$ that are not on any line in $\mathcal{M}(Lines^*)$ not equal to $\mathcal{M}(l)$ (Proposition 3.7). Let $\mathcal{N}$ be $\mathcal{M} \cup \{\langle C, c \rangle\}$, where $c$ is a point between $\mathcal{M}(A)$ and $\mathcal{M}(B)$ that was not on any line in $\mathcal{M}(Lines^*)$ not equal to $\mathcal{M}(l)$. In that case $\mathcal{N}$ is an extension of $\mathcal{M}$ that is a premodel of $E$.

   If (ii), then it is possible to find a point $b$ on the side of $\mathcal{M}(l)$ with respect to $\mathcal{M}(A)$ that does not contain $\mathcal{M}(B)$ such that $\overline{b\mathcal{M}(A)}$ is congruent to $\overline{\mathcal{M}(A)\mathcal{M}(B)}$ (Axiom III,1). In that case there is an infinite number of points between $b$ and $\mathcal{M}(A')$ that are not on any line in $\mathcal{M}(Lines^*)$ that is not equal to $\mathcal{M}(l)$ (Proposition 3.7). Let $\mathcal{N}$ be $\mathcal{M} \cup \{\langle C, c \rangle\}$, where $c$ is a point between $b$ and $\mathcal{M}(A')$ that was not on any line in $\mathcal{M}(Lines^*)$ not equal to $\mathcal{M}(l)$. In that case $\mathcal{N}$ is an extension of $\mathcal{M}$ that is a premodel of $E$.

3. (Existence of Segments*) In this case $E$ results from $D$ by Existence

of Segments to $D$, so there is a segment* $\overline{AB}$, a point* $C$ on* a line* $l$, and no indicators of type $\alpha$ in $D^4$. By Axiom III,1 there exists a point $x$ on each side of $\mathcal{M}(l)$ with respect to $\mathcal{M}(C)$ such that the segment defined by $\mathcal{M}(C)$ and $x$ is congruent to the segment defined by $\mathcal{M}(A)$ and $\mathcal{M}(B)$. If $E$ is obtainable from $D$ by Existence of Segments then $E$ is just like $D$ but for the fact that an indicator $\alpha$ indicates segments* $\overline{AB}$ and $\overline{CC'}$, for some $C'$ in $E$. Let $\mathcal{N}$ be $\mathcal{M} \cup \{\langle C, x \rangle\}$. In that case $\mathcal{N}$ is an extension of $\mathcal{M}$ that is a premodel of $E$.

($\Longrightarrow$) Suppose $\mathcal{I}$ can be extended to a model. We need to prove that $\mathcal{I}$ is 1-1, and that means that if $x \neq y$ then $\mathcal{I}(x) \neq \mathcal{I}(y)$. There are three possibilities: (1) either $x$ is a point* and $y$ is a line* or vice versa; or (2) they are both points*; or (3) they are both lines*.

1. Suppose $x$ is a point* and $y$ is a line*. Then $\mathcal{I}(x)$ is a point and $\mathcal{I}(y)$ is a line. So $\mathcal{I}(x) \neq \mathcal{I}(y)$.

2. Suppose both $x$ and $y$ are points*. We will call them $A$ and $B$. We need to prove that if $A \neq B$ then $\mathcal{I}(A) \neq \mathcal{I}(B)$. Suppose $A \neq B$. That is:

By the Principle of Line* Introduction we can obtain:

By the Principle of Point* Introduction we can obtain:

Thus, according to Definition 3.1, $\mathcal{I}(C)$ is between $\mathcal{I}(A)$ and $\mathcal{I}(B)$. Hence $\mathcal{I}(A) \neq \mathcal{I}(B)$, by Axiom II,1.

3. Suppose both $x$ and $y$ are lines*. Let us call them $l$ and $m$. We need to prove that if $l \neq m$ then $\mathcal{I}(l) \neq \mathcal{I}(m)$.

   Suppose $l \neq m$. That is:

---

[4]Notice that $C$ does not have to be distinct from $A$ or $B$, so $\mathcal{M}(C)$ can be equal to $\mathcal{M}(A)$ or $\mathcal{M}(B)$.

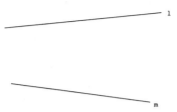

By the Principle of Point* Introduction we can obtain:

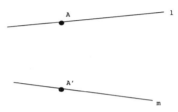

By the Principle of Line* Introduction we can obtain:

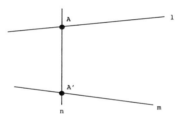

By the Principle of Existence of Segments we can obtain:

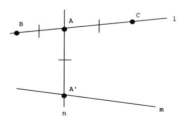

Suppose $\mathcal{I}(l) = \mathcal{I}(m)$. According to Definition 3.1 $\mathcal{I}(A)$ is on $\mathcal{I}(l)$ and $\mathcal{I}(A')$ is on $\mathcal{I}(m)$. Since $\mathcal{I}(l) = \mathcal{I}(m)$, $\mathcal{I}(A')$ is also on $\mathcal{I}(l)$. This means that $\mathcal{I}(l) = \mathcal{I}(n)$, because $\mathcal{I}(A)$ and $\mathcal{I}(A')$ are also on $\mathcal{I}(n)$ and there is at most line that goes through two different points (Axiom I-2). For each side of $\mathcal{I}(l)$ with respect to $\mathcal{I}(A)$ there is only one segment that is congruent to $\mathcal{M}(\overline{A'C})$ (see 158). So either $\mathcal{I}(B) = \mathcal{I}(A')$ or $\mathcal{I}(C) = \mathcal{I}(A')$. But that is not possible, for $\mathcal{I}$ is one-one for points*. Thus, $\mathcal{I}(l) \neq \mathcal{I}(m)$.

Since in the three possible cases we get that $\mathcal{I}(x) \neq \mathcal{I}(y)$ we can conclude that $\mathcal{I}(x) \neq \mathcal{I}(y)$. $\qquad\qquad\square$

# 4   Rules of Transformation

The transformation rules of the system allow us to obtain new diagrams from old diagrams. The new diagram obtained is an extension of the old one.

There are two ways of extending a diagram: by adding new points* or lines* or by adding only indicators. This allows us to make an important distinction. A transformation rule is called a *construction rule* if any points* or lines* (and maybe also new indicators) are added. If by applying the rule we get an extension that only has new indicators, we will say that it is an *inference* rule.

## Construction Rules

The construction rules of DS1 are just the three deduction principles we considered above, namely:

**R 4.1  Line* Introduction**

**R 4.2  Point* Introduction**

**R 4.3  Existence of Segments***

## Inference Rules

### R 4.4  Transitivity of Congruence

If $D$ is a *wfd* such that an indicator $\alpha$ indicates segments* $\overline{AB}$ and $\overline{A'B'}$ and an indicator $\beta$ indicates segments* $\overline{A'B'}$ and $\overline{A''B''}$, and if $E$ is an extension of $D$ that is just like $D$ except for the fact that $\alpha$ indicates $\overline{A''B''}$, then $E$ is obtainable from $D$.

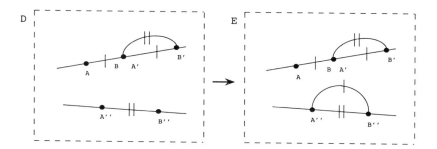

Figure 10: Diagram $E$ is obtainable from diagram $D$ by R4.

## R 4.5  Sum of Segments*

If $D$ is a *wfd* such that

1. points* $A$, $B$ and $C$ are on a line* $l$ and points* $A'$, $B'$ and $C'$ are on* a line* $l'$;

2. an indicator $\alpha$ indicates segments* $\overline{AB}$ and $\overline{A'B'}$;

3. an indicator $\beta$ indicates segments* $\overline{BC}$ and $\overline{B'C'}$; and

4. an indicator $\gamma$ indicates segment* $\overline{AC}$

and if $E$ is an extension of $D$ that is just like $D$ except for the fact that $\gamma$ indicates segment $\overline{A'C'}$, then $E$ is obtainable from $D$.

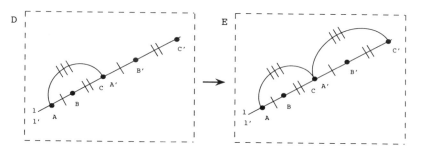

Figure 11: Diagram $E$ is obtainable from diagram $D$ by R5.

## Obtainability

### Definition 4.6

A set $S$ of diagrams is *obtainable* from $D$ ($D \rightsquigarrow S$) if and only if there is a rule of transformation $R$ such that $S$ is the disjunctive set of diagrams that is the result of applying $R$ to $D$.

# Geometric Consequence

**Definition 4.7**

Diagram $E$ is a *logical consequence* of $D$ (written $D \models E$) if and only if every model of $D$ is also a model of $E$.

This notion of logical consequence does not account for the validity of our construction rules. Take for instance rule R1. Given a diagram $D$ that has two points* $A$ and $B$, we could obtain by R1 an extension $E$ of $D$ that is just like $D$ but that has a new line $l$ such that $A$ and $B$ are on* it. It is clear that $E$ is not a logical consequence of $D$, since there are models of $D$ that are not models of $E$, namely all the models that give values to $A$ and $B$ but not to $l$.

However, since construction rules are typically involved in the informal use of diagrams in geometric proofs we need a new notion of consequence to validate them.

**Definition 4.8**

Diagram $E$ is a *geometric consequence* of $D$ (written $D \mathrel{|\!\subset} E$) if and only if every model of $D$ can be extended to a model of $E$.

**Proposition 4.9** *If $D \models E$ then $D \mathrel{|\!\subset} E$.*

The proof is based on the fact that each model is an extension of itself. We can generalize the notion of geometric consequence to sets of diagrams as follows:

**Definition 4.10**

A set $S$ of diagrams is a *geometric consequence* of $D$ (written, $D \mathrel{|\!\subset} S$) if and only if for each model $\mathcal{M}$ of $D$ there is an extension of $\mathcal{M}$ that is a model of one of the diagrams in $S$.

# Contradictory Diagrams

Sometimes one of the diagrams obtainable from a diagram by a transformation rule cannot represent any possible situation. In that case we will say that it is semantically contradictory.

**Definition 4.11** Diagram $D$ is *semantically contradictory* if and only if it does not have any models.

We need to characterize the contradictory diagrams syntactically so we can use the notion in the proofs of the system.

**Definition 4.12** Let $\overline{AB}$ be any segment* and $S_{AB}$ be the set of points* $P$ such that $P$ is $A$, $P$ is $B$, or $P$ is between* $A$ and $B$. Diagram $D$ is a *syntactically contradictory diagram* if there is an indicator that indicates both $\overline{AB}$ and $\overline{pq}$, for some $\overline{pq} \neq \overline{AB}$ and $p, q$ are in $S_{AB}$.

**Proposition 4.13** If a diagram is syntactically contradictory then it is semantically contradictory.

This proposition holds in virtue of the uniqueness of segment construction that follows from Axioms III,4 and III,5 (Hilbert [1971] p.13).

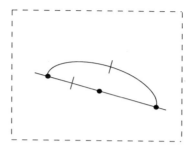

Figure 12: A syntactically contradictory diagram.

# 5    Proofs

Since they typically involve the use of enumeration of cases, geometry proofs that use diagrams cannot have the form of a sequence, like in most linguistic formal systems. In fact they will have a graph-structure.

In order to define the notion of proof in a diagrammatic inference system for geometry we will use Information Flow Graphs (IFGs) from Barwise and Etchemendy [1990] with some modifications.

**Definition 5.1** A *derivation* $\mathcal{P}$ from $D$ is a rooted, finite, directed graph such that

1. all the nodes are diagrams;

2. the initial node is $D$;

3. for all $D'$ the set of children of $D'$ is obtainable from $D'$ by one of the transformation rules.

There are two different types of terminal nodes: open and closed. A closed node is a syntactically contradictory diagram. If a terminal diagram is not closed then it is open. We represent open nodes as white circles and closed nodes as black circles.

**Definition 5.2** A sequence of derivations $\Pi = \langle \mathcal{P}_0, ..., \mathcal{P}_n \rangle$ is a *proof* of $S$ from $D$ if and only if

1. $\mathcal{P}_0 = \{D\}$;

2. for each $\mathcal{P}_m$ such that $0 \le m < n$, $\mathcal{P}_{m+1}$ is like $\mathcal{P}_m$ but for the fact that there is one and only one open terminal node in $\mathcal{P}_m$ that has children in $\mathcal{P}_{m+1}$;

3. $S$ is the set of open terminal nodes in $\mathcal{P}_n$.

**Definition 5.3** A set of diagrams $S$ is *provable* from $D$ (written $D \vdash S$) if and only if there is some proof from $D$ to $S$. (if $D \vdash \{E\}$ we can just write $D \vdash E$.)

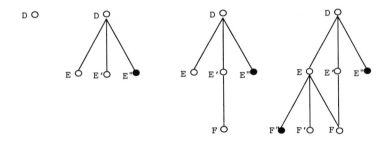

Figure 13: We can observe that $D \vdash D$, $D \vdash \{E, E'\}$, $D \vdash \{E, F\}$ and $D \vdash \{F, F'\}$.

An important difference between proofs, as defined in this chapter, and IFGs is that here the nodes *are* diagrams, instead of being just labeled by diagrams. The main advantage of having the nodes labeled by diagrams is that it allows you to have the same diagram as two different steps in your proof, as in the following derivation.

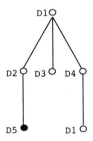

Figure 14

However that can never be the case in our system, because each step involves the application of a rule of transformation, and both inference and construction rules add new objects to the diagram. We could only obtain a diagram that is identical to one of its ancestors (like in Figure 14) if we had a rule that allowed us to erase diagrammatic objects from our diagrams, but there is no such a rule in DS1.

**Example Diagrammatic Proof 5.4 : Subtraction of Segments in DS1. We need to prove that**

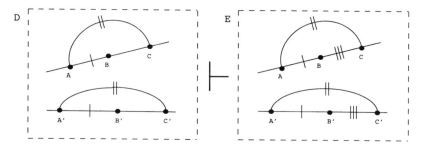

We start with $D$.

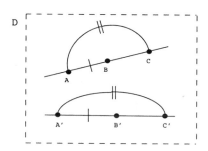

By the Rule of Existence of Segments we obtain the following set of diagrams:

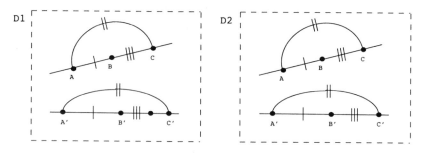

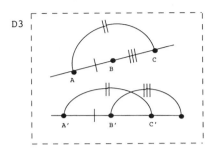

If we apply the Rule of Sum of Segments to $D_1$ we obtain the contradictory diagram $D_4$. If we apply the Rule of Sum of Segments to $D_3$ we obtain the contradictory diagram $D_5$,

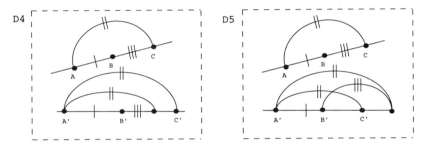

Therefore $D \vdash D_2$, since there exists the following proof from $D$ to $D_2$:

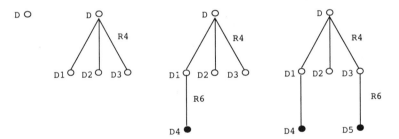

And since $D_2 = E$ we can conclude that $D \vdash E$.

# 6   Soundness

## Validity of the Rules of Transformation

**Definition 6.1** A transformation rule $R$ is *valid* if and only if, if $D \rightsquigarrow S$ by $R$, then $D \models S$.

**Lemma 6.2** *The transformation rules of the system are valid.*

For the proof, please refer to Luengo [1995].

## Proof of Soundness

**Theorem 6.3** *If $D \vdash S$ in DS1 then $D \mathrel{\Vdash} S$*

**Proof:** Suppose that $D \vdash S$. Then there is a proof $\Pi = \langle \mathcal{P}_0, ..., \mathcal{P}_n \rangle$ of $S$ from $D$. The proof will be by induction on the length of $\Pi$.

1. Basis case
   The length of $\Pi$ is 1. Then $S = \{D\}$. Therefore $D \mathrel{\Vdash} S$.

2. Inductive step
   Let $S$ be the set of open terminal nodes of $\mathcal{P}_m$ and $S'$ be the set of open terminal nodes of $\mathcal{P}_{m+1}$. We need to prove that if $D \mathrel{\Vdash} S$ then $D \mathrel{\Vdash} S'$. Suppose $D \mathrel{\Vdash} S$ and $\mathcal{M} \models D$. Then there is an extension $\mathcal{N}$ of $\mathcal{M}$ that is a model of $E$, for some $E$ in $S$ (by Definition 4.10). Therefore, either $E$ is in $S'$ or there is an $S''$ such that $E \rightsquigarrow S''$ and $S'' \subseteq S'$ (by Df. 5.2). Suppose $E$ is in $S'$. Then $D \mathrel{\Vdash} S'$. Suppose there is an $S''$ such that $E \rightsquigarrow S''$ and $S'' \subseteq S'$. Then, by Lemma 6.2, there is an extension of $\mathcal{N}$ that is a model of some $E'$ in $S''$. Hence, by transitivity, there is an extension of $\mathcal{M}$ that is a model of some $E'$ in $S'$ (since $S'' \subseteq S'$). Therefore, $D \mathrel{\Vdash} S'$.     □

## Semantic Restrictions

On defining the semantics of this system we had to consider two things: the definition would have to agree with our intuitions of what geometric diagrams represent and it would have to make certain deduction principles valid.

Take for instance clauses 3 and 4 of the definition of an interpretation function (Def. 3.1):

3. if $l$ is a line* and $A$ is a point* then $A$ is on* $l$ if and only if $\mathcal{I}(l)$ goes through $\mathcal{I}(A)$; and

4. if $A$, $B$ and $C$ are points* then $A$ is between* $B$ and $C$ if and only if $\mathcal{I}(A)$ is between $\mathcal{I}(B)$ and $\mathcal{I}(C)$.

It is seems pretty intuitive that if $A$ is on* $l$ then $\mathcal{I}(l)$ should go through $\mathcal{I}(A)$, but why the biconditional? And the corresponding question also applies to Condition 4.

**Proposition 6.4** If we replace Clause 3 in Definition 3.1 with 3b then the system is not sound.

3b. If $l$ is a line*, $A$ is a point* and $A$ is on* $l$ then $\mathcal{I}(l)$ goes through $\mathcal{I}(A)$.

**Proof:** We need to find two diagrams such that one is provable from the other and yet it is not a geometric consequence. Figure 15 shows such two diagrams.

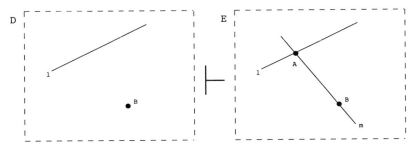

Figure 15: $D \vdash E$ by R3 and R1.

Diagram $E$ is provable from $D$ by the Rules of Point* Introduction and Line* Introduction.

If we adopt Clause 3b, it is possible to find a model $\mathcal{M}$ of $D$ such that $\mathcal{M}(B)$ is on $\mathcal{M}(l)$. By Definition 3.1, any model $\mathcal{N}$ of $E$ will have to meet the following conditions:

1. $\mathcal{N}(m) \neq \mathcal{N}(l)$, since $\mathcal{N}$ is 1-1,

2. $\mathcal{N}(B)$ is on $\mathcal{N}(m)$, and

3. $\mathcal{N}(A)$ is on $\mathcal{N}(l)$ and $\mathcal{N}(m)$

Suppose there is a model $\mathcal{N}'$ of $E$ that is an extension of $\mathcal{M}$. In that case, in addition to the three conditions listed above we know that $\mathcal{N}'(B)$ is on $\mathcal{N}'(l)$. Since two points can define only one line that means that $\mathcal{N}'(l) = \mathcal{N}'(m)$. However, that is impossible, since $\mathcal{N}$ is 1-1. Thus we can conclude that $E$ is not a logical consequence of $D$, since there is a model of $D$ that cannot be extended to a model of $E$.                           □

**Proposition 6.5** If we replace Clause 4 in Definition 3.1 with 4b then the system is not sound.

4b. If $A$, $B$ and $C$ are points* and $A$ is between* $B$ and $C$ then $\mathcal{I}(A)$ is between $\mathcal{I}(B)$ and $\mathcal{I}(C)$.

**Proof:** We need to find two diagrams such that one is provable from the other and yet it is not a geometric consequence. Figure 16 shows such two diagrams.

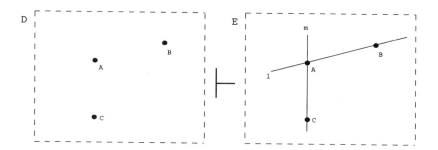

Figure 16: $D \vdash E$ by R1.

Diagram $E$ is provable from $D$ by the Rule of Line* Introduction.

If we adopt clause 4b, it is possible to find a model $\mathcal{M}$ of $D$ such that $\mathcal{M}(C)$ is between $\mathcal{M}(A)$ and $\mathcal{M}(B)$. In that case there must be a line $L$ such that $\mathcal{M}(A)$, $\mathcal{M}(B)$ and $\mathcal{M}(C)$ are on $L$.

By Definition 3.1, any model $\mathcal{N}$ of $E$ will have to meet the following conditions:

1. $\mathcal{N}(l) \neq \mathcal{N}(m)$,

2. $\mathcal{N}(A)$ and $\mathcal{N}(B)$ are on $\mathcal{N}(l)$, and

3. $\mathcal{N}(A)$ and $\mathcal{N}(C)$ are on $\mathcal{N}(m)$.

Suppose that there is an extension $\mathcal{N}'$ of $\mathcal{M}$ that is a model of $E$. In that case in addition to the three conditions listed above we know that $\mathcal{N}'(l) = L$ and $\mathcal{N}'(m) = L$. But that is impossible, since $\mathcal{N}'$ is one-one. Thus we can conclude that $E$ is not a logical consequence of $D$, since there is a model of $D$ that cannot be extended to a model of $E$.                    □

## 7  Completeness

A system is complete if, for any two diagrams $D$ and $E$, if $E$ is a consequence of $D$ then $E$ is also provable from $D$ in the system. That means that if we can find a counterexample, that is, two diagrams $D$ and $E$ such that $E$ is a consequence of $D$ and yet it is not provable from $D$ in the system then the system is not complete.

DS1 is not complete, since we can find a counterexample (Figure 17).

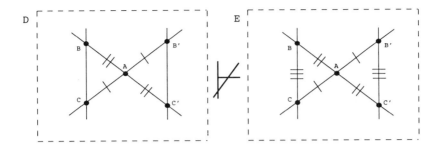

Figure 17: Counterexample.

According to Hilbert's axioms $E$ is a consequence of $D$ (Theorem 7.1), but we will show in the following pages that it is not provable from $D$ in DS1.

**Theorem 7.1** *If $B$, $A$, $C'$ are points on a line and $B'$, $A$, $C$ are also points on a line and $\overline{AB} \cong \overline{AC} \cong \overline{AB'} \cong \overline{AC'}$ then $\overline{BC} \cong \overline{B'C'}$.*

**Proof:** Angle $\angle BAB'$ is the supplement of $\angle BAC$ and also of $\angle B'AC'$. Since $\angle BAB' \cong \angle BAB'$ it follows by subtraction of angles (Theorem 15[5]. (Hilbert [1971], p.16.)) that $\angle BAC \cong \angle B'AC'$. Now we can prove that $\overline{BC} \cong \overline{B'C'}$. The proof goes as follows. By Axiom III.1 there is a point $D$ on the line defined by $C'$ and $B'$ such that $\overline{CB} \cong \overline{C'D}$. We know that $\overline{AC} \cong \overline{AB'}$, $\overline{AB} \cong \overline{AC'}$ and $\angle BAC \cong \angle B'AC'$. Then, by Axiom III.5 $\angle CBA \cong \angle B'C'A$ and $\angle BCA \cong \angle C'B'A$, and by the same axiom, $\angle BCA \cong \angle DAC'$. Then the line defined by $A$ and $B'$ is identical to the line defined by $A$ and $D$ (Axiom III.4), and since two distinct lines can intersect in at most one point (by Axioms I.1 and I.2) it follows that $B' = D$, and hence $\overline{BC} \cong \overline{B'C'}$. □

Since theorem 7.1 is a theorem of Euclidean geometry, every model of $D$ in Euclidean geometry will be extendable to a model of $E$, and therefore $E$ is a geometric consequence of $D$. However, the proof given above cannot be carried out in DS1 since it relies heavily on the notion of angle, and DS1 does not have any way of representing angles.

Just because this proof does not carry over does not mean there is no proof in DS1. We need to prove that $E$ is not provable from $D$ in DS1. The way to do that is to find another diagrammatic system $S$ such that:

1. $S$ has the same syntax as DS1;

2. $S$ has a different semantics from DS1;

---

[5]Theorem 15. Let $h$, $k$, $l$ and $h'$, $k'$, $l'$ be rays emanating from $O$ and $O'$ in the planes $\alpha$ and $\alpha'$, respectively. If the congruences $\angle(h, l) \equiv \angle(h', l')$ and $\angle(k, l) \equiv \angle(k', l')$ are satisfied then so is the congruence $\angle(h, k) \equiv \angle(h', k')$

3. $\mathcal{S}$ is sound (that is, the five transformation rules of DS1 are valid in $\mathcal{S}$); and

4. we can find a model of $D$ in $\mathcal{S}$ that cannot be extended to a model of $E$ (Figure 17).

In such a system $\mathcal{S}$, if $D \vdash E$ then $D \models E$ (soundness), however $D \not\models E$. Therefore, $D \not\vdash E$ in $\mathcal{S}$. Since DS1 and $\mathcal{S}$ are syntactically identical, we have $D \not\vdash E$ in DS1.

Where are we going to find the semantics for such system? The first idea would be to look at non-Euclidean geometries. Non-Euclidean geometries differ from Euclidean geometries in that they do not have the Axiom of Parallels as one of their axioms. However, since we are not using that axiom anywhere in the proof of Theorem 7.1 it does not seem that a non-Euclidean geometry could be the solution.

Nevertheless, it is clear that we are going to need some kind of mathematical objects in our semantics, since the transformation rules of DS1 force the interpretation of the lines* to be infinite, continuous objects. Also, because the transformation rules have to be valid, curved lines (open or closed) are ruled out since they cannot be defined by just two points. Circles cannot be considered because they make the Between* relation impossible to define.

Working in a three-dimensional space will not do, since the lines we need to use in our proof define a plane. Interpreting points* as dimensional objects does not work either, because in that case two points* could define more than one line.

So it seems that the only solution would be to give points* and lines* their standard interpretation and try and give a different interpretation to the fact that two segments* have the same indicator. In any case we will have to use indicators to represent an equivalence relation, since having a particular indicator is reflexive and symmetric for diagrammatic reasons and transitive because of R4.

## A Non-Standard Interpretation for DS1

A *non-standard interpretation* for DS1 is any sound diagrammatic system whose syntax and transformation rules are identical to those of DS1 but that has a different semantics.

In this section we are going to describe such a non-standard interpretation. We will need the notion of a *ruler*. Intuitively, a ruler is a straight line divided into portions of equal length. Formally, a ruler is a pair $\langle l, r \rangle$ where $l$ is a line and $r$ is a positive real number called the *unit* of the ruler. A *ruler-plane* is a Euclidean plane in which each line has been turned into a ruler, possibly with different units. Notice that each Euclidean plane corresponds to an infinite number of ruler-planes. We need to consider only those ruler-planes in which there is at least one ruler whose units are not congruent to the units of the other rulers. We also need to define the *pseudolength* of a segment. We will say that the quotient $u/r$ is the pseudolength of a segment on a ruler, where $r$ is the unit of the ruler and $u$ is the ordinary Euclidean length of the segment.

We are going to call *Rulers* a diagrammatic system whose syntax is just the one of DS1 and whose semantics is given by the following definition of a model:

**Definition 7.2** Function $\mathcal{R}$ is a *model* of a diagram $D$ if and only if it is a 1-1 interpretation function[6] from the diagrammatic objects of $D$ into the rulers and points of a ruler-plane $\mathcal{P}$ such that:

1. if $A$ is a point* then $\mathcal{R}(A)$ is a point;

2. if $l$ is a line* then $\mathcal{R}(l)$ is a ruler;

3. if $A$ is on* $l$ then $\mathcal{R}(A)$ is on $\mathcal{R}(l)$;

4. if $\overline{AB}$ is a segment* then $\mathcal{R}(\overline{AB})$ is the segment defined by $\mathcal{R}(A)$ and $\mathcal{R}(B)$;

5. if $A$ is between* $B$ and $C$ then $\mathcal{R}(A)$ is between $\mathcal{R}(B)$ and $\mathcal{R}(C)$; and

6. if an indicator indicates both $\overline{AB}$ and $\overline{A'B'}$ then $\mathcal{R}(\overline{AB})$ and $\mathcal{R}(\overline{A'B'})$ have the same pseudolength.

Obviously the most important difference between DS1 and *Rulers* is the interpretation of the indicators.

To prove that *Rulers* is an interpretation we need to prove that it is sound. First we need to define the notion of provability and then we need to prove that the transformation rules of the system are valid.

**Proposition 7.3** $D \vdash E$ in DS1 if and only if $D \vdash E$ in *Rulers*.

The proof follows from the fact that DS1 and *Rulers* have the same syntax and transformation rules because that is how we have defined both systems.

**Proposition 7.4** The transformation rules of *Rulers* are valid.

For the proof refer to Luengo [1995].

**Theorem 7.5** *Rulers* is sound.

---

[6]$\mathcal{R}$ has to be 1-1 if we want the transformation rules to be valid, as shown in Proposition 3.8.

**Proof:** We need to prove that if $D \vdash E$ then $D \models E$, which follows from the fact that all the transformation rules are valid (Proposition 7.4). The inductive proof is just the one we gave for Theorem 6.3.        □

**Proposition 7.6** For diagrams $D$ and $E$ in Figure 17, $D \not\models E$ in *Rulers*.

**Proof:** We need to find a model $\mathcal{R}$ of $D$ that is not a model of $E$. Suppose $\mathcal{R}$ is a model of $D$ and the units of the ruler that goes through $\mathcal{R}(B')$ and $\mathcal{R}(C')$ are not congruent to the units of any of the other rulers. By Theorem 7.1 we know that $\mathcal{R}(\overline{BC})$ is congruent to $\mathcal{R}(\overline{B'C'})$. Now, since the length of the units of $\mathcal{R}(\overline{B'C'})$ is different from that of the units of $\mathcal{R}(\overline{BC})$ it follows that $\mathcal{R}(\overline{B'C'})$ is not congruent to $\mathcal{R}(\overline{BC})$, and therefore $\mathcal{R}$ is not a model of $E$.        □

**Theorem 7.7** DS1 is incomplete.

**Proof:** Suppose DS1 is complete. Then, for any two diagrams $D$ and $E$, if $D \models E$ in DS1 then $D \vdash E$ in DS1. Thus, by contraposition, if $D \not\vdash E$ then $D \not\models E$. Now, we have proven that the two diagrams $D$ and $E$ in Figure 17 are such that $D$ is not a consequence of $E$ in *Rulers* (Proposition 7.6). Therefore, since *Rulers* is sound (Theorem 7.5), $D$ is not provable from $E$ in *Rulers*, and that means that it is not provable from $D$ in DS1 either, since both systems share the same syntax and transformation rules. However, we have proven that $E$ is a consequence of $D$ in DS1 (Theorem 7.1). Therefore, DS1 is incomplete.        □

# Part C

# Heterogeneous Systems

# Chapter VIII

# Heterogeneous Logic

JON BARWISE and JOHN ETCHEMENDY

## 1  Historical Background

A major concern to the founders of modern logic—Frege, Peirce, Russell, and Hilbert—was to give an account of the logical structure of valid reasoning. Taking valid reasoning in mathematics as paradigmatic, these pioneers led the way in developing the accounts of logic which we teach today and that underwrite the work in model theory, proof theory, and definability theory. The resulting notions of proof, model, formal system, soundness, and completeness are things that no one claiming familiarity with logic can fail to understand, and they have also played an enormous role in the revolution known as computer science.

The success of this model of inference led to an explosion of results and applications. But it also led most logicians—and those computer scientists most influenced by the logic tradition—to neglect forms of reasoning that did not fit well within this model. We are thinking, of course, of reasoning that uses devices like diagrams, graphs, charts, frames, nets, maps, and pictures.

The attitude of the traditional logician to these forms of representation is evident in the quotation of Neil Tennant in Chapter I, which expresses the standard view of the role of diagrams in geometrical proofs. One aim of our work, as explained there, is to demonstrate that this dogma is misguided. We believe that many of the problems people have putting their knowledge of logic to work, whether in machines or in their own lives, stems from the logocentricity that has pervaded its study for the past hundred years.

Recently, some researchers outside the logic tradition have explored uses of diagrams in knowledge representation and automated reasoning, finding inspiration in the work of Euler, Venn, and especially C. S. Peirce. This volume is a testament to this resurgence of interest in nonlinguistic representations in reasoning.

While we applaud this resurgence, the aim of this chapter is to strike a cautionary note or two. Enchanted by the potential of nonlinguistic representations, it is all too easy to overreact and so to repeat the errors of the past. Just as many in logic and AI once argued (and still argue) that first-order logic is a *universal* representation language, others are now striving toward a universal non-linguistic representation scheme. We want to suggest that the search for *any* universal scheme of representation— linguistic, graphical, or diagrammatic—is a mistake. Efficient reasoning is, we believe, inescapably heterogeneous (or "hybrid") in nature.

## 2   Logic and Information

We approach inference from an informational perspective. Wherever there is structure, there is information. But in order for agents (animals, people, or computers) to traffic in information, the information must in some way or other be presented to or represented by the agent. Typically, a given representation or family of representations will represent certain information explicitly, while other information will be implicit in the information explicitly represented. Inference, as we understand the term, is the task of extracting information implicit in some explicitly presented information.

This informational perspective is part of the modern, semantic approach to logic associated with names like Gödel, Tarski, Robinson, and the like. On this view, a purported rule of inference is valid or not depending on whether it in fact guarantees that the information represented by the conclusion is implicit in the information represented by the premises. But when one takes this informational perspective seriously, the logician's disdain for nonlinguistic representations seems like an oversight, a case of dogma in desperate need of reexamination. The most casual survey of the ways people actually represent information shows an enormous variety of representational devices that go beyond simple text.

In carrying out a reasoning task, part of the solution lies in figuring out how to represent the problem. In problem solving, well begun really is half done. Indeed, this is probably an understatement. Figuring out how to represent the information at hand is often the most important part of the solution. What we need to do, and need to teach students of inference to do, is to use the most appropriate form of representation for the reasoning task at hand. As long as the purported proof really does clearly demonstrate that the information represented by the conclusion is implicit in the information represented by the premises, the purported proof is valid.

Why are logicians so suspicious of diagrams and other forms of nonlinguistic representation? The answer goes back to the tradition in geometry, where diagrams were viewed with suspicion by the founders. Certain mistaken proofs were thought to result from misleading diagrams that accompanied them. So, the tradition went, the diagram should in theory be eliminable from the proof. The textual part of the proof should stand on its own two feet.

This argument is itself a nonsequitur. If we threw out every form of reasoning that could be misapplied by the careless reasoner, we would have little if anything left. Mathematical induction, for example, would certainly have to go. No, the correct response is not to throw out methods of proof that have been misapplied in the past, but rather to give a careful analysis of such methods with the aim of understanding exactly when they are valid and when they are not.

A nice case study along these lines has been carried out in Shin [1991a] and reported in Shin [1991]. In introductory logic, many people teach the method of Venn diagrams. But often they also tell their students that Venn diagrams are only a heuristic aid to giving proofs. A "real" proof has to be given in first-order logic. Shin shows that this is a mistake. She gives a rigorous analysis of Venn diagrams as a formal system, with its own syntax, semantics, and logical consequence relation. She shows that the usual rules of inference are sound with respect to this consequence relation. Furthermore, she shows that, with some trivial additional rules that had been overlooked, one can give a completeness proof for the deductive system.

An even earlier study is given in Sowa [1984]. In the early chapters of that book, Sowa gives a formal treatment of Peirce's existential graphs, including their syntax, semantics, and proof theory. This is a formalism that is expressively equivalent to first-order logic, but it is given in purely diagrammatic terms.

The importance of these results is this: they show that there is no principled distinction between inference formalisms that use text and those that use diagrams. One can have rigorous, logically sound (and complete) formal systems based on diagrams. And while Venn diagrams may seem very simple, they are probably used more frequently in real life than first-order formalisms.

# 3  Homomorphic Representations

By *homomorphic representations* we mean representations that are structurally similar to whatever it is that they represent. (These are what Myers and Konolige [1992] call "analogical" representations. We borrow the term "homomorphic" from modern algebra, though our use of the term is somewhat broader than the technical notion.) Another way to put this is that with homomorphic representations, the mapping $\phi$ between syntactic structure (that is, the structure of the representation itself) and semantic structure (that is, the structure of the object, situation, or event represented) is highly structure preserving, whereas the corresponding mapping in the case of linguistic representations is anything but structure preserving.

Here are some of the hallmarks of a homomorphic representation system:

1. Objects are typically represented by icon tokens. It is often the case that each object is represented by a unique icon token and distinct tokens represent distinct objects.

2. There is a mapping $\phi$ from icon types to properties of objects.

3. The mapping $\phi$ preserves structure. For example, one would expect that:

   (a) If one icon type is a subtype of another (as in the case of shaded squares and squares, for example), then there is a corresponding subproperty relation among the properties they represent.

   (b) If two icon types are incompatible (say squares and circles), then the properties they represent should be incompatible.

   (c) The converses of (a) and (b) frequently hold as well.

4. Certain relations among objects are represented by relations among icon tokens, with the same kinds of conditions as in (3a)–(3c).

5. Higher-order properties of relations among objects (like transitivity, asymmetry, reflexivity, and the like) are reflected by the same properties of relations among icon tokens.

6. Every possibility (involving represented object, properties, and relations) is representable. That is, there are no possible situations that are represented as impossible.

7. Every representation indicates a genuine possibility.

As these points should make clear, homomorphic representation is not an all-or-nothing affair. A given system may be more or less homomorphic. At one end are representations that are isomorphic to the target domain along certain dimensions. The limiting case of this is reasoning directly with the target domain itself. (If you can't infer which lid fits the jar from the available information, try them on in turn.) At the other extreme are things like Morse code, where the syntactic structure of the representation bears little if any discernible relationship to the structure of whatever the message is about. In between, there can be various degrees of "homomorphicity." For example, the diagrams of *Hyperproof* (see Figure 4 for a sample), while highly homomorphic, do not satisfy (3b), since there are incompatible types of icons that represent compatible properties of blocks. Circuit diagrams, by contrast, do satisfy (3b). Venn diagrams are fairly homomorphic, but they do not satisfy condition 7. Linguistic representations occasionally satisfy some of these conditions to a very limited extent, but typically they won't.

## Against universal schemes of representation

The literature on diagrammatic representations contains many discussions about why "a picture can be worth 10,000 words." A recurring theme in these discussions is that good diagrammatic representations are homomorphic to what they represent along important dimensions. The homomorphism allows the structure of the representation to carry a great deal of the inferential burden, obviating reasoning that would have to be made explicit in inferences with linguistic representations.

This observation has its up side and its down side. On the positive, we see why good diagrams help make reasoning easier. On the negative, though, they show that a search for a universal representation system in effective reasoning is misguided.

The world is a complex, multi-dimensional affair. Besides the four dimensions of space and time, there are other dimensions as well where other relations most naturally reside. The regularities that we want to exploit reside in and across these dimensions. There just aren't enough regularities in two-space (or three- or four-space) to go around to devise a universal homomorphic representation system.

Let us look at a concrete example from the field of hardware design and verification. (This example comes from Johnson, Barwise, and Allwein [1993]. See also Fisler [1994] for a follow-up development.) Think of a computer chip. There are hundreds of different relationships that figure into the design of a new chip or other electronic device. These relationships typically cluster into families, depending on what perspective one takes for the moment. It must be considered from the point of view of control, of logic gates, and of timing, to focus on just three. Each of these has complicated relations that need to be represented in the design of the device. Engineers have solved this representation problem with three separate representational systems: state charts for the representation of control, circuit diagrams for the representation of gate information, and timing diagrams for the representation of timing. Figures 1-3 show three different representations of a very simple device, a so-called unit pulser.

Diagram 1 shows a timing diagram specification for the pulser. It shows that any input pulse should turn into a unit output pulse. Figure 2 shows a state diagram for such a device with two internal states. The arcs show

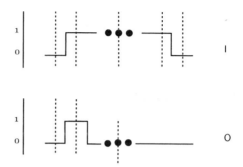

Figure 1: A timing diagram of a unit pulser

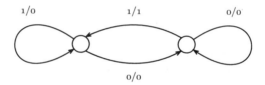

Figure 2: A state diagram of a unit pulser

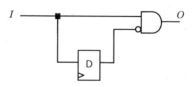

Figure 3: A circuit diagram of a unit pulser

transitions between these states. The $I/O$ arcs are labeled by pairs of zeros or ones, the first member of the pair representing input and the second output. Finally, Figure 3 shows a circuit diagram for such a device. In addition to the usual logic gates, it employs a "storage" device that holds a value for one unit of time before passing it on.

Each of these representational schemes is highly homomorphic to the aspect of hardware they represent. Certain physical relationships among lines and other sorts of tokens represent relationships among various aspects of the operating circuit. But notice that a line in one diagram has quite a different interpretation from that in the others: wiring connections between gates, transitions among states, and the value on a wire through time. When engineers design and reason about hardware, they use all three kinds of diagrams at once. This is a clear example of "heterogeneous" reasoning in real life. They simply use all three sets of conventions, and reason with all of them.

## Against an "interlingua"

People who accept the argument against a universal diagrammatic system, and so accept the idea of a heterogeneous reasoning system, often suppose that in order to have a rigorous heterogeneous system, there must be *some* system of conventions into which all the others can be embedded and compared, some sort of "interlingua" to mediate between the various systems of representations. But this is not correct. Whether it is *useful* to have an interlingua is debatable, but there is certainly no logical necessity to employ one.

The idea that an interlingua is needed to mediate between the various representations misses the crucial fact that these are representations of a single target domain. The semantic mappings that link all of them to a common target domain (circuits in our example) allow for interaction between different forms of representation. Imagine trying to design a hardware system where all three forms of information were represented in a single system. Experience shows that such a system would lose the clarity, crispness, and utility of the systems that have developed in practice. To combine these into one system, the mappings from syntax to semantics would have to be complicated to an extent that they would lose much of their homomorphic character. The more complicated this mapping becomes, the closer we come to having a notational variant of a linguistic scheme of representation, thereby losing the very representational advantages inherent in a homomorphic system.

As a case study in how one can define a useful, truly heterogeneous inference system, one where there is no single form or representation into which all the others are translated, let us consider a working heterogeneous system without an interlingua.

# 4   Hyperproof

*Hyperproof* is a computer program and textbook that we use in teaching elementary logic courses. The reasoning system it implements is heterogeneous, since it uses both the usual language of first-order logic, plus diagrams. It has all the usual rules of first-order logic, plus a number of rules for dealing with diagrams and the interplay between diagrams and sentences.

In *Hyperproof* every diagram represents partial information about some class of blocks worlds. (We will model these blocks worlds by means of set-theoretic structures below.) A sentence in the first-order language will be true in some of these worlds, false in others. It does not really sound right to say that a diagram is true or false in a world. Rather, a diagram will depict some of these worlds and conflict with others. To adopt a uniform terminology, let us say that a representation $r$ *holds* in a world $w$ if $r$ is a diagram and depicts the world $w$, or if $r$ is a sentence and is true in $w$.

When we are given both a diagram and some sentences, the combined information limits us to the worlds in which all the givens hold. Some other sentence or diagram follows from the given sentences and diagram if it holds in all the worlds in which all the given information holds.

Neither of the two forms of representation made available in *Hyperproof* is made redundant by the other. That is, there are things that can be depicted by diagrams that cannot be said in the language, and vice versa. For example, we can depict a block as being on the leftmost, front square, but there is no way to express this in the language, since the language only allows us to speak of relative positions, not absolute positions. Conversely, we can say that there is a large tetrahedron somewhere to the right of block **b**, but there is no way to depict exactly this with a diagram. Any diagram that depicts a world where there is a large tetrahedron left of **b** would depict it in some particular place, and so hold in fewer worlds than the sentence. Thus the information content of the sentence and the diagram would be different.

There is an even bigger difference between the forms of representation. If we are given a sentence $\varphi$ and a diagram $d$, we can determine whether $\varphi$ follows from $d$ by inspection. We simply look at $d$ and "see" if the sentence is true in all the worlds it depicts. There is no way to do this the other way around. We cannot "see" the worlds in which a sentence holds in the way we can with a diagram.

What accounts for this asymmetry? We will analyze this in some detail below, but here is a quick gloss of what is going on. A given diagram $d$

can be modeled in two ways. One is as a completed structure in its own right. The other is as a partial structure modeling the pictured facts of the worlds depicted by $d$. These are distinct structures. For instance, the former will have as objects various pictures of blocks. The latter will have as objects various blocks, not pictures of blocks. There is a mapping from the pictures to the blocks, though, a mapping which preserves a lot of structure. This mapping lets the user easily reinterpret the sentence $\varphi$ as though it were about the diagram itself. If $\varphi$ holds of the diagram, under this reinterpretation, then it holds in all the worlds in which the diagram holds. This reinterpretation is possible because of the homomorphic nature of the relationship between diagrams and the worlds they depict. The impossibility of going the other way around stems from a lack of a similar homomorphic relationship between sentences and world.

This asymmetry is also responsible for some of the differences in expressive power between diagrams and sentences mentioned earlier. The homomorphism from diagrams to worlds makes the diagrams better at depicting very particular facts, facts that may not be expressible in the language. Conversely, linguistic devices like quantifiers, negation, and disjunction that allow sentences to represent facts that cannot be represented diagrammatically also block any homomorphism between the sentence and the worlds in which it holds.

## Why there is no interlingua in *Hyperproof*

It is important to remember that *Hyperproof* maintains two distinct forms of representing information about blocks worlds. There is no sense in which the program has a single underlying representation into which both diagrams and sentences are translated. What holds the two together is not an underlying representation scheme, or interlingua, but simply the fact that they are both about the same worlds. It is this fact that underwrites the rules of inference which govern how we can reason with both at the same time.

This becomes clearer with some examples. Let us examine two of the most important rules of *Hyperproof*, the rules of **Observe** and **Cases Exhausted** (and a special case of the latter, **Apply**).

For any given diagram there are literally an infinite number of sentences that can be observed to hold on the basis of the diagram. The rule **Observe** allows us to extract sentential information from diagrammatic information. (**Apply** allows us to go the other way around.) **Observe** allows the user to infer any sentence which is definitely true in the partial structure that corresponds to the diagram—that is, true according to the truth evaluation schema embodied in the (weak) Kleene three-valued logic. The three values are *true*, *false*, and *unknown*. The implementation of the **Observe** rule in

*Hyperproof* is basically just the recursive definition of this Kleene three-valued evaluation scheme.

The most important features of the *Hyperproof* system are the techniques for transferring information from sentences into a range of diagrams. Thus, we are typically given a diagram $d$ and some sentences $\varphi_1, \ldots, \varphi_n$ describing the target world. Based on one of these sentences, say $\varphi$, we see that there is a range of possibilities, each of which can be embodied by fleshing out the diagram $d$ in some way. Thus we create some new diagrams $d_1, \ldots, d_k$, each an amplification of $d$ (in that it carries more information than $d$), and say that these exhaust all the possibilities, given the sentence $\varphi$. This step is valid if any way the world could be, consistent with $d$ and $\varphi$, is also consistent with at least one of these new diagrams. This is the rule of **Cases Exhaustive**.

A special instance of **Cases Exhaustive** is where $k = 1$, that is, where there is just one new diagram. Using the rule in this case means that the information added to $d$ in the new diagram $d_1$ is implicit in the sentence $\varphi$. We call this special instance **Apply**, since you can think of it as applying the information in $\varphi$ to add new information to the diagram.

There are many cases where one can infer some sentence from a diagram and other sentences, but where one cannot do this using only the rule of **Observe**. Some version of **Apply** or **Cases Exhausted** is necessary to obtain the inference. Examples of these, together with methods for knowing when they arise, are discussed in the chapter "Logic and Observation" of Barwise and Etchemendy [1994].

To see how we can implement the **Apply** rule without going through an interlingua, let us describe the algorithm. Imagine we are in the following situation. The user has a diagram $d$ and a sentence $\varphi$. She wants to apply $\varphi$ to amplify the diagram to $d'$.

Ideally, what one would like would be an algorithm that did the following: If this **Apply** is legitimate, then say so. That is, look at all diagrams $d^*$ that amplify $d$ in ways that are incompatible with $d'$, and see if any of them make $\varphi$ true. If not, accept the conclusion $d'$. Otherwise, reject it and produce a counterexample by displaying an incompatible diagram $d^*$ that amplifies $d$ but in which $\varphi$ is true.

This is a legitimate form of reasoning (as we will show later in this chapter) but it is not in general realizable in a computationally feasible manner. The reason is that it can happen that such a diagram $d^*$ would have to settle too many issues, issues which themselves can be resolved in a variety of ways. Thus one gets lost in a huge search space.

In *Hyperproof* we solve this problem by relying on partial information in two ways. First, we only search for counterexamples among those diagrams

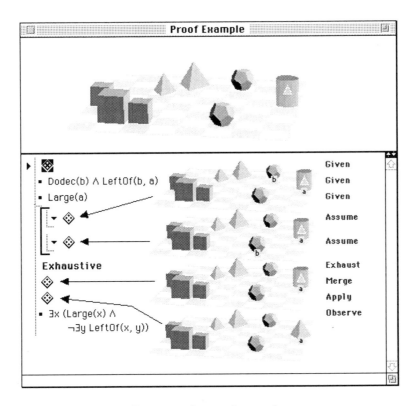

Figure 4: A sample proof.

that settle just issues raised in $d'$.[1] If we can find such a diagram in which $\varphi$ is true, then we will have found a counterexample. But we do not insist that the sentence $\varphi$ come out as true in $d^*$, only that it *not* come out as false. If it comes out as neither true nor false in a diagram $d^*$ which is incompatible with $d'$ and which settles all issues raised in $d'$, we call this a possible counterexample, and give it to the user as a possibility that needs to be considered explicitly. In this way, the search space is greatly reduced and the rule is sound, in that it never ratifies an invalid use of **Apply**. The algorithm is not complete, in that it will not be able to recognize some valid uses of **Apply**, but in such cases it returns a possible counterexample for the user to consider.

The point of describing the algorithms that implement the **Observe** and **Apply** rules is to stress the claim made above about there being no

---

[1]For example, if $d'$ settles the size of a single block $b$, and that is all, then the only issue we consider is the size of that block. All other amplifications of $d$ are ignored.

need for an interlingua to mediate between the two forms of representation. The rules are sound because of the semantics that relate the two forms of representation, but the semantics itself is not in any sense internal to the program.

## 5   Towards a Mathematical Analysis of *Hyperproof*

In this section we provide a mathematical framework for *Hyperproof* in which to make some of the above claims more rigorous. Our aim here to to carry the development just far enough to put some logical meat on the bones of the informal argument given in the first half of this chapter. In particular, we want to give a rigorous analysis of the *Hyperproof* rules of **Observe** and **Apply**. The logically-minded reader should be able to carry the development further if so inclined.

### Syntax

We begin by constructing models of the representations used in *Hyperproof*, namely, the sentences and the diagrams. We start with a standard recursive definition of the sentences.

**Definition 5.1** (Sentences) The *predicates* of our language consist of the following:

- Unary: **Small, Medium, Large, Tet, Cube, Dodec**

- Binary: **=, Larger, LeftOf, FrontOf, Adjoins, SameSize, SameShape, SameRow, SameColumn**

- Ternary: **Between**

- The *variables* of our language consist of $v_1, v_2, \ldots$

We define the *wffs* as follows:

- The atomic wffs are formed as usual from the variables, names, and predicates.

- The compound wffs are formed recursively as usual from the atomic wffs using $\neg, \wedge, \vee, \rightarrow, \leftrightarrow, \forall, \exists$.

The *sentences* consist of those wffs with no free variables.

By contrast, the syntax of our diagrammatic representations are not presented recursively.

$$\Delta^{0,j} \qquad \Delta^{1,j} \qquad \Delta^{2,j} \qquad \Delta^{3,j}$$

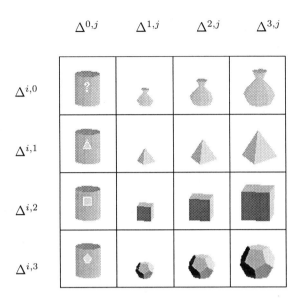

Table 1: Icon types in *Hyperproof*.

**Definition 5.2** (Syntax of Diagrams) (Icon types) There are sixteen icon types in our system. For ease of type setting, we refer to these as $\Delta^{i,j}$ for $0 \leq i,j \leq 3$. See Table 1 for the form these icons take in *Hyperproof*.

(Icon tokens) We assume that there are an infinite number of icon tokens of each icon type. We indicate an icon token of type $\Delta^{i,j}$ by adding a numerical subscript: $\Delta^{i,j}_n$. We assume that you can always recover the type from any of its tokens, and we refer to the type of token $\tau$ as $Type(\tau)$.

(The Grid) We also assume the existence of a *grid* of size $k \times k$. We refer to a grid position by means of a pair $\langle x, y \rangle$ where $1 \leq x, y \leq k$.

(Diagrams) A *diagram d* consists of a triple $\langle Tokens^d, Pos^d, Label^d \rangle$ satisfying the following conditions.

1. $Tokens^d$ is a finite set of icon tokens.

2. $Pos^d$ is a partial, one-to-one function from $Tokens^d$ into grid positions. If $Pos^d(\tau) = \langle x, y \rangle$ we say that the icon token $\tau$ has position $\langle x, y \rangle$ on the grid. If $\tau \notin dom(Pos^d)$, then we say that $\tau$ is unlocated in $d$. (In the implementation of *Hyperproof*, unlocated tokens sit off to the right of the grid.)

3. $Label^d$ is a partial function from the set of names into the set $Tokens^d$ of tokens of $d$. If $Label^d(\mathbf{n})$ is defined, then we say that the name $\mathbf{n}$ *labels* the token $Label^d(\mathbf{n})$ in diagram $d$.

It should be clear from the definitions of world, sentence, and diagram, that there is a much higher degree of structural similarity between diagrams and worlds than there is between sentences and worlds. We will spell out this similarity in some detail in our discussion of the semantics to follow, since it is this similarity which makes our diagrams a homomorphic representation system.

A proof in the *Hyperproof* system typically involves a sequence of diagrams, not just one. We need to decide how to think about the identity of tokens in different diagrams appearing in the course of a proof. Suppose, for example, that during a proof we have a token $\tau$ of type $\Delta^{0,1}$ (representing a tetrahedron of unknown size) with no grid position (representing a lack of information about where the tetrahedron is located) in a diagram $d$. Suppose further that by means of a valid use of the **Apply** rule, we replace this token by the token $\tau'$ of type $\Delta^{1,1}$ (representing a small tetrahedron), and locate it on the grid at some location, obtaining a new diagram $d'$. Since these tokens are of different types, they are distinct tokens, but they represent the same block. It is only the dynamic aspect of the proof that indicates that the two tokens are being used to represent the same block. To model this history, we follow Shin [1991a] by introducing the notion of counterpart tokens.

**Definition 5.3** (Counterparts)

- A *counterpart structure* $U = \langle U, \equiv \rangle$ consists of a universe $U$ of icon tokens and some equivalence relation $\equiv$ on $U$. Tokens $\tau, \tau' \in U$ are *counterparts* iff $\tau \equiv \tau'$.

- $U$ *respects* the diagram $d$ if $U$ contains all the icon tokens of $d$ but no two of them are counterparts in $U$.

- Diagrams $d$ and $d'$ are *counterpart diagrams* (relative to $U$) if every token in $Tokens^d$ has a counterpart in $Tokens^{d'}$ and vice versa.

In what follows, we work relative to some fixed counterpart structure $U$. (In order to make the proofs of some of our results go through, we assume that each equivalence class of $U$ is infinite. This is basically the assumption that given any finite set $D$ of diagrams, we can find a new token which is a counterpart of the tokens which have counterparts in $D$.) We restrict attention to diagrams respected by this counterpart structure. We will not be discussing proofs explicitly, but if we did, we would insist that all diagrams in any proof be counterparts of one another relative to $U$. This reflects the fact that the counterpart structure models the process of modifying diagrams in a proof by replacing tokens with more specific tokens. To make this idea more rigorous, we next capture the idea of one token being more specific than another and, using that, the idea that some *Hyperproof* diagrams carry more information than others, not just quantitatively, but qualitatively. This is captured by the notion of one diagram "extending" another.

**Definition 5.4** (Specificity of icons)

- Icon type $\Delta^{i,j}$ is at least as *informative* as $\Delta^{i',j'}$, written $\Delta^{i,j} \geq \Delta^{i',j'}$, iff $i' = 0$ or $i' = i$ and $j' = 0$ or $j' = j$.

- One token is as informative as another if the corresponding relation holds of their types.

**Definition 5.5** (Extension of diagrams) We say that diagram $d$ is an *extension* of $d_0$ just in case the following conditions hold:

- $d$ and $d_0$ are counterpart diagrams.

- Each icon token in $d$ is at least as informative as its counterpart in $d_0$.

- The function $Loc^d$ extends the function $Loc^{d_0}$, in the sense that if $Loc^{d_0}(\tau')$ is defined then $Loc^d(\tau) = Loc^{d_0}(\tau')$, where $\tau$ and $\tau'$ are counterparts.

- The function $Label^d$ extends the function $Label^{d_0}$, in the sense that if $Label^{d_0}(\mathbf{n})$ is defined then $Label^d(\mathbf{n})$ and $Label^{d_0}(\mathbf{n})$ are counterparts.

## Semantics

We next turn to modeling the blocks worlds in which both sentences and diagrams hold.

**Definition 5.6** (Worlds) We assume the existence of an infinite supply of *blocks*, an infinite supply of *names*, and a finite number of possible *locations* arranged in a $k \times k$ array. We refer to a location by means of a pair $\langle x, y \rangle$ where $0 < x, y \leq k$.

A *world $w$* consists of a tuple $\langle B^w, N^w, Sz^w, Sh^w, Loc^w, Den^w \rangle$ satisfying the following conditions.

1. $B^w$ is a non-empty set of blocks, called the *domain* of $w$.

2. $N^w$ is a non-empty set of names, called the *names* of $w$.

3. $Sz^w$ is a function from $B^w$ into the set {Small, Medium, Large} of sizes; $Sz^w(b)$ is called the *size* of the block $b$.

4. $Sh^w$ is a function from $B^w$ into the set {Tetrahedron, Dodecahedron, Cube} of shapes; $Sh^w(b)$ is called the *shape* of the block $b$.

5. $Loc^w$ is a one-to-one function from $B^w$ into the set of locations; $Loc^w(b)$ is called the *location* of the block $b$.

6. $Den^w$ is a function from $U \cup N^w$ into $B^w$; $Den^w(x)$ is called the *denotation* of $x$. If $x$ is an icon token (name) then $x$ is said to *depict* (*name*, resp.) the block $Den^w(x)$. Among icon tokens, we require that $Den^w$ respect the counterpart relation; that is, if $\tau \equiv \tau'$, then $Den^w(\tau) = Den^w(\tau')$

**Definition 5.7** (Semantics of sentences) Let $w$ be a blocks world. A *variable assignment* $f$ is a function from the set of variables into $B^w$. We extend $f$ to a function on names and variables by letting $f(\mathbf{n}) = Den^w(\mathbf{n})$ for each name $\mathbf{n}$. We define the notion of $f$ satisfying the wff $\varphi$ in $w$, written $w \models \varphi[f]$, by recursion. We give a few examples of the clauses here.

1. (Atomic)

$w \models \mathbf{Small(t)}\ [f]$ iff $Sz^w(f(\mathbf{t})) = \text{Small}$.
$w \models \mathbf{Tet(t)}\ [f]$ iff $Sh^w(f(\mathbf{t})) = \text{Tetrahedron}$.
$w \models \mathbf{LeftOf(t, t')}\ [f]$ iff $x < x'$ where $x$ is the first co-ordinate of $Loc^w(f(\mathbf{t}))$ and $x'$ is the first coordinate of $Loc^w(f(\mathbf{t'}))$.

2. (Negation) $w \models \neg\varphi\ [f]$ iff $w \not\models \varphi\ [f]$.

3. (Conjunction) $w \models \varphi \wedge \psi\ [f]$ iff $w \models \varphi\ [f]$ and $w \models \psi\ [f]$.

4. (Universal quantifier) $w \models \forall \mathbf{v}_i \varphi\ [f]$ iff for all assignments $f'$ that agree with $f$ except possibly on $\mathbf{v}_i$, $w \models \varphi\ [f']$.

If $\varphi$ is a sentence (i.e. a wff with no free variables) we say that $\varphi$ *holds* in $w$ if $\varphi$ is satisfied by any assignment $f$.

**Definition 5.8** (Semantics of diagrams) Let $w$ be a blocks world and let $d$ be a diagram. We say that $d$ *holds* in $w$ if the following conditions obtain:

1. Every block in $w$ is denoted by some icon token in $d$.

2. For any icon token $\tau = \Delta_n^{i,j}$ of $d$:

   if $i = 1$ (2, 3) then the size of the block $Den^w(\tau)$ in $w$ is Small (resp. Medium, Large).
   if $j = 1$ (2, 3) then the shape of the block $Den^w(\tau)$ in $w$ is Tetrahedron (resp. Cube, Dodecahedron).
   if $Pos^d(\tau)$ is defined, say $=\langle x, y \rangle$, then the location of the block $Den^w(\tau)$ in $w$ is $\langle x, y \rangle$.

3. If a name is used to label an icon token $\tau$ in $d$, then the block denoted by $\tau$ must have that name in $w$. That is, if $Label^d(\mathbf{n}) = \tau$, then $Den^w(\tau) = Den^w(\mathbf{n})$.

## Logical notions defined

Our earlier definitions now allow us to define the main logical notions.

**Definition 5.9** (Logical consequence)

- Let us call any well-formed sentence or diagram a *Hyperproof representation.*

- Let $P$ be a set of representations and $q$ be a single representation. We say that $q$ is a *logical consequence* of $P$, written $P \models q$, if every blocks world in which every representation in $P$ holds is also one in which $q$ holds.

- We say that a set $P$ of representations is *consistent* if there is a blocks world in which all the representations in $P$ hold.

The following is an easy consequence of our definitions.

**Proposition 5.10** (Autoconsistency) Every diagram is consistent.

We do not present proofs of the results claimed here. None of them are at all difficult, but presenting the details would use up more space than we have at our disposal.

**Corollary 5.11** Let $d$ be any diagram and let $T$ be any set of sentences all of which are logical consequences of $d$. Then $T \cup \{d\}$ is consistent.

A hint that something interesting is going on with the diagrams is given by the following simple, but important, result.

**Proposition 5.12** If $d$ and $d'$ are logical consequences of one another then $d = d'$. Hence, the logical consequence relation, restricted to single diagrams, is a partial ordering.

We write $d \geq d'$ for $d \models d'$ when we want to stress the fact that it is a partial ordering. The following result shows that this relation has a syntactic characterization, modulo the question of which icon tokens are counterparts of one another.

**Proposition 5.13** Given diagrams $d$ and $d'$, the following are equivalent:

1. $d \geq d'$.

2. $d$ is an extension of $d'$.

This ordering is what rests behind *Hyperproof*'s rule of **Merge**, a rule that lets the user extract all the information common to an exhaustive set of diagrams.

**Proposition 5.14** (Merge) Let $D$ be a finite set of diagrams. The following are equivalent:

1. There is a single diagram $d$ which is the greatest lower bound of the diagrams in $D$ (that is, $d$ is a logical consequence of each diagram in $D$, and it entails any other diagram $d'$ entailed by every diagram in $D$).

2. All the diagrams in $D$ are counterparts of one another.

## On the Observe and Apply rules

We conclude our discussion by making precise our earlier claims about the validity of the **Observe** and **Apply** rules. We begin by getting clearer about what we mean when we say we can "see" what is true in a diagram.

We can think of diagrams as first-order structures in their own right. The domain of a diagram $d$ is just the set of icon tokens in the diagram. We can use these structures to give non-standard interpretations of our language. This, in turn, can be used to understand both the cognitive and logical utility of the **Observe** rule of *Hyperproof*.

**Definition 5.15** A *diagrammatic interpretation* $I$ of our language is a function that assigns to each diagram $d$ and each name and predicate of our language an object as follows.

- If **P** is an $n$-ary predicate, then $I(d, \mathbf{P})$ is a pair $\langle T, F \rangle$ of sets of $n$-tuples of icon tokens in $Tokens^d$ satisfying the conditions that if $\langle \tau_1, \ldots, \tau_n \rangle$ is in $T$ (resp. is in $F$) then for any model $w$ of $d$, the $n$-tuple
$$\langle Den^w(\tau_1), \ldots, Den^w(\tau_n) \rangle$$
satisfies (resp. does not satisfy) the predicate **P** in $w$. The set $T$ (resp. $F$) is called the extension (resp. anti-extension) of **P** under the interpretation $I$.

- If **n** is a name and $I(d, \mathbf{n})$ is defined then its value is an icon token $\tau$ labeled by **n**. (Equivalently, $\tau$ denotes the same thing as **n** in any world which in which $d$ is true.)

The function $I$ is required to be monotone in the following sense.

1. If $d'$ extends $d$ and $\langle \tau_1, \ldots, \tau_n \rangle$ is in the extension (resp. anti-extension) of **P** in $d$ under $I$ then $\langle \tau_1', \ldots, \tau_n' \rangle$ is in the extension (resp. anti-extension) of **P** in $d'$ under $I$, where $\tau_i'$ is the $d'$-counterpart of $\tau_i$.

2. Similarly, if **n** is a name with an interpretation in $d$ under $I$, then it also has an interpretation in $d'$ under $I$ (in which case both interpretations will have to be icon tokens labeled by **n**).

Let's give an example. It is natural to reinterpret **Tet** in $d$ by taking its extension to be the set of icon tokens of type $\Delta^{i,1}$ for any $i$, and its anti-extension to be the set of icon tokens of type $\Delta^{i,j}$ for any $i$ and any $j > 1$. A less natural reinterpretation, but a reinterpretation none-the-less, would be to take the extension of **Tet** in $d$ to be the set of icon tokens of type $\Delta^{1,1}$, and the anti-extension to be those of type $\Delta^{3,3}$.

A diagrammatic interpretation $I$ gives us a way to associate a partial model of our language with any diagram $d$. Let us write $d \mathrel{\vDash}_I \varphi$ if $\varphi$ evaluates as true using the weak Kleene evaluation scheme, when the predicates of $\varphi$ are reinterpreted according to $I$.

**Proposition 5.16** (Depiction Lemma) Suppose we have a blocks world $w$ and a diagram $d$ that is true in $w$. For any sentence $\varphi$, if $d \mathrel{\vDash}_I \varphi$ then $w \models \varphi$.

**Corollary 5.17** (Observe) If $d \mathrel{\vDash}_I \varphi$ then $d \models \varphi$.

**Definition 5.18** A reinterpretation $I$ *captures* $\mathbf{P}$ if whenever $d$ is a maximal diagram, $I(d, \mathbf{P})$ is total. That is, the extension and anti-extension of $\mathbf{P}$ are complements of one another. Similarly, $I$ *captures* $\mathbf{n}$ if whenever $d$ is a maximal diagram, then $I(d, \mathbf{n})$ is defined.

**Proposition 5.19** Suppose $w \models d$. There is an extension $d'$ of $d$ such that $d' \mathrel{\vDash}_I \varphi$ for every sentence $\varphi$ all of whose names and predicates are fully captured by $I$.

**Corollary 5.20** Suppose we have a sentence $\varphi$ such that all the names and predicates in $\varphi$ are captured by $I$. If $d$ is consistent with $\varphi$ then there is an extension $d'$ of $d$ such that $d' \mathrel{\vDash}_I \varphi$.

This result shows that any sentence which is consistent with a diagram and a set of sentences can be shown to be consistent within the *Hyperproof* system. This is one of the features we hoped for earlier in a homomorphic system of representation. It likewise shows that non-consequence results can be proven within the system. This is in marked contrast to linguistic systems.

Following the standard terminology in partial orders, we say that two diagrams are *incompatible* if they have no common extension. While this definition makes it look as though it would be computationally difficult to check whether two diagrams were incompatible, the following observation shows that for the *Hyperproof* system, this property is easily checked by reference to the two diagrams in question, without any search over other diagrams. Types $\Delta^{i,j}$ and $\Delta^{i',j'}$ are *incompatible* if $i$ and $i'$ are distinct and non-zero (representing incompatible information about size) or if $j$ and $j'$ are distinct and non-zero (representing incompatible information about shape).

**Proposition 5.21** (Incompatibility check) Diagrams $d$ and $d'$ are incompatible iff there are counterpart tokens in the diagrams which are of incompatible types or located at different positions on the grid, or if there is a name that labels tokens that are not counterparts.

This result, while simple, is quite important in making the notion of proof decidable, and even tractable. Using it, we can now state the result which justifies the rule **Apply**.

**Proposition 5.22** (Apply Lemma) Given a sentence $\varphi$ and two diagrams $d$ and $d' \geq d$, exactly one of the following holds:

1. $d'$ is a logical consequence of $d$ and $\varphi$.

2. There is a diagram $d^*$ which extends $d$ but is incompatible with $d'$ such that $d^* \not\approx_I \varphi$.

In particular, if there is no diagram $d^*$ as in (2), then (1).

As we mentioned earlier, the implementation of this rule in *Hyperproof* is weaker than this for the sake of tractability. Let us conclude by justifying the *Hyperproof* version of **Apply**.

**Corollary 5.23** (Tractable Apply Lemma) Given a sentence $\varphi$ and two diagrams $d$ and $d' \geq d$, at least one of the following holds:

1. $d'$ is a logical consequence of $d$ and $\varphi$.

2. There is a diagram $d^*$ which extends $d$ but is incompatible with $d'$ such that not $d^* \approx_I \neg\varphi$.

In particular, if there is no diagram $d^*$ as in (2), then (1).

We hope it is clear from this discussion that we could give a similar justification for *Hyperproof*'s most important rule, that of **Cases Exhausted.**

Eberle [1995] has developed an alternative analysis of the syntax and semantics of *Hyperproof*, and used it to formalize *Hyperproof*'s notion of proof. Using this, she has shown the soundness of the *Hyperproof* system, and explored the senses in which the *Hyperproof* system is complete.

# 6 Conclusions

In this chapter we have argued against the idea of a universal diagrammatic system, and against the idea that a system with multiple forms of representation needs some underlying "interlingua" to tie the representations together. On a more positive note, we have argued that *Hyperproof* shows that one can have a effective heterogeneous reasoning system without an interlingua, and we have developed enough of an analysis of the system to show why this is the case. In particular, we have shown how to give rigorous justifications for some of the rules of *Hyperproof* involving both sentences and diagrams without any such interlingua.

*Chapter IX*

# Toward the Rigorous Use of Diagrams in Reasoning about Hardware

Steven D. Johnson, Jon Barwise, and Gerard Allwein

## 1 Introduction

The logician's conventional notion of proof has grown increasingly anachronistic through the twentieth century as computing capabilities have advanced. Classical proof theory provides a partial model of actual mathematical reasoning. When we move away from mathematics toward reasoning in engineering and computation, its limitations are even more pronounced. The standard idea of a formal system seems frozen in the information technology of Frege's time; it is decidedly quaint in the presence of today's desk-top computer.

Contrary to formalists' dogma, experience suggests that pictures, diagrams, charts, and graphs are important tools in human reasoning, not mere illustrations as traditional logic would have us believe. Nor is the computer merely an optimized Turing machine. The computer's graphical capabilities have advanced to the point that diagrams can be manipulated in sophisticated ways, and it is time to exploit this capability in the analysis of reasoning, and in the design of new reasoning aids.

In this chapter, we propose a new understanding of the role of various sorts of diagrams in the specification and design of computational hardware. This proposal stems from a larger project, initiated by Barwise and Etchemendy [1991a], the goals of which are to develop a mathematical basis from which to understand the substantive logical relationships between diagrams and sentences, and to develop a new generation of automated reasoning tools from that basis.

Microelectronic CAD systems are among the supreme examples of visualized reasoning environments. Their tools are highly oriented toward diagrams, are quite sophisticated, and are comparatively well integrated. These systems also integrate logical and physical design, providing a strong coherence between specification and implementation views. Formalized reasoning meshes poorly with these working frameworks. Although it provides needed rigor for today's highly complex design challenges, its preoccupation with formulas at the expense of diagrams is simply too cumbersome. We should attempt to draw lessons from these advanced design environments, making the reasoning rigorous without subverting their character.

This chapter is built around a simple design example, a synchronizing circuit. Our purposes are, first, to illustrate heterogeneous use of pictoral "formalisms" in design, and second, to expose basic questions for the logical analysis that follows. We will develop a mathematical basis in which the example can be analyzed. These are admittedly modest beginnings, but we hope that they start to put to rest the idea that only formulas can be used in formal reasoning about hardware.

# 2   The Circuitproof Project

The foundations of the research described here arose from previous work in information theoretic aspects of logic: *Turing's World*, a program for building and running Turing machines using only graphical representations for them in Barwise and Etchemendy [1986], and *Tarski's World*, a program to teach the language of first-order logic in Barwise and Etchemendy [1991b]. The success of these programs shows the power of graphical designs in reasoning in logic, but it also raises a host of new theoretical issues and possibilities.

Exploring these has led to the development of *Hyperproof*, a specialized heterogeneous reasoning system described in chapter VIII of this volume (see also Barwise and Etchemendy [1994]. This program is now being used to teach basic reasoning skills to students in a way that makes crucial use of visualization of information.

*Hyperproof* is a formalism for use in reasoning about blocks worlds which using a combination of diagrams and sentences of first-order logic. Partial knowledge is used to discover facts about a situation. There is significant interplay between the information system represented by the picture and the proof manager. For instance, information in the picture is used to determine whether case analyses are exhaustive; in fact, cases themselves may be represented by hypothetical board configurations.

*Hyperproof* is very specialized and could not be applied to hardware description. However, there are some important lessons to be learned from *Hyperproof*, lessons which have informed the project initiated here, and which we summarize very briefly now.

The first lesson—which is hardly new but seems to be ignored in the standard logical formalisms—is that finding the best representation of a problem is often the most important step in solving the problem. The reason engineers use various sorts of diagrams is because diagrams are efficient representational schemes. The second lesson learned from *Hyperproof* is that "heterogeneous" systems, systems in which two or more different types of representation are used side by side, are able to integrate the strengths of types into a complete system. Typically different formalisms will be better for talking about different aspects of the problem or device under consideration. As long as there is a common subject matter, this subject matter will tie the various formalisms together, giving us a notion of valid inference. Finally, *Hyperproof* shows that we need a "hyperstructure," a global place where proofs are given using a mixture of the various formalisms.

Circuitproof is a pilot study with three goals. The first is to examine engineering practice in order to develop a suite of integrated reasoning tools which are useful in circuit-design applications. Some tools are based on sentences and some tools are based on diagrams. In this chapter, we will configure such a suite containing finite state diagrams, circuit schematics, timing diagrams, as well as second order logic. The second goal is to do research in the formal-methods area, where there is an abundance of visually oriented design tools for logicians to study. Finally, we want to inform the engineering community that automated reasoning of the kind that is entailed in hardware design is not *necessarily* textual. Logicians bear as much responsibility as tool developers to bridge the gap between practice and formalism.

# 3 Diagrams and Hardware Description

It is hard to write, talk, or think about hardware without using diagrams. Virtually all articles about formalizing hardware description make heavy, though usually intuitive, use of schematics, physical drawings, timing diagrams, state machines, and so on. It is so common that we may regard it as vital. Structural qualities of the circuits may justify the use of diagrams, but the correlation between a physical circuit and its schematic is difficult to pin down. Often, these differ dramatically.

There must be other reasons for the ubiquitous use of diagrams. As in many realms of mathematical discourse, the interaction of a narrative argument and a circuit diagram yields an efficient mode of explanation.

The following excerpt from Davis [1989] is typical:

... When $A = B$ either the
N-types will be turned on or
the P-types. They will clamp
the input to the strong (S)
inverter, overpower the weak
(W) inverter, and the output
will change to the proper
level. When $A$ and $B$ are
different neither a pull-down
or a pull-up path will exist
and the previous output will
be maintained by the latch
formed by the $W$ and and $S$
inverters. ...

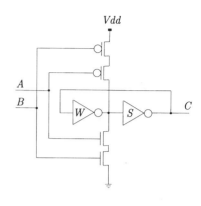

A conventional formalization of this argument represents the diagram as a sentence. In predicate logic, for example, one would employ relations for devices, variables for wires, and conjunction for composition following Gordon [1986]. The narrative sketches a proof, "this circuit is a C-element," listing relevant facts that can be extracted from such a formula and which, taken together, should imply the behavioral properties of a C-element. This regimen for verification raises several questions, but foremost is its denial at the outset that the diagram itself is serving any purpose. We can see that it serves at least as a referent to the narrative. Once everything is distilled to sentences it is hard to see how to recover this manner of reference. Discovered properties like "pull-down path" and "latch" emerge as syntactic qualities of the diagram, but would otherwise have to be indirectly developed in the course of a formal deduction.

Hunt [1992] offers a radical statement of purist objectives:

> We envision providing a mathematical statement which we call a *formula manual* [Hunt's italics], that completely specifies the operation of a hardware component. With respect to digital systems, we want to: [1] Completely replace programmer's manuals, timing diagrams, interface specifications, power requirements, etc. with clear precise formulas. [2] Provide a perfectly clear foundation upon which systems can be built.

Surely this is not the world to which we really aspire, for while the programmer's manual may convey information imperfectly, it conveys that imperfect information rather efficiently in human terms. Hunt is justifiably calling for greater rigor in the description of hardware, but his formula manual, as described, would be of marginal benefit to the human user.

Cohn [1989] poses the central problem in her summary of the VIPER verification project :

> The first task in the [block level] verification effort is to derive a functional expression of the block model in a formal logic which is suitable for reasoning and proof. This is necessary because it is difficult to reason formally about a schematic diagram indicating [information flow]. It is possible to imagine doing this by reasoning about sequences of annotated pictures, but the real problem is not so much the obvious awkwardness of such a method as the lack of a formal semantics of pictures.
> . . .

A reasoning system based purely on pictures would, of course, be awkward, but, on the other hand, so is purely textual reasoning, judging from the experience gained to date. Given the human tendencies for using both forms, it is worth investigating a middle ground.

A notable example of work connecting diagramatic representation with formal proof is the *LAMBDA* system of Fourman and others describing Mayger, et. al. [1989]. A schematic-entry facility called *DIALOG* associates graphical symbols with HOL proof tactics, which are invoked as new components are connected. These tactics generate proof obligations, which may be resolved by either graphical or textual interactions with the system. We think the claim that such tools make "[formal methods] accessible to design engineers" is a valid one. For this reason, serious attention should be paid by logicians—and the implementers of automated reasoning systems—to what have heretofore been regarded as mere human-interface issues.

In the remainder of this chapter, we examine some of the questions that arise when diagrams are used in hardware design. We cannot offer comprehensive answers to any of these questions, nor yet a system to implement these paradigms. However, we strongly believe that the formal-methods community should engage itself with questions of this nature, in order to help establish a new foundation for logic applied to hardware.

Also, in the sequel, we assume a globally clocked, synchronous design technology. This is not an inherent part of our philosophy towards hardware design; we make it merely to simplify exposition and expect our philosophy to carry well beyond its confines.

# 4    The Single-Pulser Example

To illustrate a perspective on design, let us consider a simple example, drawn from the textbook Winkel and Prosser [1989]. We will present the example as it might be developed in an actual design class, with all the diagrams one would naturally use. Our claim is relatively simple: *properly understood, this design process is a logically rigorous piece of reasoning as it stands.* There is no need to (and every reason not to) reduce the diagrams used in the reasoning into some more standard formal system.

Suppose one wants to design a device with a single one-bit input and a single one-bit output:

SP's external behavior is stated informally as follows:

*"SP emits a single-pulse on o for each pulse received on i."*

This specification, of course, leaves many things open, things which would have to be settled in the design of an actual device. The timing diagram given below provides a somewhat more exacting specification of SP's behavior by requiring that the output pulse occur in the neighborhood of its corresponding input pulse.

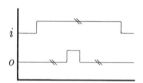

This specification is still fairly open to interpretation. Any simple implementation in hardware would determine where in the interval to generate the output pulse.

Let us think of this timing diagram as a "requirements specification." The state-machine diagram below can be thought of as a design specification:

0/1

(S0)

0/1   0/1

(S1)

0/1

Using a standard interpretation as an $\omega$-automaton of some kind, a device is described with two states and a specific input/output behavior in each of these states.

Our first observation is that any device described by this Mealy machine diagram has an input-output behavior that satisfies the requirement specification. Indeed, we can say more, since it will have a behavior that is described by the following timing diagram.

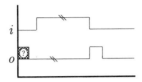

At a purely logical level, this can be made perfectly rigorous, every bit as rigorous as the fact that $A(f(3))$ follows from $\forall x A(x)$, as we will show. This diagram reflects an undetermined choice of the starting state for the machine: we cannot know whether a pulse is issued at "time zero." But given the condition that input $i$ is initially zero, the machine settles into a desirable behavior, generating its output pulse at the end of the input pulse.

Whether this output pulse lies within the "neighborhood" specified by our earlier timing diagram can only be settled by giving a rigorous semantics, including a precise meaning to the "ellipsis" symbols (the small double slashes) on the waveforms.

So much for the purely logical aspects of this step of the exercise. Let us look ahead to a future where there is computational support for such reasoning. Perhaps we can build a simulator/verifier to certify the following relationship:

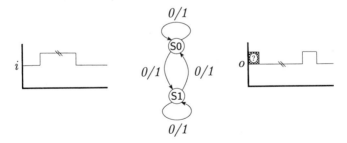

This is plausible given recent developments in symbolic simulation and inductive theorem proving. It should be at least as practical as automated proofs by induction, since there is a very simple instance of induction to verify that a simulation relationship holds.

Moving on in the design process, let us construct a circuit to implement the state machine. The circuit diagram below is obtained by a (well know, but see Johnson, Barwise, and Allwein [1993]) general construction based on a "one-hot" representation of control. Briefly, in a one-hot controller there is one d-flipflop for each state of the machine.

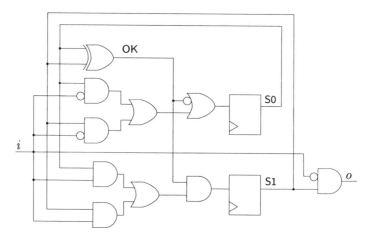

The signal OK (which in this case should be viewed as an artifact of the formalization discussed later) assures that the circuit is always in a valid state: having exactly one of S0 and S1 asserted at any time. Under the assumption OK = 1, which must obtain except possibly at "time 0", the circuit can be simplified a great deal. First, we can simplify the selection of the next-state inputs part of the diagram to:

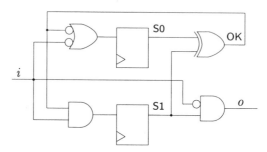

We obtained this circuit with equivalence preserving transformations, subject to valid side-conditions; since the initial circuit has the input-output behavior specified by the Mealy-machine diagram, this derivation is a proof of implementation since we build a circuit directly from this diagram.

If the signal OK is invariantly equal to 1, then the two gates feeding the registers are not needed, and if those gates are not needed, neither is the signal OK, hence neither is S0. A different possible optimization is suggested:

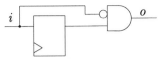

This reduction is not always valid but it is justified in this case because condition OK is equivalent to $S0 = \overline{S1}$. Rather than working out a proof of this claim, let us simply verify the circuit by checking that it, too, conforms to the state-machine. This might be accomplished, as before, by some form of simulation:

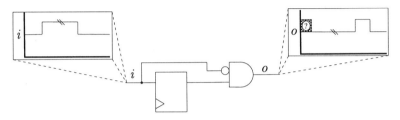

## Analysis

This method of approaching design is, we believe, reflective of practice. Our main point is that, properly understood, it is every bit as logically rigorous as any other form of proof. Furthermore, it is computationally tractable, at least for this small example.

It is clear that the diagrams are integral to this particular solution. But are English sentences integral or eliminable? In this example, the English discourse is little more than a narration of the design process, although it does occasionally point out features of the diagrams it threads together. It is playing the illustrative role that is traditionally attributed to the pictures. The succession of drawings contains the substance of the design, so it is these drawings that should be connected by a rigorous semantics. However, it is almost certain that an optimal suite of formalisms would also include classical formal systems so that we can express in logic some of what we have expressed in English in our example.

Obviously we are dealing with several distinct graphical idioms, and also—although it may not be as obvious from this example—with a number of possible language dialects. These must be united in a way that secures a relationship among them. What relates them, of course, is that they are all ways of describing various aspects of the same object. That is, they have a common semantics.

One way to approach a semantics would be to insist on a translation of all our diagrams into a common-denominator formalism with a well understood semantics. Higher-order logic is often proposed for this purpose. Under this approach a timing diagram, for example, would just be a convenient encoding for this formula. An alternative is to treat all the participating formalisms as on a par. This is the approach we have chosen. Although there are a number of reasons for this decision, we will only discuss two of the more important, connected to two of our originally stated goals.

The first reason is that a reduction to a linguistic formalism unjustifiably elevates sentential calculus to a preferred status. Nothing forces one to do this, and doing it violates the basic engineering practice we seek to understand. This practice uses a system in which textual formalisms interact with diagramtic formalisms as peers. We want our theoretical development to reflect this balance. Although a proper formula might specify the same relation, we do not think it shares all the inferential properties of a diagram.

The second reason has to do with our objective for diagram-based design tools. We do not regard formal systems—as they are currently understood—to be sufficiently powerful engines to drive automated reasoning. A lesson learned from *Hyperproof* is that systems that treat diagrams and sentences on a par, admitting rules of inference that explicitly relate the two, are more natural and powerful than either alone. Purely syntactic rules of inference are not enough to prove things proficiently. For example, it would be unreasonable to perform the generalized simulation

as a purely textual deduction.

# 5    A Mathematical Basis

Let us develop a possible basis to support these preliminary explorations. We do not prescribe a model and, in fact, believe that a practical system might have to support a variety of models for different levels of description. However, we do ground our semantics in a particular domain, giving a basis for relating the various visual idioms. The formalization in this section develops toward a globally clocked, synchronous implementation technology, and involves other simplifying assumptions along the way.

To reason about any device, we need at least to know how it is connected to its environment. All of our diagrams implicitly or explicitly refer to this external view, or *signature*. The single-pulser had external ports I and O.

**Definition 5.1** A *signature* is a finite set $\Sigma = \{N_1, \ldots, N_n\}$ of *names*.

For the remainder of this section, let $\Sigma$ be a fixed general signature,

$$\Sigma = \{N_1, \ldots, N_n\}$$

For generality we will develop our semantics in ways that do not impose a direction on information flow. However, directionality is an important quality, so we shall introduce terminology for it along the way. When directionality is considered, a given signature will be composed of two disjoint, possibly empty, subsets: $\Sigma^{\text{inp}}$ of *inputs* and $\Sigma^{\text{out}}$ of *outputs*.

$$\Sigma = \{\ \overbrace{I_1, \ldots, I_p}^{\Sigma^{\text{inp}}};\ \overbrace{O_1, \ldots, O_q}^{\Sigma^{\text{out}}}\ \}$$

The partitioning could involve other attributes, such as "internal" and "bidirectional," but these two are enough for our present discussions.

For now assume that each signal can hold only a 1 or a 0 at any time. Let us represent the contents of a signal as a function from $Z$ to $\{0, 1\}$, $Z$ being the set of (both positive and negative) integers. Such a function is called a *simple sequence*. We allow time to flow infinitely in two directions in order to avoid talking about initialization, resets, and so forth.

**Definition 5.2** A $\Sigma$-*sequence* is a set of simple sequences $\{F_{N_1}, \ldots, F_{N_n}\}$. A $\Sigma$-*profile* is a set of $\Sigma$-sequences.

A $\Sigma$-sequence represents a single, infinite run of some device, $F_{N_i}(t)$ being the value on signal named $N_i$ at time $t$. If the context permits it we will use the same variable for both the name of a signal and the function associated with that name, and so write $N_i(t)$. Intuitively, a given device will admit certain sequences, but not others, and so determine a unique profile.

We frequently need to define an association, or *binding*, between names in $\Sigma$ and values in some other set.

**Definition 5.3** A $\Sigma$-*binding in S* is a mapping from $\Sigma$ to a set of values, $S$.

Thus, a $\Sigma$-sequence is just a $\Sigma$-binding to the class of simple sequences over $\{1, 0\}$.

In many of the definitions that follow, bindings are represented by a string of values corresponding to some implicit ordering of $\Sigma$. If $\Sigma$ is given as $\{N_1, \ldots, N_n\}$, then the string $V_1 \cdots V_n$ binds each $N_i$ to $V_i$.

A partial ordering on signatures can be based on set containment, and extends in the usual way to sequences and profiles.

**Definition 5.4** A subset $\Sigma \subseteq \Sigma'$ is called a *reduct of* $\Sigma'$. A $\Sigma$-sequence $W$ is a *reduct* of a $\Sigma'$-sequence $W'$ iff the functions in $W$ are identical to those in $W'$ to which they correspond by name. Finally, a class $P$ of $\Sigma$-sequences is the *projection* (onto $\Sigma$) of a class $P'$ of $\Sigma'$-sequences if $P$ is the set of all reducts of sequences in $P'$ relative to $\Sigma$. For $P$ we write $P'|\Sigma$.

We will require that projections preserve directionality; so if $\Sigma$ is a reduct of $\Sigma'$, we must also have $\Sigma^{\mathrm{inp}} \subseteq \Sigma'^{\mathrm{inp}}$, and $\Sigma^{\mathrm{out}} \subseteq \Sigma'^{\mathrm{out}}$.

$\Sigma$-profiles will provide the semantic domain for assigning meaning to diagrams. If diagrams $D_i$ have signatures $\Sigma_i$ and profiles $\mathcal{D}_i$, then $D_1$ is *consistent* with $D_2$ if $\mathcal{D}_1 \cap \mathcal{D}_2 \neq \emptyset$. $D_1$ *entails* $D_2$ iff $\mathcal{D}_1 \subseteq \mathcal{D}_2$. $D_1$ is *logically equivalent* to $D_2$ iff $\mathcal{D}_1 = \mathcal{D}_2$. A transformation from one diagram to another is *universally valid* iff the two diagrams are logically equivalent.

None of the logical qualities above captures the notion of *implementation*. As a first attempt, we might say that a diagram $D_1$ is an implementation of diagram $D_2$ if $\mathcal{D}_2 = \mathcal{D}_1|\Sigma_2$. This is too strong if we want to say, for example, that a particular single-pulser circuit implements the single-pulser specification, since there would be sequences that fit the specification but which would not be accepted by the circuit.

Alternatively, we might say that $\mathcal{D}_1|\Sigma_2 \subseteq \mathcal{D}_2$, corresponding to the standard representation of "implements" by "implies" in formal methods. But as citeweise89 and many others have explained, this is too weak, since, for example, the empty set becomes an implementation profile of any specification.

"Implementation" involves both entailment and consistency. In the directional case, we can say that any input accepted by the specification must also be accepted by the implementation. Formally, $D_1$ implements $D_2$ if $\Sigma_2$ is a reduct of $\Sigma_1$, $\mathcal{D}_1|\Sigma_2 \subseteq \mathcal{D}_2$, and for all $\sigma$ in $\mathcal{D}_2$ there exists a $\sigma'$ in $\mathcal{D}_1$ such that

$$\sigma'|\Sigma_2^{\mathrm{inp}} = \sigma|\Sigma_2^{\mathrm{inp}}$$

In the following sections we develop what might be called an abstract syntax for the various forms of diagrams we have seen earlier. We are not specifically concerned with how diagrams are rendered but with their underlying information structures. However, it should of course be possible to render diagrams without too much human intervention.

## Circuit diagrams

We are given a number of icon types, $D$, each having an arity, $\ell(D) > 0$. For each icon type there is an infinite set of *icon tokens*, each associated with a signature $\Sigma_D$ of size $\ell(D)$. Examples of tokens include the gates and storage elements seen in the previous section

as well as higher level symbols, such as

Each token must have a signature, whether or not it is revealed by its graphics. Where necessary, we will let the set $\{1, 2, \ldots, n\}$ stand for the generic signature of arity $n = \ell(D)$. A generic token of type $D$ could be drawn

Circuit diagrams are represented as hypergraphs in which the nodes stand for connections and the hyperedges are associated with components. For example our SP diagram,

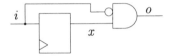

would have node set $\{i, x, o\}$, with two hyperedges: one for the d-flipflop connecting i and x and the other for the and-gate connecting i, x, and o:

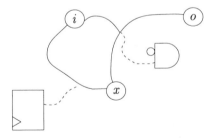

**Definition 5.5** A $\Sigma$-*circuit graph* is a hypergraph structure $\langle \Sigma, E, R \rangle$, where $E$ is a set of icon tokens, and the relation $R \subseteq E \times \Sigma^*$ respects arities. That is, if $(e, N_1 N_2 \cdots N_n) \in R$ and $e$ is a token of type $D$, then $\ell(D) = n$.

Our semantics will interpret the string $N_1 N_2 \cdots N_n$ as a $\Sigma_D$-binding (Definition 5.3). Intuitively, we want to associate a circuit graph with the set of $\Sigma$ sequences that is simultaneously determined by its components. For example, define the *and-profile* to be the set of $\{A, B; Z\}$-sequences in which $Z(t) = A(t) \cdot B(t)$ for all $t$; and similarly for other Boolean gates (recall that we are using the same variable for the name and its function). A storage element with signature $\{D;\ Q\}$ has a profile whose sequences satisfy $Q(t+1) = D(t)$.

Composite profiles for circuit graphs are built from the families of profiles associated with the graph's hyperedges. Thus, a consistent family of sequences for our single-pulser, shown above, is $\{I; X, O\}$ where for all $t \in Z$, $X(t+1) = I(t)$ and $O(t) = X(t) \cdot \overline{I(t)}$. The set of all such $\{I, X, O\}$-sequences would comprise a "fine-grained" profile for the circuit; and the $\{I, O\}$-projection would be a "course grained" profile, which hides internal signals.

For device type $D$ let $\Sigma_D = \{1, 2, \ldots, \ell(D)\}$ represent the class of all signatures that can be affiliated with D. The semantics assigns as given a $\Sigma_D$-profile, written $Profile(D)$.

**Definition 5.6** Let $\Sigma = \{N_1, \ldots, N_n\}$ and let $G$ be a $\Sigma$-circuit graph. A $\Sigma$-sequence $\{F_1, \ldots, F_n\}$ is *consistent* with $G$ if whenever $G$ contains an edge $(e, N_{e_1} \cdots N_{e_k})$, in which $e$ has device type $D$, then the $\Sigma_D$-sequence

$$\{F_{e_1}, \ldots, F_{e_k}\} \in Profile(D)$$

The *G-profile* is the collection of all $\Sigma$-sequences that are consistent with $G$.

By calling $\{F_{e_1}, \ldots, F_{e_k}\}$ a $\Sigma_D$-binding we affiliate each $F_{e_j}$ with $j$ in the generic signature. In other words, the connection of component $e$ to the signal nodes $N_{e_j}$ is fully determined.

When directionality is considered, we would like circuit-graphs to act as functions from (the individual sequences associated with) inputs to outputs. We can develop this notion by generalizing to a *directional* $\Sigma$-circuit graph in which icons have fixed input and output arities and these are respected by the relation $R$ of Definition 5.5. The storage elements of a digital circuit induce a directionality with respect to time. To be *properly formed*, several structural conditions would have to be met. Initial nodes come from $\Sigma^{in}$; terminal nodes must come from $\Sigma^{out}$ (but outputs may participate in cycles and hence not be terminal); in $R$, each node is associated with at most one component output; and every cycle includes an edge associated with a storage-element icon.

A standard result—though not a trivial one to prove considering these structural conditions—is that a directional circuit graph is *functional*: that is, its profile represents a well-defined, total function from its input signals to its output signals, as desired.

**Proposition 5.7** If directed $\Sigma$-circuit graph $G$ is properly formed and if its components are functional, then so is $G$.

## State diagrams

For behavioral specification we will use finite-state automata (FSAs, or "state-machines") whose inputs and outputs fit some particular signature. Our diagrams will associate some outputs with machine states ("Moore outputs") and others with state transitions ("Mealy outputs"), although our formalization will include only the latter. For example, the single-pulser state machine in the previous section had only Mealy outputs, but suppose we add a light to indicate when the machine is waiting for a pulse. We might specify this enhanced single-pulser in one of two ways, the difference being a matter of notation.

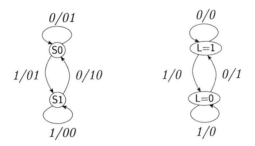

The diagrams need an explicit association to tell which values go with which terminals. In this example, the state labels hold the value of the light, $L$, and the edge labels hold the values of $I$ and $O$. We can eliminate the state labels by adding them to all edges leaving the state, as shown in the diagram on the left above. Let us adopt this simplification in defining state machines.

**Definition 5.8** A *state-machine graph* for signature $\Sigma = \{N_1, \ldots, N_n\}$ is a directed graph, with edges labeled by $\Sigma$-bindings to $\{0, 1\}$.

For example, the state machine shown to the left above refers to signature $\{I;\ O,\ L\}$, and the $\{I;\ O,\ L\}$-binding associates the first digit of each label with input $I$, the second with output $O$, and the third with output $L$.

The notion of a machine $M$ accepting a $\Sigma$-sequence is simply that a series of states exists whose transition labels agree with the sequence. For example, a $\{I;\ O,\ L\}$-sequence is accepted by the machine shown above provided the following conditions are satisfied:

1. $O(t) = 1$ iff $I(t-1) = 1$ and $I(t) = 0$; that is, the machine is in state S1 and detects a 0 on $I$.

2. For all $t \in Z$, if $I(t) = 0$ then $L(t+1) = 1$

These are simply the sequences that accept complete (infinite in both directions) runs of the machine. In general, given any $\Sigma$ state-machine $M$, we associate a $\Sigma$-profile with it as follows.

**Definition 5.9** A $\Sigma$-sequence $\{N_1, \ldots, N_n\}$ is *accepted* by state machine $M$ provided there is a sequence of states $s_i$, for $i \in Z$, such that for each $i$, there is a unique edge from $s_i$ labeled by the string $N_1(i) \cdots N_n(i)$ and leading to $s_{i+1}$. By the *profile* of a machine $M$ we mean the set of all $\Sigma$-sequences accepted by $M$.

We want machines which at all times respond to all possible input stimuli. Assuming $\Sigma^{\text{inp}} = \{I_1, \ldots, I_k\}$, the state-machine graph is said to be *reactive* if for every state $s$ and string $b_1 \cdots b_k$, there is an edge whose label maps $I_j$ to $b_j$ for $i \leq j \leq k$.

**Proposition 5.10** Deterministic reactive state machines are functional.

## Timing diagrams

In contrast to the circuits and state machines we have looked at so far, a semantics for timing diagrams seems more subtle. One reason for this subtlety may be that the diagrams are partial descriptions, while, typically, circuit and machine diagrams fully determine the objects they describe. Another reason may be the context-sensitive quality of these kinds of diagrams, which often express controlling relationships among events.

We begin with the notion that a conventional timing diagram is really a collection of diagrams which happen to share a common reference to the time line.

**Definition 5.11** A *time scale* $\delta = \langle V, \preceq, s \rangle$ consists of a set $V$ of *time variables*, a linear ordering $\preceq$ of $V$, and a partial *successor* function $s$ on $V$. Whenever $\mathsf{t} \in \text{dom}(s)$, then $s(\mathsf{t})$ must be the immediate successor of $\mathsf{t}$ in the ordering $\preceq$ (but the converse is not required).

We sometimes refer to the time variables as "ticks" on the time line, since this is the way they are rendered in simple diagrams. Intuitively, the ticks stand for arbitrary times as constrained by the ordering and the successor function. Temporal orderings assigned to $V$ must preserve $\preceq$; and in addition, the successor function constrains two consecutive times to be just one unit apart (recall that we are modeling time with the set of integers, $Z$). These notions are formalized in the next definition.

**Definition 5.12** Let $\delta = \langle V, \preceq, s \rangle$ be a time scale. A *timing assignment* for $\delta$ is a function $\tau: V \to Z$ satisfying the following two conditions:

1. $\tau$ is strictly order preserving: $\mathsf{t} \preceq \mathsf{t}'$ implies $\tau(\mathsf{t}) \leq \tau(\mathsf{t}')$,

2. for all $\mathsf{t} \in \text{dom}(s)$ $\tau(s(\mathsf{t})) = \tau(\mathsf{t}) + 1$.

**Definition 5.13** A *waveform* consists of a time scale $\delta$ together with a partial function $\nu$ from $V_\delta$ into the values $\{0, 1, \phi\}$. A timing assignment for a wave form is just a timing assignment for its time scale.

If $\nu(t) = 1$, this represents a value of 1 on the wave form over the interval starting at time $t$ and ending at (just before) the next tick on the scale. Similarly for $\nu(t) = 0$. We will use $\nu(t) = \phi$ to mean that the value over the interval starting at tick $t$ is undetermined. This is made precise by the following definition.

**Definition 5.14** Let $W = \langle \delta, \nu \rangle$ be a waveform, and let $\tau$ be a timing assignment for $W$. A function $X \in 2^Z$ is said to *conform to $W$ relative to $\tau$* provided the following conditions hold:

1. for all ticks $t \in V_\delta$ $X(\tau(t)) = \nu(t)$ unless $\nu(t) = \phi$.

2. if $t$ is a non-final tick, and $t'$ is its immediate successor under the ordering $\preceq$, then $X$ is constant on the half-open interval $\big[\tau(t), \tau(t')\big)$.

A $\Sigma$-timing diagram will contain one waveform for each name in $\Sigma$. A $\Sigma$-sequence conforms to a $\Sigma$-timing diagram if its individual sequences conform to their associated wave forms *for a particular set of timing assignments*. The subtlety of the definition lies in how valid timing assignments are chosen.

Timing diagrams contain dependence information which gives a notion of relevance or "control". It is this implicative information that allows us to specify which $\Sigma$-sequences lie in the profile of a diagram. The function $R$ in the next definition represents the "control arrows" that one might find in a timing diagram, in that $R(\sigma)$ denotes the set of all wave forms that participate in controlling $\sigma$.

**Definition 5.15** A $\Sigma$-*timing diagram* $D = \langle \delta, f, R \rangle$ is a time scale $\delta$, a $\Sigma$-binding $f$ to wave forms on $\delta$, and a $\Sigma$-binding $R$ to $2^\Sigma$.

For $\sigma \in \Sigma$, we will write $D_\sigma$ for the wave form $f(\sigma)$. Given a $\Sigma$-sequence $X$, we will write $X_\sigma$ for the elementary sequence associated with the name $\sigma$. We will say that $\sigma$ *depends on* $\sigma'$ if $\sigma' \in R(\sigma)$.

We now extend the notion of conforming from a single wave form to an arbitrary timing diagram.

**Definition 5.16** Let $D$ be a timing diagram with time scale $\delta$. A $\Sigma$-sequence $X$ *conforms* to $D$ provided the following holds for each $\sigma \in \Sigma$: for each timing assignment $\tau$, if $X_{\sigma_0}$ conforms to $D_{\sigma_0}$ relative to $\tau$ for each $\sigma_0$ on which $\sigma$ depends, then $X_\sigma$ conforms to $D_\sigma$ relative to $\tau$. The *profile* of a timing diagram is the set of all $\Sigma$-sequences that conform to it.

In fact, a weaker definition may be needed in practice, based on a natural partial ordering on time scales. Given time scales $\delta_1, \delta_2$, we say that $\delta_2$ is an *extension* of $\delta_1$ if $V_1 \subseteq V_2$, $\preceq_1$ is the restriction of $\preceq_2$ to $V_1$, and $s_1$ is a subfunction of $s_2$. Write $\delta_1 \sqsubseteq \delta_2$ for this relationship, which is a partial ordering. We may say that various time scales are *compatible* if they have an upper bound in this ordering. Intuitively, this means that the constraints imposed by each are compatible with one another. If we need to build timing diagrams not only by "stacking up" wave forms, but also by concatenating them, then it may be better to allow for compatible time scales, rather than identical time scales, in Definition 5.15.

## A Formal Language for Hardware

Our representative formal language is a version of two-sorted second order logic, with sorts *Integer* ($Z$, representing time) and *Boole* ($B$). It is composed from the following alphabet:

1. individual variables of sort $Z$,

2. binary constants 0 and 1 of sort $B$, no constants of sort $Z$,

3. unary function constant '$-$' of sort $B \rightarrow B$,

4. binary function constants '$*$' and '$+$' of sort $B \times B \rightarrow B$,

5. unary signal function symbols $F, G, H, \ldots$ of sort $Z \rightarrow B$, some of these are treated as constants, others as variables, and

6. function constants $f, g, \ldots$ of sort $Z \rightarrow Z$, (all we need for our examples is the successor function).

**Definition 5.17** *Time terms* will consist of variables and expressions of the form $f(t_1, \ldots, t_n)$ where $t_1 \ldots t_n$ are time terms and $f$ is a function symbol of sort $Z \rightarrow Z$.

**Definition 5.18** A *value term* is either a binary constant, a term of the form $F(t)$ where $F$ is a signal function symbol and $t$ is a time term, or a compound term involving $*$, $+$, and $-$, whose proper subterms are value terms.

**Definition 5.19** The *atomic wffs* are of the form: $t_1 \leq t_2$ and $t_1 = t_2$, where $t_1$ and $t_2$ are time terms; and $b_1 = b_2$, where $b_1$ and $b_2$ are value terms.

**Definition 5.20** *Wffs* include the atomic wffs and are closed under the standard connectives $\wedge$, $\vee$, $\neg$, $\rightarrow$, $\forall x$, $\exists x$, $\forall F$, and $\exists F$, where $x$ is a time variable and $F$ is a function variable.

We write $\exists x \in [y, z] : \mathcal{G}$ for $\exists x : (y \leq x \wedge x \leq z) \wedge \mathcal{G}$, and similarly for $\forall$. And we will permit metalinguistic definitions. As an example, we will develop some sentences about single-pulser. First, we capture the notion of a "pulse."

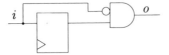

$$\mathsf{pulse}(F,n,m) \quad \equiv_{\mathsf{df}} \quad n < m$$
$$\wedge\ F(n-1) = 0$$
$$\wedge\ F(m) = 0$$
$$\wedge\ \forall x \in [n, m-1]\ :\ (F(x) = 1)$$

The SP specification below narrows the original English description, "For every input pulse there is an single pulse on output," which is inadequate in many respects. Like the initial timing diagram, it requires the output pulse to occur in the neighborhood of the input pulse. The other conjuncts exclude spurious output pulses and infinite input pulses.

$$\mathsf{spec}(I,O) \equiv_{\mathsf{df}} \forall n, m :\ \mathsf{pulse}(I,n,m) \Rightarrow$$
$$(\exists!\, k \in [n, m] :\ O(k) = 1)\ \wedge$$
$$[\forall k :\ O(k) = 1\ \Rightarrow$$
$$(\mathsf{pulse}(O, k, k+1)\ \wedge$$
$$(\exists n, m :\ n \le k \le m\ \wedge\ \mathsf{pulse}(I,n,m)))]$$

Of course, we can also associate a formula with the SP circuit:

$$\mathsf{imp}_1(I,O) \equiv_{\mathsf{df}} \exists X\ :\ \mathsf{delay}(I,X)\ \wedge\ \mathsf{and}^{\circ}_{\bullet}(X,I,O)$$

Expanding the component definitions yields

$$\mathsf{imp}_2(I,O) \equiv_{\mathsf{df}} \exists X\ \big(\forall n\ :\ I(n) = X(n+1)\ \wedge\ O(n) = -I(n) * X(n)\big)$$

To carry out a proof of this implementation we must make the additional assumption that there have been no infinite pulses. This is a consequence of the fact that our circuit is not really a pulse detector but is instead an "edge" detector. Define

$$\mathsf{env}(I,O) \equiv_{\mathsf{df}} \quad \forall t\ \exists t' < t : I(t') = 0$$
$$\wedge\ \forall t\ \exists t' > t : I(t') = 0$$

Our implementation theorem[1] is

$$\forall\, I, O\ :\ \big(\mathsf{env}(I,O) \wedge \mathsf{imp}_2(I,O)\big)\ \Rightarrow\ \mathsf{spec}(I,O)$$

---

[1] Proved by Paul Miner using Owre, Rushby, and Shankar[1992], a prototype verification system.

A *wff* $W$, which is closed with respect to its time variables, can be associated with a signature $\Sigma_W$, consisting of $W$'s free signal variables. Any $\Sigma_W$-sequence provides an assignment under which $W$ can be interpreted.

**Definition 5.21** The *profile* for wff $W$ is the set of all $\Sigma_W$-sequences which make $W$ true.

## Relating the idioms

Figure 1 illustrates the relative expressiveness of the visual idioms we have developed so far.

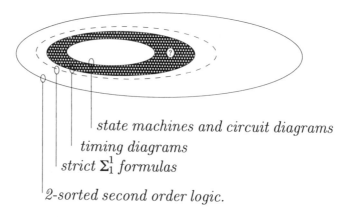

*state machines and circuit diagrams*
*timing diagrams*
*strict $\Sigma_1^1$ formulas*
*2-sorted second order logic.*

Figure 1: Relative expressiveness of the visual idioms

Since there are constructions that produce circuits from state machines and state machines from circuits these two diagramantic forms are equivalent with respect to the class of profiles they can describe.

Timing diagrams are properly more expressive than circuit diagrams and machine diagrams. For instance, our single-pulser *specification*,

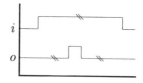

would include a device which generates its output pulse at the midpoint of every input pulse; and no circuit could realize that implementation.

It is also apparent that the full second-order logic is properly more expressive than any of the visual forms because restricted, and properly less expressive, dialects of this language can characterize each kind of diagram.

This is well known for circuit diagrams, hence also state machines. We believe that the following sublanguage encompasses timing diagrams.

**Definition 5.22** The *strict* $\Sigma_1^1$ formulas form the smallest collection of *wffs* containing all atomic and negated atomic wffs and closed under $\wedge$, $\vee$, $\forall x$, $\exists x \in [t_1, t_2]$, $\exists F$.

Our conjecture is that every timing diagram (in our current model of these) specifies a profile that can be defined by a strict $\Sigma_1^1$ wff.

# 6   Conclusions

We have illustrated the case for the use of diagrams in reasoning systems. Hardware design is a rich domain to consider these questions; our example and the work of Fisler [1994] reveal a deeply woven interplay among visual idioms. It is relatively easy to assign a semantics to the visual forms, a semantics which ties them to a common domain of meaning as profiles. However, this is only the first step toward integrating the diagramatic reasoning systems.

Our visual forms reflect three of the four principal aspects of hardware design proclaimed by Melham [1990]. Circuit diagrams deal with the design *structure*; state machines deal with design *behavior*; and timing diagrams deal with the aspect of *timing* which includes not only real-time constraints but also protocol and communcation. The missing aspect is *typing*, or data abstraction, which would inevitably arise as larger examples are considered. The examples differ from conventional formal treatments in that the visual idioms, although related by a common design instance, are not required to coexist in a common linguistic framework.

Maintaining distinct views of an evolving design and reasoning in a fashion that integrates them are not just problems for visual-inference research. They confront any attempt to apply formalized reasoning to nontrivial design problems. An important contribution of visual-inference research is its attention to human reasoning processes, not only to the form of expression but also to underlying organization of thought.

One of the advantages of a diagram is that it is similar to what it represents along some dimensions, enough so that one can simply "read off" facts about the represented object from the representation. This is Shimojima's notion of a *free ride* (Shimojima [1995]). A diagram $\mathcal{D}$ of an object $\mathcal{S}$ is useful if there is a *structure preserving* map $h: \mathcal{D} \to \mathcal{S}$ where what we mean by "structure preserving" is support for logical inference. In the *Hyperproof* system (discussed in Section 1) for example, an observe inference rule ($\approx$) is used to justify facts that can be directly extracted from the visual scene:

The representations we have developed bear similar relationships to the real circuits to which they refer—as we should expect—and therefore permit certain facts to be inferred by observation. An important question is the following: among our four kinds of representations, $S$ for state-machine, $C$ for circuit, $T$ for timing, and $F$ for formulas, for which pairs do we have an **observe** relation between them? $F$ does not stand on the left of any such relation. $T \approx\!\!\!\models F$ makes sense and can be defined for a wide class of $W$'s and all $T$'s. $C \approx\!\!\!\models S$ makes sense: we can read off facts about the state diagram from the circuit, under the assumption that each state has a known assignment of values to the storage elements. $S \approx\!\!\!\models C$ does not seem to work, although we do have a form of inference which allows us to construct a $C$ from an $S$. $S \approx\!\!\!\models T$, and by transitivity broadly construed, $C \approx\!\!\!\models F$ should make sense.

On the other hand, there are significant differences between *Hyperproof* and *Circuitproof* as it is developed so far. The notion of proof in *Circuitproof* is essentially a sequence of reasoning steps about a process from the outside, we look at the circuit as being the closed form of the transfer function from inputs to outputs. We tend to prove global properties about the transfer function, not local properties. This is somewhat at variance with *Hyperproof* where one is concerned with local properties of the situation. *Circuitproof* has no situational aspect as yet and this greatly complicates the comparison of the two systems.

One way to support the notion of a local semantics is to involve hierarchy. The examples we have been working with are at too low a level to exercise much hierarchical decomposition. Again, the presence of several distinct diagrammatic forms, each contributing its own sense of a "black box", greatly complicates the organization of an argument. However, it is evident that the human designer is adept at managing these contending hierarchies: this skill deserves support in the reasoning tools and study by logicians.

Our tentative formalization of diagrams is deficient in its handling of abstraction, as discussed briefly in the previous section. It is also lacking a coherent treatment of relevance as one would see in relevance logic. Typically, there is some direct connection between inputs and outputs in a circuit, i.e., we rarely design a circuit where changes in the inputs are not relevant or do not induce some changes in the output. Perhaps the simplest notion of relevance is directionality: our attempt to develop a nondirectional semantics faltered on at least three occasions. The first was our attempt to characterize "implementation," the purely logical notions of entailment and consistency seeming to bracket a range of possible relationships. The second minor problem arose in the discussion of state diagrams. Finally, our attempt to fix a semantics for timing diagrams exposed a substantive issue of relevant control.

Of course, directionality is the simplest manifestation of relevance. The single-faceted view provided by one of the diagram idioms represses the fact that there are other dependent views. Similarly, focusing on a single design module supresses the constraints offered by the rest of the design. Conversely we do not expect one part of a specification containing a contradiction to induce logical nonsense in another unconnected part. Relevant connections can be handled at a logical level and ought to be if rigorous formalism is to contribute to engineering practice.

# 7  Acknowledgments

We thank Kathi Fisler and Paul Miner for many helpful discussions and other contributions to this chapter

*Chapter X*

# Exploiting the Potential of Diagrams in Guiding Hardware Reasoning

KATHI D. FISLER

## 1  Introduction

> Formal methods offer much more to computer science than just
> "proofs of correctness" for programs and digital circuits. Many
> of the problems in software and hardware design are due to
> imprecision, ambiguity, incompleteness, misunderstanding, and
> just plain mistakes in the statement of top-level requirements,
> in the description of intermediate designs, or in the specification
> of components and interfaces.
>
> Rushby [1993]

Desire for correctness proofs of systems spawned the research area
known as "formal methods". Today's systems are of sufficient complexity that testing is infeasible, both computationally and financially. As an
alternative, formal methods promote mathematical analysis of a system as
a means of locating inconsistencies and other design errors. Techniques
used can range from writing system descriptions in a formal notation to
verification that the designed system satisfies a particular behavioral specification. A good general introduction to formal methods appears in Rushby
[1993].

Ideally, using formal methods increases our assurance in and understanding of our designs. Assurance results from proof, while understanding results from the process of producing the proof. Successful use of formal methods therefore requires powerful proof techniques and clear logical
notations. The verification research community has paid considerable attention to the former. Current techniques, many of which can be fully
automated, handle sufficiently complex systems that formal methods are

now being adopted (albeit slowly) in industry. In our drive to provide powerful proof methods, however, we have overlooked the latter requirement. Research has focused on proof without paying sufficient attention to reasoning. Current tools are often criticized as too hard to use, despite their computational power. Most designers, not having been trained as logicians, find the methodologies and notations very unnatural. Industrial sites, starting out with formal methods, must often rely on external verification professionals to help them use these tools effectively (NASA [1995]). Tools that are not supportive of reasoning therefore fail to provide the full benefits of formal methods. We can augment our current methodologies to address this problem, but we first need to understand reasoning and its role in hardware design.

Barwise and Etchemendy [199+] view valid reasoning as "the exploration of a space of possibilities" defined by the given information and the desired reasoning task. Under this definition, the more clearly a representation system allows for the exploration of this space, the more naturally reasoning can be conducted within this representation. They note that reasoning is a *heterogeneous* activity—people use multiple representations of information while reasoning, and those representations are often non-sentential forms such as diagrams. This is consistent with what occurs in hardware reasoning, in which a combination of state machines, circuit diagrams, timing diagrams, and sentential languages (such as VHDL) are often used.

We believe that diagrams naturally support such exploration, and therefore have the potential to bridge the proof-versus-reasoning gap. Diagrams are usually cast aside as informal notations, but they can be made rigorous. Some people view diagrams as too specialized to be suitable for formal methods; certainly, if we were to construct a tool out of only one style of diagram, this would be a legitimate concern. The key to using diagrammatic representations effectively is to use different styles simultaneously. Multiple representations of information interact formally in *heterogeneous logics*, an introduction to which appears in Barwise and Etchemendy [1991a].

We have developed a heterogeneous hardware logic that encompasses diagrammatic and sentential representations. Section 2 develops a simple example to illustrate hardware reasoning with diagrams. Section 3 defines our proposed logic, which supports circuit diagrams, timing diagrams, a variant of state machines, and second-order logic. Section 4 contains additional examples, intended to illustrate how the logic supports various styles of hardware reasoning.

# 2  Contrasting Diagrammatic and Sentential Representations

Consider a simple physical device, a single pulser $(SP)$. A single pulser converts each input pulse of arbitrary but finite duration into an output pulse of unit duration. There are many possible implementations of a single pulser; we propose one which generates its output pulse in the clock cycle following the fall of the input. Two views of the implementation, one diagrammatic and one sentential, can be given as follows:

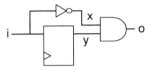

$$SP(I, O) \equiv \exists x \exists y : delay(I, x) \wedge not(I, y) \wedge and(y, x, O)$$
$$delay(I, O) \equiv \forall t : O(t + 1) = I(t)$$
$$not(I, O) \equiv \forall t : O(t) = 1 - I(t)$$
$$and(I_1, I_2, O) \equiv \forall t : O(t) = I_1(t) \times I_2(t)$$

Notice that, up to a level of abstraction that ignores the lengths of the lines in the diagram, both representations contain the same information. However, the presentation of that information is crucial to how easily we can reason about it. For example, suppose we want to determine whether the output of the circuit can ever be high when the input is high. Reasoning about this on the schematic is straightforward: looking at the diagram, we see that the input value is inverted and passed to an **and** gate which computes the output value. Given that a high **and** gate output requires two high inputs, it is easy to conclude that the input cannot be high when the output is to be high.

We will now attempt to reason about the same question using the sentential representation. Assuming the input is high (where high corresponds to numeric value 1 and logical true), we can rewrite (either in our heads or on paper) the definitions to determine that both the *delay* predicate and the *not* predicate have high as their first argument. This in turn produces a value for the second argument of the *not* predicate, binding $y$ to 0. We can now replace occurrences of $y$ with 0, from which we conclude that the output of the **and** gate is 0. Returning to the definition of SP, we see that the output of the **and** gate is the output of SP; again, we conclude that the input cannot be high when the output is high.

Although we arrive at the same conclusion using each representation, one could reasonably argue that reasoning about the diagram is clearer than reasoning about the sentences. In this case, we suggest that the qualitative difference lies in how each representation maintains the connections between the components of the circuit. The diagram maintains the connections explicitly; in the sentential representation, the user has to connect mentally the components via the common wire names and concentrate on rewriting values based on those connections. The diagram frees the user from having to reconstruct connection information, thereby allowing the user to concentrate on the reasoning rather than on the representation. This is a very small example, yet it illustrates our point nicely: using diagrams for reasoning about circuit and value problems is advantageous.

Diagrams can also play a role in the specification and verification of systems. Timing diagrams are becoming a more popular notation for expressing behavioral specifications (Schlör and Damm [1993], Khordoc, et. al., [1993]) presumably because people find them clearer to use than formalisms such as temporal logic. To contrast methods, we present the behavioral specification of the single pulser in three representations: second-order logic, temporal logic, and timing diagrams. In each case, we want to specify that the pulser produces an output pulse for each input pulse, it produces only one output pulse for each input pulse, and all output pulses are of unit duration.

### Higher-Order Logic:

$spec1(i, O) = (\forall n, m : Pulse(i, n, m) \supset$
$$\exists k : n \leq k \wedge k \leq m \wedge O(k) = 1 \wedge$$
$$(\forall j : (n \leq j \wedge j \leq m \wedge O(j) = 1 \supset j = k))$$

$spec2(i, O) = (\forall k : O(k) = 1 \supset$
$$SinglePulse(O, k) \wedge$$
$$(\exists n, m : n \leq k \wedge k \leq m \wedge Pulse(i, n, m)))$$

$Pulse(f, n, m) = (n < m \wedge f(n - 1) = 0 \wedge f(m) = 0 \wedge$
$$(\forall t : (n \leq t \wedge t < m \supset f(t) = 1)))$$

$SinglePulse(O, k) = O(k) \wedge \neg O(k - 1) \wedge \neg O(k + 1)$

### Temporal Logic:

$$rising\_edge \equiv \neg i \wedge \bigcirc i$$
$$\Box (rising\_edge \rightarrow \bigcirc(\neg rising\_edge \,\mathcal{U}\, o))$$
$$\Box (rising\_edge \rightarrow \Diamond o)$$
$$\Box (o \rightarrow \bigcirc(\neg o))$$
$$\Box (o \rightarrow \bigcirc(\neg o \,\mathcal{U}\, rising\_edge))$$

**Timing Diagrams:**

The temporal logic representation uses the usual operators: next ($\bigcirc$), henceforth($\square$), eventually ($\diamond$), and until ($\mathcal{U}$). The timing diagram notations will be explained in detail in section 3. In this timing diagram, the dashed arrow indicates that any appearance of the second event must be preceded by the first (safety). The solid arrow indicates that the edge is not only safe, but, in addition, any occurrence of the first event must eventually be followed by the second event (liveness). The $= 1$ constrains the amount of time (in this case, one clock cycle) that must elapse between the two events.

We claim that the timing diagram is the clearest of these behavioral specifications for purposes of human reasoning. Specifications need to be easily understandable since systems are often built based on a designer's interpretation of them. The meaning of neither sentential specification is immediately clear, despite the fact that each is written in a well-known logical notation. In fact, the average person might construct a diagrammatic depiction of the sentential specifications in the process of understanding their full meanings. As in the case of the circuit diagram example, the important information—here, the relationship between timing events—is made more explicit by the diagram than by the other two representations. Timing diagrams therefore seem a good candidate for expressing event-based behavioral specifications.

To illustrate heterogeneous reasoning, we complete the single pulser example by proving diagrammatically that the proposed circuit diagram satisfies the specification expressed in the timing diagram. The steps taken here, although appearing informal, are consequences of inference rules in the logic; these rules are presented formally in section 3.

We start by assuming the implementation shown above and an input pulse of unspecified duration on $i$:

The circuit indicates the functional relationship between signals $i$, $y$, and $x$; the timing diagram for $i$ can be extended to reflect these relationships; the resulting diagram appears below on the left. Given the waveforms for $y$ and $x$, the diagram can be further extended to display information about signal *o* as in the diagram on the right:

Looking at the specification, one of our goals is to relate the events on *i* and *o*. We can relate the rising edge on *i* to the rising edge on *o* based on an implicit edge between each pair of events on signal *x*. Another implicit edge on *x* allows us to relate the falling edge on *o* and the second rising edge on *i*. The top diagram shows the implicit edges and the lower two diagrams the inferences on signals *i* and *o*.

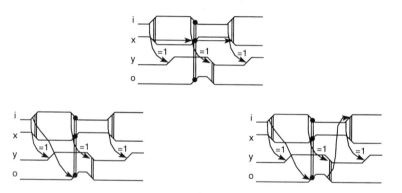

Comparing the specification we are trying to prove with our current derived timing diagram, we note that we are missing constraints between the rising and falling events on *o*. We note that each of these events is synchronous with another event and that an edge denoting duration one exists between the other two events. We therefore add an edge to obtain the following diagram:

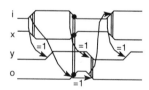

The diagram now contains quite a bit of information, much of which has been subsumed by inference steps. We can always remove information from the timing diagram (though doing so might weaken the information content):

Note that this diagram differs from the desired diagram only in the style of the arrow relating the rising edge on $o$ to the rising edge on $i$. Our informal definition of the edge types indicates that the solid arrow subsumes the dashed arrow; we can weaken the existing arrow to a dashed arrow, thus completing the proof.

The purpose of this example is not to advocate this style of deductive hardware verification; automatic verification techniques are capable of handling large classes of circuits without the need for such low level human intervention. Our intent is to demonstrate that there is a formal structure to how we reason with diagrams and that that structure lends a certain degree of natural clarity to the reasoning process.

What remains is to formalize diagrammatic reasoning methods like the ones used above in a logic suitable for hardware design. That task is the focus of the next section. Although the focus of this section is on the merits of diagrammatic representations, we do not mean to suggest that traditional, sentential representations have no role to play. Indeed, we believe that for a hardware reasoning system to be suitably flexible, sentential as well as diagrammatic representations need to be included. We suspect that sentential representations will be particularly crucial for mathematical reasoning, although we save exploration of that issue for later research.

# 3   Heterogeneous Hardware Logic

Our logic supports four representations: circuit diagrams, timing diagrams, algorithmic state machines (ASMs), and higher-order sentential logic. The diagrammatic portion of heterogeneous hardware logic was first presented in Fisler [1994]. This chapter redefines the syntax and semantics for timing diagrams originally presented in Fisler [1994]; in addition, the sentential portion of the logic is formally presented for the first time. The circuit diagram and ASM portions of the logic are unchanged from Fisler [1994], but are provided here for reference. We first define a model of physical devices, which will serve as a common semantic basis for the four syntactic representations. The syntax and semantics of each representation is presented in turn in subsections 3 through 3. A discussion of logical consequence and presentation of inference rules are provided in section 3.

## Physical Devices

Our model of physical hardware is defined in two stages. First, we capture the structural aspects of a device along with its interface with the external environment. Later, we augment this model so that it can express how a device behaves over time while interacting with the environment. We assume that wires in devices can carry values in $\{0, 1\}$. Ports are primitive objects providing connection points for wires. We choose to associate voltage values with ports rather than wires; the term *assignment* will refer to a total function from a set of ports to the set $\{0, 1\}$.

We assume that devices are composed only of wires and *basic components*: binary and and or gates, inverters, and unit delay elements. Specifically, a basic component is a tuple $\langle I, O, F, D \rangle$ where $I$ and $O$ are disjoint sets of input ports and output ports; $F$ is a function which assigns each $p \in O$ a function $F_p$ from assignments on $I$ into $\{0, 1\}$; and $D$ is a function from $O$ to the non-negative integers indicating the delay of the component. We assume that delay elements have $d = 1$ and all other basic components have $d = 0$.

An *abstract device* is a 5-tuple $D = \langle I, O, B, W, c \rangle$ capturing the structure of a component where $I$ and $O$ are disjoint sets of ports providing the external input and output interface to $D$, $B$ is a set of basic components, $W$ is a set of wires, and $c$ is a wiring function from $W$ to sets of ports. We assume that all ports in a device are distinct and that the sets $c(w)$ partition the ports of $D$. Any ports in $I \cup O$ are called *interface ports*; all other ports are *internal*.

Although any abstract device corresponds to a piece of physical hardware, we are only interested in considering those that meet certain well-formedness conditions. In defining those conditions, we need to be able to talk about paths between ports within a device. Given an abstract device $D$, there is a *connecting step* from port $p_i$ to port $p_j$, denoted $p_i \rightsquigarrow p_j$, iff either $p_i$ and $p_j$ are respectively an input and an output port to some basic component, or $p_i$ is an internal output port or input interface port, $p_j$ is an internal input port or output interface port, and $\{p_i, p_j\} \subseteq c(w)$ for some wire $w$. A finite transitive chain of connecting steps forms a *connecting path*, denoted $p_0 \rightsquigarrow^* p_n$; a device contains a connecting cycle if $p \rightsquigarrow^* p$ for some port $p$. We call a device *well-connected* if treating the basic components as nodes and the wiring function as giving rise to edges yields a connected graph, if for each internal port $p$ in $D$ there exists a connecting path from $p$ to an element of $O$, and if every connecting cycle in $D$ passes through a delay element.

In order to consider an abstract device in mid-computation, we need to know the values on the ports of the device. A tuple $\langle D, i \rangle$ consisting of an abstract device and an assignment for its ports will be called a *concrete device*. We require that all assignments included as part of a concrete device are consistent with the structure of the device. That is, given $\langle D, i \rangle$, for all gates $g$ in $D$, the value in $i$ on the output port of $g$ is consistent with the values in $i$ for the input ports of $g$ and the function associated with $g$. The set of all possible assignments to the delay output ports in a device forms its *possible states*. A concrete device is well-connected if the abstract device it contains is well-connected.

We are interested in determining when two devices exhibit the same external behavior. This requires that we be able to operate our devices over time. Given a well-connected concrete device $C = \langle D, i \rangle$ and an assignment $a$ to the input ports of $D$, there is a unique *derived assignment* $i'$ such that $\langle D, i' \rangle$ is a concrete device where $i'$ is defined as follows: if $p$ is an interface input port of $D$, then $i'(p) = a(p)$; if $p$ is an output port to a delay element with input port $p_{\text{in}}$, then $i'(p) = i(p_{\text{in}})$; if $p$ is an output port of some gate $g$, then $i'(p)$ is $F_p$ applied to the restriction of $i'$ to the input ports of $g$; and if $p$ is any other port, $i'(p) = i'(q)$ where $q$ is the unique internal output port or input interface port wired to $p$.[1] Concrete device $\langle D, i' \rangle$ is said to *follow from* $C$ given $a$, where $i'$ is the derived assignment from $\langle D, i \rangle$ and $a$.

A sequence of assignments $i_1, i_2, \ldots, i_k$ to the interface input ports of a device is called an *assignment sequence*. Given concrete device $C = \langle D, i \rangle$ and assignment sequence $\langle i_1, i_2, \ldots, i_k \rangle$, a *run* of $C$ is a sequence $r = \langle C_0, C_1, \ldots, C_k \rangle$ of concrete devices such that $C_0 = C$ and, for each $1 \leq j \leq k$, $C_j$ is the concrete device that follows from $C_{j-1}$ given $i_j$. The *output* of a concrete device $\langle D, i \rangle$ is the restriction of $i$ to the interface output ports $O$ of $D$. The output of a run $r = \langle C_0, C_1, \ldots, C_k \rangle$ of a concrete device is a sequence $\langle O_0, O_1, \ldots, O_k \rangle$ where each $O_i$ is the output of $C_i$. The state of devices and runs are similarly defined by restricting assignments to the delay output ports. For port $p$, the *run-valuation* of $p$ is the restriction of these assignments to $p$.

Concrete devices $C_1 = \langle D_1, i_1 \rangle$ and $C_2 = \langle D_2, i_2 \rangle$ are *behaviorally equivalent* if $D_1$ and $D_2$ have the same sets of input and output interface ports and for every assignment sequence $a$ for $D_1$, the output of the run of $C_1$ under $a$ is the same as the output of the run of $C_2$ under $a$. Abstract devices $D_1$ and $D_2$ are behaviorally equivalent if for every $\langle D_1, i_1 \rangle$ there exists an $i_2$ such that $\langle D_1, i_1 \rangle$ and $\langle D_2, i_2 \rangle$ are behaviorally equivalent, and vice versa.

---

[1] The proof of uniqueness appears in Fisler [1994].

## Circuit Diagrams

In this logic, we consider circuit diagrams composed of icons representing binary and and or gates, unit delay elements, inverters, and wires. We use a set-theoretic model to capture the syntactic information contained in a given circuit diagram. In this model, we represent a wire line as an ordered pair of the points it connects; a binary gate icon is modelled as an ordered triple $\langle x, y, z \rangle$, indicating that the icon connects $x$ and $y$ on the left, in that order, from top to bottom, with $z$ on the right. Unary icons are similarly represented with an ordered pair.

Specifically, a *circuit sketch* is a tuple $\langle P, I, O, W, N, D, A, R \rangle$ where $P$ is a set of objects called the *connection points* of $s$, $I$ and $O$ are disjoint subsets of $P$ called the input points and output points of $s$, $W$, $N$, and $D$ are disjoint subsets of $P \times P$ called the *wire lines, negation icons,* and *delay icons,* and $A$ and $R$ are disjoint subsets of $P \times P \times P$ called the **and gate icons** and **or gate icons**. A wire $w = \langle p_a, p_b \rangle$ is *branch-free* iff $w$ is the unique wire with $p_a$ as its first component; otherwise $w$ is a *branching* wire. We use the term *circuit sketch*, as opposed to *circuit diagram*, so that we may reserve the latter term for only those diagrams which are well-formed. A formal definition of this term will be presented shortly.

**Definition 3.1** Let $s$ be a circuit sketch and $D$ be an abstract device.

1. A *depiction map* from $s$ to $D$ is an injective function $\phi$ from the connection points of $s$ into the ports of $D$ such that for all $p \in s_P$:

    (a) $p \in s_I \rightarrow \phi(p) \in D_I$.

    (b) $p \in s_O \rightarrow \phi(p) \in D_O$.

    (c) If $l = \langle p_a, p_b \rangle$ is a wire line of $s$, then $\phi(p_a)$ and $\phi(p_b)$ are wired together by some wire $w \in D_W$; $\phi(p_a)$ must be an input interface port or internal output port and $\phi(p_b)$ must be an output interface port or internal input port.

    (d) If $n = \langle p_a, p_b \rangle$ is a negation icon of $s$ then $\phi(p_a)$ is connected to the input port and $\phi(p_b)$ is connected to the output port of some inverter in $D_G$.

    (e) If $d = \langle p_a, p_b \rangle$ is a delay icon of $s$ then $\phi(p_a)$ is connected to the input port and $\phi(p_b)$ is connected to the output port of some delay element in $D_R$.

    (f) If $g = \langle p_a, p_b, p_c \rangle$ is an and-gate icon of $s$ then $\phi(p_a)$ and $\phi(p_b)$ are connected to the input ports and $\phi(p_b)$ is connected to the output port of some and-gate in $D_G$.

    (g) If $g = \langle p_a, p_b, p_c \rangle$ is an or-gate icon of $s$ then $\phi(p_a)$ and $\phi(p_b)$ are connected to the input ports and $\phi(p_b)$ is connected to the output port of some or-gate in $D_G$.

2. $D$ is a *structural implementation of* $s$ if there is a surjective depiction map from $s$ to $D$ and the converse of requirements 1c through 1g in the definition of a depiction map holds. This is written $D \models_s s$.

3. $D$ is a *behavioral implementation of* $s$ if $D$ is behaviorally equivalent to some device $D'$ which is a structural implementation of $s$. This is written $D \models_b s$.

**Lemma 3.2** *For any device $D$ there exists a circuit sketch $C$ that is unique up to isomorphism on circuit sketches such that $D \models_s C$. For any circuit sketch $C$ there exists a device $D$ that is unique up to isomorphism on devices such that $D \models_s C$.*

We use this lemma to make a deferred definition: a *circuit diagram* is any circuit sketch $s$ for which the device $D$ such that $D \models_s s$ is well-connected. For the remainder of this work, we assume we are dealing only with circuit diagrams, as opposed to circuit sketches.

## ASM Charts

ASM charts are a variant of state machines that combine the traditional Mealy and Moore machines. They have an appearance reminiscent of flow-charts: rectangles denote states, diamonds represent conditional branches, and ovals represent conditional (Mealy) outputs. Moore outputs are desig-nated by assigning a variable a value (either T or F) within a state rectan-gle. Each conditional branch diamond contains the name of a single signal to be tested and has two paths leaving it, one labeled T and one labeled F (where T and F are relative to the value of the signal tested in the dia-mond). Each conditional oval contains one or more variable names to be assigned T when control reaches the oval. Examples of ASM charts appear in Figure 5 (page 248) and more extensive discussion appears in Winkel and Prosser [1989]. As in the section on circuit diagrams, we will reserve the term *ASM chart* for what we wish to consider well-formed diagrams, using the term *ASM graph* for the general case.

An *ASM graph* $g$ is a tuple $\langle S, B, O, N, R, P \rangle$ where $S$ is a set of state objects, $B$ is a set of conditional branch objects, and $O$ is a set of conditional output objects such that $S$, $B$, and $O$ are all pairwise disjoint. We will refer to the union of these sets as the *objects* of $g$. $N$ is a set of signal names. $R$ is a subset of $S \times S \times \mathcal{P}(N) \times \mathcal{P}(N)$ called the *next state transitions* of $g$.[2] The first and second elements of these tuples are called the *source state* and *target state*, respectively. The third and fourth elements are called the *true conditions* and the *false conditions*, respectively. Finally, $P$ is a subset of $S \times N \times U \times \mathcal{P}(N) \times \mathcal{P}(N)$ called the *output conditions* of $g$. The first two

---

[2]The notation $\mathcal{P}(N)$ represents the powerset of $N$.

elements are called the *asserting state* and *asserted variable*, respectively. The third element is called the *assignment value* and is a member $\{T, F\}$. The last two elements are called the *true conditions* and the *false conditions*, respectively. We will use the term *external signal* for those elements of $N$ that appear in the true or false conditions of some element of $R \cup P$ but are not the asserted variable for any output condition; non-external signals are classified as *internal*.

In order to relate ASM graphs to devices, we need to be able to talk about their computational behavior. A *signal-value assignment* for an ASM graph is a function from the names $N$ to the set $\{T, F\}$. An *external signal-value assignment* is the restriction of a signal-value assignment to the external signals. $\langle g, s \rangle$ is an *executing ASM graph* where $g$ is an ASM graph and $s$ is some state in $g$. The following symbol, when placed near state $s$ in ASM graph $g$, denotes that $\langle g, s \rangle$ is executing at time $t$.

Given executing ASM graph $\langle g, s \rangle$ and a signal-value assignment $i$ for $g$, a next-state transition $\langle t_s, t_t, c_t, c_f \rangle \in R$ is *satisfied by s and i* if $t_s = s$, $i(n) = T$ for all names in $c_t$, and $i(n) = F$ for all names in $c_f$. If there is exactly one such transition satisfied by $s$ and $i$, that transition is called the *next state of g under s and i*. We say that output condition $\langle t_s, n, u, c_t, c_f \rangle \in P$ is *satisfied by s and i* if $t_s = s$, $i(v) = T$ for all names $v$ in $c_t$, and $i(v) = F$ for all names $v$ in $c_f$. Let $i'$ be the unique signal-value assignment such that for all output conditions $\langle t_s, n, u, c_t, c_f \rangle$ satisfied by $s$ and $i$, $i'(n) = u$, $i'(x) = i(x)$ if $x$ is an external signal, and $i'(x) = F$ for all other signals $x$. $i'$ is called the *signal update of g under s and i*.[3]

An ASM graph $g$ is *deterministic* if no two next state transitions are satisfied by the same state $s$ and signal-value assignment $i$; it is called *transitionally complete* if for all states $s$ and all signal-value assignments $i$ there exists a next-state transition that is satisfied by $s$ and $i$. An ASM graph that is both deterministic and transitionally complete will be called an *ASM chart*. This corresponds to a well-formedness definition on ASM graphs.

We have established sufficient framework to discuss when a given ASM chart describes a given physical device and when a given device implements the algorithm depicted in an ASM chart. Given ASM chart $g$ and abstract device $D$, a *state map* from $g$ to $D$ is a function from the states $S$ of $g$ to the possible states of $D$. Function $\phi$ from the signal names of $g$ to the ports

---

[3]We are using $F$ as the global default value for signals, though defaults could be assigned in various other ways.

of $D$ is called a *signal map* iff $\phi$ maps each external signal in $g$ to an input interface port of $D$ and each internal signal in $g$ to an internal output port in $D$. $\phi$ is called a *complete signal map* iff it is a signal map with every interface port (input and output) of $D$ in its co-domain.

We will establish relationships between ASM graphs and devices by simulating each on the same inputs and seeing how closely the state transitions and output behaviors correspond. Doing this requires that we know when a signal-value assignment and a port assignment are reflecting the same values. Given a signal map $\phi$ and signal-value assignment $i$, assignment $a$ for $D$ is *compatible* with $\phi$ and $i$ iff $a(p) = i(\phi^{-1}(p))$ for all ports $p$ in the co-domain of $\phi$. A state map $\phi_s$ and a signal map $\phi_n$ are said to be *feasible for $g$ and $D$* if for all signal-value assignments $i$ for $g$ and all states $s$ in $g$ there exists an assignment $a$ for $D$ which is compatible with $\phi_n$ and $i$ and reflects state $\phi_s(s)$ such that:

1. If $s'$ is the next state of $g$ under $s$ and $i$, then $\phi_s(s')$ is the next state of $D$ under $\phi_s(s)$ and $a$.

2. If $i'$ is the signal update of $g$ under $s$ and $i$, then assignment $a'$ derived from $\langle D, a \rangle$ is compatible with $i'$.

If $\phi_s$ and $\phi_n$ are feasible for $g$ and $D$ and the converse of requirement 1 holds for all $i$ and $s$, we say that $\phi_s$ and $\phi_n$ *capture $g$ and $D$*.

As in the section on circuit diagrams, we now define three relationships between ASM graphs and devices that capture the various granularities of relationships between them.

**Definition 3.3**

1. *$g$ describes $D$* if there exists a state map and a signal map that are feasible for $g$ and $D$.

2. $D$ is a *structural implementation of $g$* iff there exists a surjective state map and a complete signal map that capture $g$ and $D$. This is written $D \models_s g$.

3. $D$ is a *behavioral implementation of $g$* if $D$ is behaviorally equivalent to some device $D'$ which is a structural implementation of $g$. This is written $D \models_b g$.

## Timing Diagrams

The timing diagram syntax and semantics originally presented in Fisler [1994] is too restricted to be able to represent general timing relationships. We have updated our syntax and semantics to follow the much more flexible system of Schlör and Damm [1993]. A timing diagram is a collection of

Safe Edge     Live Edge     Combined Edge     Simultaneous Edge     Conflict Edge

Figure 1: Notations and definitions from the work of Schlör and Damm [1993].

individual waveforms whose events are related by a series of edges between them. The types and notations for edges are given in Figure 1 and include notations for safety requirements, liveness requirements, and coincidence requirements. Safe edges require the source event to occur before or simultaneously with the target event. Live edges require the target event to occur after the source event. Combined edges are used when safe and live edges are needed between the same two events. Simultaneous edges require the events to happen concurrently, while conflict edges do not permit the events to occur simultaneously. In order to draw simultaneous edges, it is often necessary to cross events that should not be synchronized. In the event that a synchronization line applies to only some of the events it crosses, those events it relates will be attached to the line using a dark circle.

A timing level is an element of the set {high, low, don't-care, rising, falling}. We define a *timing pattern* as a pair $\langle s, c \rangle$ where $s$ is a sequence of timing levels and $c$ is a color used to indicate the role of the signal in the system as one of input, output, or internal. A timing pattern is *well-formed* if high is never immediately followed by low or rising, low is never immediately followed by high or falling, rising is never immediately followed by rising or falling, and falling is never immediately followed by rising or falling. A *timing event* is defined as a tuple $\langle p, i \rangle$ where $p$ is a timing pattern and $i$ is an index into $p_s$ such that $i$ is no larger than the length of $p_s$. We will write $p(i)$ to refer to the timing level in $p_s$ at time $i$.

Given a collection $C$ of timing patterns, an *edge* on those patterns is a pair of the form $\langle e_1, e_2 \rangle$ where $e_1$ and $e_2$ are timing events on patterns in $C$. An edge may be annotated with a duration marker consisting of a positive integer or integer variable and one of the symbols $+, -, =$; these markers specify bounds on the amount of time that may pass between the two events. A partial function mapping edges to duration markers is a *duration mapping*. We consider a *timing diagram* to be a tuple $\langle N, P, E_S, E_L, E_M, E_C, \phi \rangle$ in which $N$ is a set of names, $P$ is a function from $N$ to timing patterns, $E_S$ is a set of safe edges, $E_L$ is a set of live edges, $E_M$ is a set of simultaneous edges, $E_C$ is a set of conflict edges, and $\phi$ is a duration mapping on $E_S \cup E_L$.

In comparing devices and timing diagrams, a timing value $v_t$ and a numeric device value $v_d$ are said to *correspond* if $v_t$ is high and $v_d = 1$ or if $v_t$ is low and $v_d = 0$. If $v_t$ is don't-care, then it corresponds to any value of $v_d$. We relate the signal names in a timing diagram $T$ to the ports of a device $D$ using an injective function called a *waveform map* in which input signals in $T$ map to input interface ports of $D$, output signals in $T$ map to output interface ports of $D$, and internal signals in $T$ map to internal output ports of $D$. The *defining indices* of a timing pattern are those that map to values in {high, low, don't-care}.

Given a run $R = \langle D, a_0 \rangle, \langle D, a_1 \rangle, \ldots, \langle D, a_n \rangle$ of a concrete device, a timing event $\langle p, i \rangle$, and a port $s$ in $D$, $\langle p, i \rangle$ *matches* $s$ in $C_j$ iff if $i$ is a defining index of $p$ then $p(i)$ corresponds to $a_j(s)$, if $p(i) =$ rising then $a_j(s) = 0$ and $a_{j+1}(s) = 1$, and if $p(i) =$ falling then $a_j(s) = 1$ and $a_{j+1}(s) = 0$. A timing diagram $T$ is *valid* for $R$ under waveform map $\phi$ between $T$ and $D$ iff

1. For every signal $s \in T$, there exists a monotonic function $f$ from the indices of $s$ to $\{0, \ldots, n\}$ such that for all defining indices $i$, the value of $\phi(s)$ in $R_{f(i)}$ corresponds to $s(i)$.[4]

2. For every $\langle \langle s_1, i_1 \rangle, \langle s_2, i_2 \rangle \rangle \in E_S$ and for all $j$, $0 \le j \le n$, if $\langle s_2, i_2 \rangle$ matches $\phi(s_2)$ in $R_j$, then there must exist $k$, $0 \le k \le j$, such that $\langle s_1, i_1 \rangle$ matches $\phi(s_1)$ in $R_k$.

3. For every $\langle \langle s_1, i_1 \rangle, \langle s_2, i_2 \rangle \rangle \in E_L$ and for all $j$, $0 \le j \le n$, if $\langle s_1, i_1 \rangle$ matches $\phi(s_1)$ in $R_j$, then there must exist $k$, $j \le k \le n$, such that $\langle s_2, i_2 \rangle$ matches $\phi(s_2)$ in $R_k$.

4. For every $\langle \langle s_1, i_1 \rangle, \langle s_2, i_2 \rangle \rangle \in E_M$, if $\langle s_1, i_1 \rangle$ matches $\phi(s_1)$ in $R_j$, then $\langle s_2, i_2 \rangle$ matches $\phi(s_2)$ in $R_j$.

5. For every $\langle \langle s_1, i_1 \rangle, \langle s_2, i_2 \rangle \rangle \in E_C$, if $\langle s_1, i_1 \rangle$ matches $\phi(s_1)$ in $R_j$, then $\langle s_2, i_2 \rangle$ does not match $\phi(s_2)$ in $R_j$.

**Definition 3.4** Let $T$ be a timing diagram and let $D$ be a device.

1. $T$ *describes* $D$, written $D \models T$, if there is a waveform map $\phi$ from $T$ to $D$ such that for all runs $R$ of $D$, $T$ is valid for $R$ under $\phi$.

2. $D$ is a *structural implementation of* $T$ if $T$ describes $D$ using a surjective waveform map. This is written $D \models_s T$.

3. $D$ is a *behavioral implementation of* $T$ if $D$ is behaviorally equivalent to some device $D'$ which is a structural implementation of $T$. This is written $D \models_b T$.

---

[4]This function $f$ is not necessarily unique.

## Sentential Logic

Our sentential logic is second-order logic augmented with arithmetic operations. We assume the existence of a sort $N$ of natural numbers and a sort $B$ of booleans with boolean constants $\mathbf{f}$ and $\mathbf{t}$. We also assume we have temporal variables $t_1, t_2, \ldots$, temporal constants $\bar{0}, \bar{1}, \ldots$ for each number $k$ in $N$, and function constants $\bar{f}$ for every function from $N$ to $N$. Given a concrete device $C$ and an assignment sequence $A$, we associate with each port $p$ in $C$ a *port function constant* $\bar{p}$ from $N$ to $B$; for each $i$ up to the length of $A$, $\bar{p}(i)$ returns the value on $p$ in device $C_i$ in the run of $C$ on $A$, and for all other $i$, $\bar{p}(i)$ returns $\mathbf{f}$. Port value 0 is equivalent to boolean constant $\mathbf{f}$ and port value 1 is equivalent to boolean constant $\mathbf{t}$. We will assume the existence of port function variables $W, X, Y$.

The class of *temporal terms* is the smallest class containing the temporal variables and constants and closed under the following operation: if $t$ is a temporal term and $\bar{f}$ is a function from $N$ to $N$, then $\bar{f}(t)$ is a temporal term. Given a function $\phi$ mapping temporal variables into $N$, we extend $\phi$ to a function mapping all temporal terms $t$ into $N$ in the obvious way by recursion on terms:

$$\phi(\bar{k}) = k$$
$$\phi(\bar{f}(t)) = f(\phi(t))$$

We also have a set $L$ of *value terms*, defined as the smallest set containing $\mathbf{t}$, $\mathbf{f}$, $F(t)$ for each temporal term $t$ and $F \in N \to B$, $X(t)$ for each temporal term $t$ and port function variable $X$, and closed under the following: if $l_1, l_2 \in L$, then $\neg l_1$ and $(l_1 \wedge l_2)$ are in $L$. We assume that $\vee$ is defined as usual from $\neg$ and $\wedge$.

Given any function $\phi$ from temporal variables into $N$ and port function variables into $N \to B$, and any value term $l$, we define $l[\phi]$ to be the boolean value that $l$ takes on under the mapping $\phi$. This is defined by recursion as follows:

$$\mathbf{t}[\phi] = \text{true}$$
$$\mathbf{f}[\phi] = \text{false}$$
$$F(t)[\phi] = F(\phi(t))$$
$$X(t)[\phi] = \phi(X)(\phi(t))$$
$$(\neg l)[\phi] = \neg(l[\phi])$$
$$(l_1 \wedge l_2)[\phi] = (l_1[\phi] \wedge l_2[\phi])$$

The *atomic formulae* are the expressions of the form $t_1 \leq t_2$, $t_1 = t_2$ for temporal terms $t_1$ and $t_2$, and $l_1 = l_2$ for value terms $l_1$ and $l_2$. The set of formulae of our language is the smallest set containing the atomic formulae and closed under the following: if $B_1$ and $B_2$ are formulae, then so are $\neg B_1$, $(B_1 \wedge B_2)$, $\forall X B_1$, and $\forall t B_1$; $\vee$ and $\exists$ are assumed to be defined as usual from these connectives.

We define the semantics of formulae in terms of concrete devices and assignments to variables, as one would expect. For any formula $E$, we define $C, A \models E[\phi]$ recursively on $E$, where $C = \langle D, i \rangle$ is a concrete device and $A$ is an assignment sequence of length $k$ for $D$. $\phi$ maps temporal variables into temporal constants $\overline{0} \ldots \overline{k}$ and port function variables into port function constants. The notation $B_1[X/\overline{p}]$ denotes the substitution of $\overline{p}$ for $X$ in $B_1$; $B_1[t/t_i]$ is defined analogously.

$$C, A \not\models \mathbf{f}[\phi]$$
$$C, A \models \mathbf{t}[\phi]$$
$$C, A \models (t_1 = t_2)[\phi] \text{ iff } \phi(t_1) = \phi(t_2)$$
$$C, A \models (t_1 \leq t_2)[\phi] \text{ iff } \phi(t_1) \leq \phi(t_2)$$
$$C, A \models (l_1 = l_2)[\phi] \text{ iff } \phi(l_1) = \phi(l_2)$$
$$C, A \models \neg B_1[\phi] \text{ iff } C, A \not\models B_1[\phi]$$
$$C, A \models (B_1 \wedge B_2)[\phi] \text{ iff } C, A \models B_1[\phi] \text{ and } C, A \models B_2[\phi]$$
$$C, A \models (\forall X B_1)[\phi] \text{ iff } C, A \models (B_1[X/\overline{p}])[\phi]$$
$$\text{for each port function constant associated}$$
$$\text{with a port in } C$$
$$C, A \models (\forall t B_1)[\phi] \text{ iff } C, A \models (B_1[t/t_c])[\phi]$$
$$\text{for each temporal constant } t_c \in \overline{0} \ldots \overline{k}$$

**Definition 3.5** Let $C = \langle D, i \rangle$ be a concrete device and $E$ be a formula in our sentential language. $E$ *describes* $C$, written $C \models E$, if for all assignment sequences $A$ for $D$, there exists a function $\phi$ mapping port function variables into port function constants for $C$ and temporal variables into temporal constants $\overline{0} \ldots \overline{k}$, where $k$ is the length of $A$, such that $C, A \models E[\phi]$. We say that $E$ *describes* $D$, written $D \models E$ if for all assignments $i$, $\langle D, i \rangle \models E$.

## Rules of Inference and Methods of Proof

Although a general discussion of the theory of heterogeneous inference is out of the scope of this chapter, our presentation is motivated by the work of Barwise and Etchemendy [1990]. When stating these rules, we use the term *representation* as opposed to the more traditional term *formula* to avoid the sentential connotations associated with the latter. In general, a rule can be formulated to infer representation $G$ from a set of representations $S$ if it is the case that whenever a device $D$ models every element of $S$, $D$ also models $G$; in this case $G$ is said to be a logical consequence of $S$. While this requirement does not dictate which of the modeling relationships (structural or behavioral) should be used in defining rules of inference, we use behavioral modeling to create rules between diagrams of the same type and structural modeling to create rules between diagrams of different types.

There are a number of inference rules for the full logic; only a subset are relevant to the examples presented in this chapter. Rules are presented with their diagrammatic depictions where feasible. We do not present the standard inference rules of higher-order logic or the rules of arithmetic, but assume they are defined within the system.

We start by defining some general methods of proof. In these definitions, we consider a *proof* to be a sequence of representations such that each element of the sequence is either a single representation or another proof; each proof appearing as a complete element of a proof $P$ is a *direct subproof* of $P$. Each proof starts with a series of representations called the *initial assumptions* of the proof. The *context* for an element of a proof is the set of elements that have preceded it in the proof. We will consider a proof to be *valid* if every element that is not an initial assumption is the logical consequence of its context. A *goal* is a representation that we wish to prove from the set of initial assumptions. The goal is satisfied if it is the last representation in a valid proof.

In the course of producing a proof, it is often the case that there are many possible cases that need to be considered in order to complete the next proof step; a simple example of this from sentential logic arises when working with disjunctions. In this case, it is common to consider each possibility in turn and then to prove that the desired goal is satisfied in each case. The following rule generalizes this notion of breaking into a set of cases:

**Rule 3.6 (Condition Exhaustive)** Let $C_1, \ldots, C_n$ be a set of direct subproofs of a proof $P$, let $R$ be some representation, and let $A$ be some property that can be associated with $R$. $C_1, \ldots, C_n$ are *exhaustive with respect to* $A$ iff every context in which $R$ has property $A$ is subsumed by some $C_i$.

As an example of how this rule can be instantiated for a particular property, we define a rule for breaking into cases based on the states of an ASM chart that assert a particular variable.

**Rule 3.7 (Asserting States Exhaustive)** Let $A$ be an ASM chart, let $v$ be any signal in $A$, and let $u$ be a truth value. Let $S$ be the set of all states $s$ such that $\langle s, v, u, c_t, c_f \rangle$ is an output condition in $A$. Direct subproofs $C_1, \ldots, C_n$ are *Asserting States Exhaustive* if each element of $S$ is the state of $A$ in the initial assumptions of some $C_i$.

Usually, our goal in splitting into cases is to derive some particular representation from each case so that the representation may be extracted from the cases and asserted at the level containing the subproofs. We express this in our logic using the following rule:

**Rule 3.8 (Merge)** Let $P$ be a proof containing an exhaustive set of cases

$C_1, \ldots, C_n$ and let $R$ be a representation that is satisfied in every $C_i$, $1 \leq i \leq n$. $R$ is true in $P$ by the *Merge* rule.

We now turn to rules that are particular to the different types of representations. We begin with four rules related to ASM charts.

**Rule 3.9 (Asserting State)** Let $A$ be an ASM chart, let $v$ be any signal in $A$, and let $u$ be a truth value such that there exists a unique state $s \in A$ that can be the asserting state for $v$ with value $u$ in the current context. If $t$ is a time variable such that $v(t) = u$, then it follows by the rule of *Asserting State* that $\langle A, s \rangle$ is executing at time $t$.

**Rule 3.10 (Value in State)** Let $\langle A, s \rangle$ be executing at time $t$. Given output condition $\langle s, n, u, c_t, c_f \rangle$, if every element of $c_t$ is true in the current context and every element of $c_f$ is false in the current context, then $n(t) = u$ follows by *Value in State*.

**Rule 3.11 (State Transition)** Let $\langle A, s \rangle$ be executing at time $t$. Given next state transition $\langle s, s', c_t, c_f \rangle$, if every element of $c_t$ is true in the current context and every element of $c_f$ is false in the current context, then $\langle A, s' \rangle$ is executing at time $t + 1$ by the rule of *State Transition*.

**Rule 3.12 (Looping)** Let $\langle A, s \rangle$ be executing at time $t$ with a next-state transition $\langle s, s, c_t, c_f \rangle$ such that there is exactly one signal in $c_t \cup c_f$. Let $v$ name this signal.

1. If $v \in c_t$, $\exists t_1 \; t_1 > t \wedge \neg v(t_1)$ is true in the current context, and $t_1$ is the smallest such time, then $\langle A, s' \rangle$ is executing at time $t_1 + 1$ under the *looping* rule, where $\langle s, s', \{\}, \{v\} \rangle$ is a next-state transition in $A$.

2. If $v \in c_f$, $\exists t_1 \; t_1 > t \wedge v(t_1)$ is true in the current context, and $t_1$ is the smallest such time, then $\langle A, s' \rangle$ is executing at time $t_1 + 1$ under the *looping* rule, where $\langle s, s', \{v\}, \{\} \rangle$ is a next-state transition in $A$.

We now present some rules associated with circuit diagrams. It is straightforward to define the rules of boolean algebra in terms of their associated circuit diagram representations; as a result, we give only one example of such a rule here, although the full set of boolean algebra rules are defined within the logic. We define one instance of the distributive law below; its diagrammatic representation appears in Figure 2.

**Rule 3.13 (Distributivity)** Given circuit diagram $C$ with a branch-free wire $w$ connecting the output of an **or** gate $r$ to the input of an **and** gate $a$, circuit diagram $C'$ is derived by means of *distributivity* by adding new **and** gates $a_1$ and $a_2$, adding new **or** gate $r_1$, wiring the output of $r_1$ to the output of $a$, wiring the non-$w$ input to $a$ to an input port of each of $a_1$ and $a_2$, wiring one input of $r$ to the unused input port on $a_1$ and the other

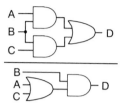

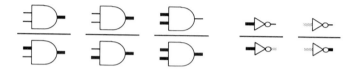

Figure 2: Inference rule corresponding to distributivity.

Figure 3: The simulation rules on circuit diagrams; high voltages are denoted in black and low voltages are denoted in grey. Thin wires are considered to have unknown/don't-care voltage. Other rules on **and** gates, such as those involving low voltages, can be derived from the existing **and** rules. Rules for **or** gates can be derived from both the **and** rules and the inverter rules.

input of $r$ to the unused input port on $a_2$, wiring the outputs of $a_1$ and $a_2$ to the input of $r_1$, and removing $a$, $w$, and $r$.

In addition to the boolean algebra rules, we define what can be thought of as simulation rules on circuit diagrams—rules that allow us to infer the propagation of voltage levels on wires across gates. These rules should be intuitively clear. A collection of these rules appears in Figure 3; the formal definition of the first rule can be given as:

**Rule 3.14 (And High Output)** Let $a$ be an **and** gate whose output voltage is known to be high. It follows that the voltage on either input must also be high.

We use a variety of timing diagram inference rules in this chapter: some between timing diagrams and other timing diagrams, some between timing diagrams and circuit diagrams, and some between timing diagrams and sentential logic. The first two types of rules were used in the single pulser discussion in section 2. The rules are now presented formally; the reader is referred back to the single pulser discussion for examples of using the rules.

**Rule 3.15 (Edge Transitivity)** Let $T$ be a timing diagram with edges $\langle e_1, e_2 \rangle$ and $\langle e_2, e_3 \rangle$ of the same type. Unless $\langle e_1, e_2 \rangle$ and $\langle e_2, e_3 \rangle$ are conflict edges, timing diagram $T'$ is derived from $T$ by means of *edge transitivity* by adding new edge $\langle e_1, e_3 \rangle$ of the same type as $\langle e_1, e_2 \rangle$ and $\langle e_2, e_3 \rangle$.

**Rule 3.16 (Weakening)** Let $T$ be a timing diagram. Timing diagram $T'$ is derived from $T$ by means of *weakening* by either removing an edge from $E_S$, $E_L$, $E_M$, or $E_C$, or by removing a timing pattern $p$ from the range of $P$ and removing all edges from $E_S$, $E_L$, $E_M$, and $E_C$ containing an event on $p$.

**Rule 3.17 (Time Equality)** Let $T$ be a timing diagram with edges $\langle e_1, e_2 \rangle, \langle e_3, e_4 \rangle \in E_M$ and edge $\langle e_1, e_3 \rangle$ of any type. Timing diagram $T'$ is derived by means of *time equality* by adding edge $\langle e_2, e_4 \rangle$ of the same type as $\langle e_1, e_3 \rangle$. If $\langle e_1, e_3 \rangle \in E_S \cup E_L$, then $\phi(\langle e_2, e_4 \rangle) = \phi(\langle e_1, e_3 \rangle)$.

The next definition gives an example of how we infer additional timing diagram information from a timing diagram and a circuit diagram. In this definition, we define the *flip* $s'$ of a sequence $s$ of timing levels such that $s'(i) =$ high if $s(i) =$ low, $s'(i) =$ low if $s(i) =$ high, $s'(i) =$ rising if $s(i) =$ falling, and $s'(i) =$ falling if $s(i) =$ rising.

**Rule 3.18 (Waveform Negation)** Let $T$ be a timing diagram, let $C$ be a circuit diagram, and let $D$ be a device such that $D \models T$ and $D \models_s C$. Let $\langle p_a, p_b \rangle$ be an inverter in $C$ such that $T$ contains a timing pattern $p = \langle s, c \rangle$ for the signal name corresponding to $p_a$. Timing diagram $T'$ follows by means of *waveform negation* by adding a new timing pattern $p' = \langle s', c' \rangle$ such that $s'$ is the flip of $s$ and $c'$ is the color associated with the function of $p_b$ in $C$, and for each $i$ up to the length of $s$, $\langle \langle p, i \rangle, \langle p', i \rangle \rangle \in E_M$.

In the next section, we will use rules between timing diagrams and sentential logic. Unlike most of the other rules in the system, these are essentially translation rules. One example is the rule that produces a live edge from a sentential formula:

$$\forall t \, (\neg A(t) \wedge A(t+1) \rightarrow \exists t' \; t' \geq t \wedge \neg B(t') \wedge B(t'+1))$$

# 4  The Island Traffic Light Controller

We are now ready to demonstrate the flexibility of the logic on an example. Assume that we want to design a controller for the traffic lights at a one lane tunnel connecting the mainland to a small island as pictured below. There is a traffic light at each end of the tunnel; there are also four sensors for detecting the presence of vehicles: one at tunnel entrance on the island side (IE), one at tunnel exit on the island side (IX), one at tunnel entrance on the mainland side (ME), and one at tunnel exit on the mainland side (MX).

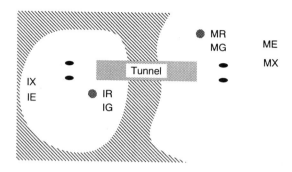

In addition, there is a constraint that at most sixteen cars may be on the island at any time. We make the environmental assumptions that all cars are finite in length, that no car gets stuck in the tunnel, that cars do not exit the tunnel before entering the tunnel, and that cars do not leave the tunnel entrance without traveling through the tunnel.

The solution discussed here consists of three communicating controllers: one for the island lights, one for the mainland lights, and one tunnel controller that processes the requests for access issued by the other two controllers. State machines depicting each of the three controllers are provided in Figures 5 and 4. We would like to establish that our solution has at least the following properties:

1. Cars never travel both directions in the tunnel at the same time.

2. Access to the tunnel is not granted until the tunnel is empty.

3. Lights do not turn green until access is granted.

4. The tunnel is used once granted.

5. Requests for the tunnel are eventually granted.

6. Once a car arrives at an entrance, the light at that entrance eventually turns green.

7. All commands to yield the tunnel are acknowledged by the island and mainland controllers.

8. There are never more than sixteen cars on the island.

9. Counters are only changed once per car.

10. Counters do not move if increment and decrement signals are asserted simultaneously.

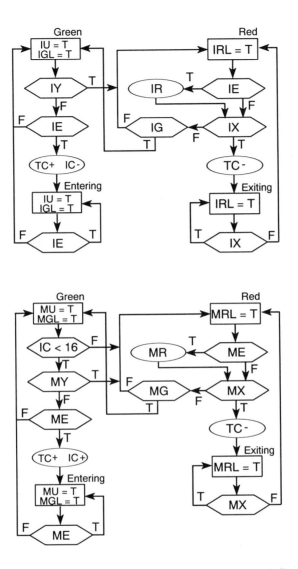

Figure 4: ASM charts for the island (top) and mainland (bottom) light controllers. IGL and IRL are the green and red lights for the island, IU indicates that the island is using the tunnel, IR indicates that the island is requesting the tunnel, IY indicates that the island is being instructed to release control of the tunnel, and IG indicates that the island has been granted control of the tunnel; a similar set of signals has been defined for the mainland. TC is a count of the number of cars presently inside the tunnel, and IC is a count of the number of cars presently on the island.

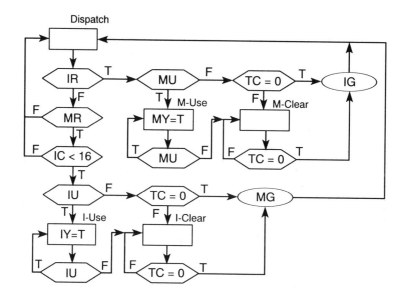

Figure 5: ASM chart for the tunnel controller.

Some of these properties, such as 2–7, are natural candidates for finite-state verification techniques, others, such as 10, are easier to reason about once an implementation of the system is designed; we will demonstrate how our logic supports reasoning at each of these levels. As an example of verification at the state-machine level, consider the condition that all yields issued by the tunnel controller should eventually be acknowledged; many of the other conditions above could also be verified in a similar manner. Assuming the island controller is being asked to yield, this can be expressed using timing diagram

$$\forall t \exists t_1 \, t_1 > t \wedge \neg IE(t_1) \wedge \forall t_2 \, t_1 > t_2 \geq t \rightarrow IE(t_2)$$

$$\forall t \exists t_1 \, t_1 > t \wedge IE(t_1) \wedge \forall t_2 \, t_1 > t_2 \geq t \rightarrow \neg IE(t_2)$$

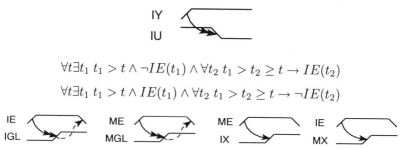

Figure 6: Representations of the environmental assumptions.

We now provide a proof, using the inference rules presented in Section 3, that this timing diagram is a logical consequence of the three controller diagrams and the environmental assumptions. Formally, we represent the environmental assumptions as shown in Figure 6. The proof is given in natural deduction style. Ideally we would develop this proof in an animated system (akin to *Hyperproof*) that updated each representation with the information from the current context as the proof progressed; lacking animation in this presentation, we provide the diagrams corresponding to each step explicitly. To keep the proof compact, rather than insert the state machine diagrams into the lines of the proof, we insert a grey icon indicating that the formula at a given step is a diagram; the diagrams corresponding to each step are numbered and are provided following the proof. We use a black rectangular icon to stand for the goal diagram on the appropriate lines. First we provide the statecharts.

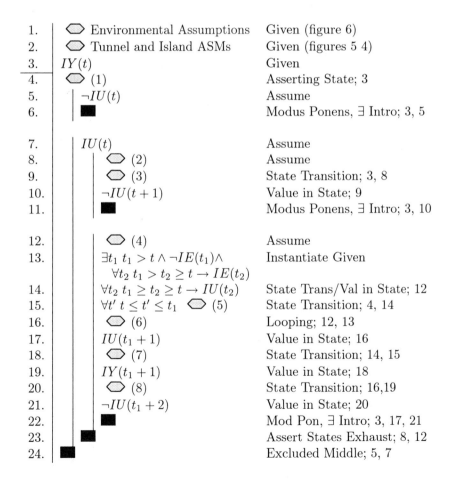

| | | |
|---|---|---|
| 1. | ◇ Environmental Assumptions | Given (figure 6) |
| 2. | ◇ Tunnel and Island ASMs | Given (figures 5 4) |
| 3. | $IY(t)$ | Given |
| 4. | ◇ (1) | Asserting State; 3 |
| 5. | $\neg IU(t)$ | Assume |
| 6. | ■ | Modus Ponens, $\exists$ Intro; 3, 5 |
| | | |
| 7. | $IU(t)$ | Assume |
| 8. | ◇ (2) | Assume |
| 9. | ◇ (3) | State Transition; 3, 8 |
| 10. | $\neg IU(t+1)$ | Value in State; 9 |
| 11. | ■ | Modus Ponens, $\exists$ Intro; 3, 10 |
| | | |
| 12. | ◇ (4) | Assume |
| 13. | $\exists t_1\ t_1 > t \wedge \neg IE(t_1) \wedge$ $\forall t_2\ t_1 > t_2 \geq t \to IE(t_2)$ | Instantiate Given |
| 14. | $\forall t_2\ t_1 \geq t_2 \geq t \to IU(t_2)$ | State Trans/Val in State; 12 |
| 15. | $\forall t'\ t \leq t' \leq t_1$ ◇ (5) | State Transition; 4, 14 |
| 16. | ◇ (6) | Looping; 12, 13 |
| 17. | $IU(t_1+1)$ | Value in State; 16 |
| 18. | ◇ (7) | State Transition; 14, 15 |
| 19. | $IY(t_1+1)$ | Value in State; 18 |
| 20. | ◇ (8) | State Transition; 16,19 |
| 21. | $\neg IU(t_1+2)$ | Value in State; 20 |
| 22. | ■ | Mod Pon, $\exists$ Intro; 3, 17, 21 |
| 23. | ■ | Assert States Exhaust; 8, 12 |
| 24. | ■ | Excluded Middle; 5, 7 |

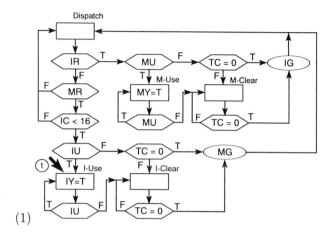

(1)

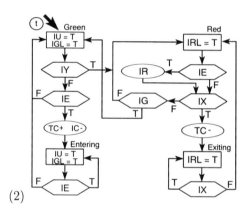

(2)

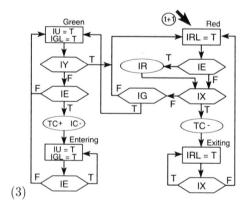

(3)

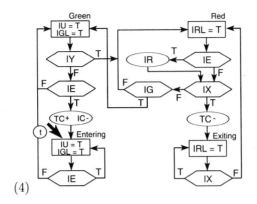

(4)

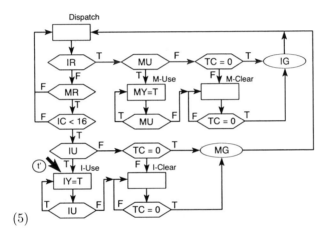

(5)

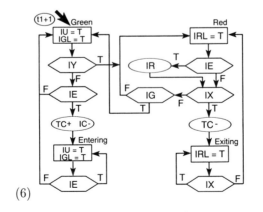

(6)

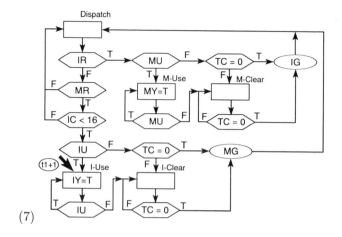

(7)

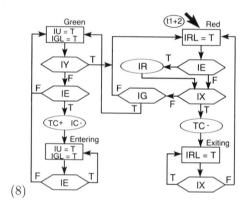

(8)

Assuming we are satisfied with the state-level design, the next step becomes designing an implementation of the system. This too can be done using the inference rules of the logic. There are several algorithms for converting a state machine into physical hardware (Winkel and Prosser [1989]); for this example we will take a state-encoded approach to the design. The circuit diagrams provided in Figure 7 for the island light controller can be shown to be logical consequences of the associated state machine in Figure 4. Although the logic includes a rule for inferring implementations from ASM charts, that rule is not presented here.

The diagrams in Figure 7 suggest how the logic can be used for design. Assuming we derive the top diagram under an inference rule for state-encoded implementations of state machines, there are a number of optimizations we could make to minimize the number of gates in the circuit.

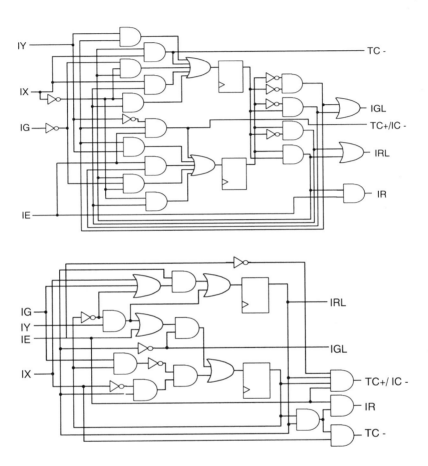

Figure 7: Circuit diagrams for the island light controller. The top diagram is naïvely produced using a state-encoding of green=00, entering=01, exiting=10, and red=11. The simplified yet behaviorally equivalent bottom diagram is derived from the first using the boolean algebra based circuit diagram inference rules .

The bottom diagram reflects one possible minimized circuit obtained from the original by means of the boolean algebra based circuit diagram inference rules. The soundness of these rules, established but not proven here, is sufficient to assure us that the two circuits are behaviorally equivalent. We are in the process of proving a completeness result based on a canonical form for circuit diagrams (Fisler [1995]); this would enable us to transform any two behaviorally equivalent circuit diagrams into one another using the inference rules.

Given implementations of the three controllers, all that remains is to design the components necessary to interface the three implementations. While some of the interface consists only of wires, additional logic is required to integrate the counters and the needed comparator into the final design. This brings us back to the issue of verification, as we would like to formally establish the correctness of the interface logic.

As an example, consider the logic required to interface to the counter TC that records how many cars are currently in the tunnel. Assume we have chosen to use a LS191 up-down counter (NSC [1987]) in our implementation. This counter has an enable signal and a single signal for indicating whether the counter should count up or count down. When the enable signal is low, a low voltage on the up/down line causes counting upwards and a high voltage on the up/down line causes counting downwards; no counting occurs when the enable line voltage is high. Once we interface the controller implementations with the counter, we must verify that our interface logic routes signals properly to the LS191. Assume that we used the following interface logic, where I-TCIncr is the signal TC+ from the island light controller and the remaining signals are analogously defined.

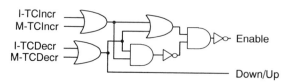

We can use the simulation style inference rules on circuit diagrams to verify that our interface logic behaves as desired. As an example proof, consider the case when the island controller issues a tunnel counter increment and the mainland controller issues a tunnel counter decrement.[5] In this case the counter should hold its current value. The following proof consists of two diagrams. In the first, we assume that both I-TCIncr and M-TCDecr are asserted simultaneously. The second diagram shows the resulting asserted signals once the simulation rules are applied to the first diagram.

---

[5]This combination is possible in our proposed state machines.

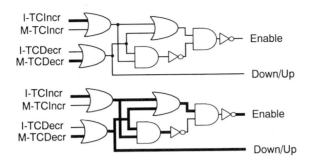

# 5 Conclusions

Diagrams are a powerful—and underutilized—notation. They are good representations for hardware reasoning because they are specialized to particular properties of systems. Combining specialized representations within a heterogeneous logic provides a powerful paradigm for supporting reasoning in addition to proof. A heterogeneous hardware logic that includes diagrams therefore suggests a possible solution to the usability problem in formal methods.

Our heterogeneous logic approach has been criticized as being unnecessarily complex (Review [1995]); traditional, sentential logics are argued to be simpler and more flexible because they can model many properties using a single notation (Gordon [1986]). Such generality comes at a cost with respect to natural reasoning. We feel that complexity in the underlying system is a suitable tradeoff for greater usability.

Other researchers have explored formal usage of diagrams in limited situations in hardware reasoning. Timing diagrams have received the most attention, being cited as a more natural formalism for use in place of temporal logic (Schlör and Damm [1993] Khordoc, et. al., [1993]). Other systems have employed more general usage of diagrammatic representations (Dillon, et. al., [1993] Srivas and Bickford [1991] Finn, et. al., [1990]). All of these systems formalize diagrams by translating them into known sentential logics; proofs in these systems are carried out in the sentential logic, with the diagrams serving as interface tools.

The translation approach is reasonable when using a single diagrammatic notation. In order to use this approach to define inference rules in our heterogeneous framework, we would have to either translate all of the representations into a common sentential logic or establish formal connections between multiple existing sentential logics. Rather than risk adding logical errors via the translation process, we define our rules directly on the diagrams.

There are additional advantages to our approach. Diagrams often encode substantial amounts of detailed information that may or may not be relevant to a verification effort. Translation, unable to filter what information to capture and what to ignore, might produce a considerably larger specification than is actually necessary. Our approach is also highly modular; adding a new representation does not involve integration of additional underlying logics.

Additional research is required before we can construct a tool based upon our logic. We need to extend it with support for making abstractions (Melham [1990]) and with better support for automatic verification methods. Automatic methods are required for handling large examples. One might question why, if we intend to automate the logic, we are concerned with how well the logic supports human reasoning. Automatic methods cannot fully handle many industrial size examples due to complexity bounds. Human reasoning is often needed in order to decompose a problem into pieces that are sufficiently small for automatic methods. In addition, the decidable logics underlying automatic methods are necessarily limited in expressibility; human reasoning is required for problems falling outside of these limitations. Addressing these two issues would yield a prototype system geared towards proof and reasoning that will help bring formal methods closer to designers.

# 6  Acknowledgements

The author thanks Jon Barwise, Shriram Krishnamurthi, Steve Johnson, Gerard Allwein, and several anonymous reviewers for useful discussions and comments on this project.

# Bibliography

BARWISE, JON

1974    *Axioms for abstract model theory.* **Annals of Mathematical Logic**, 7 (1974): 221-65.

1989    **The Situation in Logic.** Lecture Notes. CSLI Publications, Stanford, 1989.

1991    *Information links in domain theory.* **Proceedings of the Mathematical Foundations of Programming Semantics Conference (1991)**, S. Brooks, M. Main, A. Melton, M. Mislove, and D. Schmidt, editors, Springer Verlag, 1992.

1993    *Constraints, channels, and the flow of information.* **Situation Theory and Its Applications, Volume 3**, Peter Aczel, David Israel, Yasuhiro Katagiri, and Stanley Peters, editors, pages 3–27. CSLI Publications, Stanford, 1993.

1993a   *Heterogeneous reasoning.* **Conceptual Graphs and Knowledge Representation**, G. Mineau, B. Moulin, and J. Sowa, editors, New York: Springer Verlag, 1993.

BARWISE, JON and JOHN ETCHEMENDY

1986    **Turing's World.** Academic Courseware Exchange, 1986.

1990    *Information, infons, and inference.* **Situation theory and its applications, I**, Robin Cooper, Kuniaki Mukai, and John Perry, editors, University of Chicago Press, 1990.

1991    **Tarski's World 3.0.** CSLI Lecture Notes. Cambridge, MA: Cambridge Univ. Press, 1991.

1991a   *Visual information and valid reasoning.* **Visualization in Teaching and Learning Mathematics**, W. Zimmerman and S. Cunningham, editors, Washington: Mathematical Association of America, 1991. 9-24. (Also Chapter I of this volume).

1991b   **The Language of First-order logic, with Tarski's World 3.0.** CLSI Lecture Notes, 2nd edition, 1992.

1994    **Hyperproof.** CSLI Lecture Notes, University of Chicago Press, 1994.

1995    *Heterogeneous logic.* **Diagrammatic Reasoning: Cognitive and Computational Perspective**, J. I. Glasgow, N. H. Narayanan and B. Chandrasekaran editors, Menlo Park: AAAI Press and Cambridge, MA: MIT Press, (1995) 209–232.

199+    *Logic, proof, and reasoning.* **Companion to Logic**, Alan Makinowski, editor, . Blackwell, to appear.

BARWISE, JON, DOV GABBAY, and CHRYSAFIS HARTONAS

1995    *Information flow and the lambek calculus.* **Language, Logic and Computation: The 1994 Moraga Proceedings**, Dag Weståhl and Jerry Seligman, editors, . CSLI Publications, Stanford, 1995.

BARWISE, JON and JOHN PERRY

1983    **Situations and Attitudes.** Cambridge, MA: Bradford-MIT, 1983.

BARWISE, JON and JERRY SELIGMAN

1995    *Classification and information.* Unpublished, 1994.

BARWISE, JON and ASUSHI SHIMOJIMA

1995    *Surrogate reasoning.* **Cognitive Studies: Bulletin of Japanese Cognitive Science Society**, 1995.

COHN, AVRA

1989    *Correctness properties of the viper block model: the second level..* **Current Trends in Hardware Verification and Automated Theorem Proving**, G. Birtwistle and P. A. Subrahmanyam, editors, pages 1–91, New York, 1989. Springer.

DAVIS, A.L.

1989    *What do computer architects design anyway?.* **Current Trends in Hardware Verification and Automated Theorem Proving**, G. Birtwistle and P. A. Subrahmanyam, editors, pages 463–479. Springer, New York, 1989.

DEVLIN, KEITH

1991    **Logic and Information.** Cambridge University Press, Cambridge, England, 1991.

DILLON, L.K., G. KUTTY, L.E. MOSER, P.M. MELLIAR-SMITH, and Y.S. RAMAKRISHNA

1993    *A graphical interval logic for specifying concurrent systems.* Technical Report, UCSB, 1993.

EBERLE, R.

1995 *Diagrams in Natural Deduction.* Ph.D. diss. Visual Inference Laborarty and Department of Philosophy, Indiana University, 1995(in progress).

FINN, SIMON, MICHAEL P. FOURMAN, MICHAEL FRANCIS, and ROBERT HARRIS

1990 *Formal system design — Interactive synthesis on computer-assisted formal reasoning.* **Formal VLSI Specification and Synthesis: VLSI Design-Methods-I**, Luc Claesen, editor, North-Holland, 1990.

FISLER, K.

1994 *A logical formalization of hardware design diagrams.* Indiana University Technical Report TR416 September 1994.

1995 *A canonical form for circuit diagrams.* Indiana University Department of Computer Science Technical Report TR432, May 1995.

GARDNER, M.

1982 **Logic Machines and Diagrams.** 1982, [1958]. 2nd ed. Chicago: Univeristy of Chicago Press.

GOBERT, JANICE D. and CARL H. FREFERIKSEN

1992 *The comprehension of architectural plans by expert and sub-expert architects.* Unpublished (1992).

GORDON, MIKE

1986 *Why higher-order logic is a good formalism for specifying and verifying hardware.* **Formal Aspects of VLSI Design**, G. J. Milne and P. A. Subrahmanyam, editors, pages 153–177, Amsterdam, 1986. North-Holland.

HAMMER, ERIC

1995 *Reasoning with sentences and diagrams.* **The Notre Dame Journal of Formal Logic**, To appear.

1995a *Representing relations diagrammatically.* In review.

HAMMER, ERIC and NORMAN DANNER

1995 *Towards a model theory of diagrams.* In review. (Also Chapter V of this volume.)

HAMMER, ERIC and SUN-JOO SHIN

1995    *Euler and the role of visualization in logic.* **Language, Logic and Computation: The 1994 Moraga Proceedings**, Dag Westeståhl and Jerry Seligman, editors, CSLI Publications, Stanford, 1995.

HAREL, DAVID

1987    *On the formal semantics of statecharts.* **Proc. of the Second Annual IEEE Symposium on Logic in Computer Science**, Ithaca, 1987.

1987a    *On visual formalisms.* Carnegie Mellon University Computer Science tech. report 87-126, 1987.

HILBERT, DAVID

1971    **Foundations of Geometry.** Open Court Classics. La Salle, Il (1971).

HUNT, WARREN A.

1992    *A formal HDL and its use in the FM9001 verification.* Second NASA Formal Methods Workshop 1992, NASA Conference Publication 10110, Langley Research Center, Hampton Virginia. From an oral presentation.

ISRAEL, DAVID, JOHN PERRY, and SYUN TUTIYA

1991    *Actions and movements.* **IJCAI-91: Proceedings of the Twelfth International Conference on Artificial Intelligence, Volume 2**, John Mylopoulos and Ray Reiter, editors, pages 1060–1065. Morgan Kaufman Publishers, San Mateo, California, 1991.

1993    *Executions, motivations, and accomplishments.* **The Philosophical Review**, 102(4):515–540, 1993.

JOHNSON, STEVEN, JON BARWISE, and GERARD ALLWEIN

1993    *Toward the rigorous use of diagrams in hardware synthesis and verification.* **Logic and Diagrams: Working Papers**, Visual Inference Lab, Indiana University, 1993. (Shortened version Chapter IX of this volume.)

JOHNSON-LAIRD, PHILIP N. and RUTH M. J. BYRNE

1991    **Deduction.** Hillsdale (1991).

KHORDOC,K., M. DUFRESNE, E. CERNY, P. BABKINE, and A. BSILBURT

1993 *Integrating behavior and timing in executable specifications.* **Proceedings, Computer Hardware Description Languages and their Applications**, pp. 385–402, April 1993.

KINDFIELD, ANN C. H.

1992 *Expert Diagrammatic reasoning in biology.* **Proceedings of the Symposium on Reasoning with Diagrammatic Representations**, Stanford University (1992). 41-46.

KOEDINGER, KENNETH R. and JOHN R. ANDERSON

1990 *Abstract planning and perceptual chunks: elements of expertise in geometry.* **Cognitive Science**, 14 (1990). 511-550.

1991 *Interaction of Deductive and Inductive Reasoning Strategies in Geometry Novices.* **Proceedings of the Thirteenth Anual Conference of the Cognitive Science Society**, (1991).

KOSSLYN, S. M.

1980 **Image and Mind.** Harvard University Press, 1980.

LARKIN, JILL H. and HERBERT A. SIMON

1987 *Why a Diagram Is (Sometimes) worth Ten Thousand Words.* **Cognitive Science**, 11 (1987) 65-100.

LINDSAY, ROBERT K.

1988 *Images and Inference.* **Cognition**, (1988) 229-250.

LUENGO, ISABEL

1995 *Diagrams in Geometry.* Visual Inference Laboratory and Philosophy Department, Indiana University

1996 *A diagrammatic subsystem of Hilbert's geometry.* **Logic and Diagrams: Working Papers**, Visual Inference Lab, Indiana University, 1993. (Also Chapter VII in this volume.)

MAC LANE, SAUNDERS

1971 **Categories for the Working Mathematician**, Springer-Verlag, 1971.

MAYGER, E. M., M.D. FRANCIS, R.L. HARRIS, G. MUSGRAVE, and M. P. FOURMSN

1989 *Dialog – linking formal proof to the design environment.* **Abstract Hardware Ltd. report**, 1989, Uxbridge, U. K.

MAXWELL, E. A.

1959   **Fallacies in Mathematics.** Cambridge University Press (1959).

MELHAM, THOMAS F.

1990   *Formalizing Abstraction Mechanisms for Hardware Verification in Higher Order Logic.* **Computer Laboratory Technical Report No. 201**, PhD thesis, University of Cambridge, August 1990.

MORE, TRENCHARD

1959   *On the Construction of Venn Diagrams.* **Journal of Symbolic Logic**, 24 (1959): 303-304.

MYERS, KAREN and KURT KONOLIGE

1992   *Integrating sentential reasoning for perception.* **Proc. of AAAI Symposium on Reasoning with Diagrammatic Representations**, 25-27 March 1992. Stanford: Stanford U, 1992.

NASA

1995   NASA Langley Formal Methods Workshop. Panel Sessions and Discussions. May, 1995.

NSC

1987   **LS/S/TTL Logic Databook**, National Semiconductor Corporation, 1987.

OWRE, S., J.M. RUSHBY, and N. SHANKAR

1992   *PVS: a prototype verification system.* **11th International Conference on Automated Deduction (CADE), Volume 607 of Springer Lecture Notes in Artificial Intelligence**, Deepak Kapur, editor, pages 748–752. Springer, 1992.

PEIRCE, CHARLES S.

1933   **The Collected Papers of Charles S. Peirce, volume 4.** Charles Hartshorne and Paul Weiss, editors, Cambridge: Harvard University Press, 1933.

POLYTHRESS, V. and H. SUN

1972   *A method to construct convex, connected venn diagrams for any finite number of sets.* **Pentagon**, 1972.

REVIEW

1995    Reviewers' Comments on papers submitted to **Theorem Provers
        and Circuit Design 1994** and **Computer Hardware De-
        scription Languages and Their Applications**, 1995.

ROBERTS, DON

1933    **The Existential Graphs of Charles S. Peirce.** The Hague:
        Mouton and Co., 1973.

RUSHBY, JOHN

1993    **Formal Methods and Digital Systems Validation for Air-
        borne Systems.** NASA Langley Contractor Report 4551, De-
        cember 1993.

SCHLÖR, RAINER and WERNER DAMM

1993    *Specification and verification of system-level hardware designs us-
        ing timing diagrams.* **Proceedings of the European Confer-
        ence on Design and Automation**, February 1993.

SHIMOJIMA, ATSUSHI

1995    *Reasoning with diagrams and geometrical constraints.* **Language,
        Logic and Computation: The 1994 Moraga Proceedings**,
        Dag Westeståhl and Jerry Seligman, editors, CSLI Publications,
        Stanford, 1995.

SHIN, SUN-JOO

1990    *An analysis of inference involving Venn Diagrams.* ms., Stanford
        University.

1991    *A situation-theoretic account of valid reasoning with Venn dia-
        grams.* **Situation Theory and Its Applications, Vol. 2**, J.
        Barwise et al, editors, Stanford: CSLI, 1991. (Also Chapter IV of
        this volume.)

1991a   *Valid Reasoning and Visual Representation..* **Dissertation
        Stanford University**, 1991. Also forthcoming book by Cam-
        bridge University Press.

1994    **The Logical Status of Diagrams.** Cambridge University
        Press, 1994.

SOWA, JOHN

1984    **Conceptual Structures: Information Processing in Mind
        and Machine.** Addison–Wesley, 1984.

SRIVAS, MANDAYAM and MARK BICKFORD

1991    **SPECTOOL: A Computer-Aided Verification Tool for Hardware Designs, Vol I. Rome Laboratory Technical Report RL-TR-91-339**, Griffiss Air Force Base, NY, December 1991.

STENNING, KEITH

1977    *On remembering how to get there: how we might want something like a map.* **Cognitive Psychology and Instruction**, A. M. Lesgold, J. W. Pellegrino, S. W. Fokkema, and R. Glaser, editors, 1977.

STENNING, KEITH and JON OBERLANDER

1991    *Reasoning with words, pictures, and calculi: computation versus justification.* **Situation Theory and its Applications, vol. 2, CSLI Lecture Notes No. 26**, (1991) 607-621.

STIGLER, JAMES

1984    *'Mental Abacus': The effect of abacus training on Chinese children's mental arithmetic.* **Cognitive Psychology**, 16 (1984) 145-176.

TENNANT, NEIL

1984    *The withering away of formal semantics.* **Mind and Language,,** Vol. 1, No. 4, 1986, pp. 302–318.

TUFTE, EDWARD R.

1984    **Envisioning Information.** Graphics Press, Cheshire, Connecticut, 1990.

TVERSKI, BARBARA

1991    *Spatial mental models.* **The Psychology of Learning and Motivation**, 27 (1991). 109-145.

VENN, JOHN

1971    **Symbolic Logic.** 2nd ed. New York: Burt Franklin, 1971.

WALLACE, EDWARD C. and STEPHEN F. WEST

1992    **Roads to Geometry.** Prentice Hall (1992).

WEISE, DANIEL

1989    *Constraints, abstraction and verification.* **Hardware Specification, Verification and Synthesis: Mathematical Aspects**, M. Leeser and G. Brown, editors, pages 25–39, Berlin, 1989.

Springer, Mathematical Sciences Institute Workshop, Cornell University.

WHITE, RICHARD

1984 *Peirce's alpha graphs: the completeness of propositional logic and the fast simplification of truth functions.* **Transactions of the Charles S. Peirce Society**, 20, 1984.

WINKEL, DAVID and FRANKLIN PROSSER

1989 **The Art of Digital Design.** Prentice-Hall, Englewood Cliffs, New Jersey, 2nd edition, 1989.

WITTGENSTEIN, LUDWIG

1978 **Remarks on the Foundations of Mathematics.** Von Wright, Rhees and Anscombe eds, translated by Anscombe, The M.I.T. Press (1978).

ZEMAN, J. JAY

1964 *The Graphical Logic of C.S. Peirce.* Disseratation, University of Chicago, 1964.

# Index